Crack!

and

Thump

With a Combat Infantry Officer
in World War II

Captain Charles Scheffel
with **Barry Basden**

Camroc Press, LLC

Llano, Texas

First published in 2007 by
Camroc Press, LLC
PO Box 801
Llano, TX 78643
www.camrocpress.com

9 8 7 6 5 4 3 2

ISBN 978-0-9754503-6-9

Library of Congress Control Number: 2006936457

Printed in the United States of America

Front Cover Photo: Courtesy National Archives (111-SC-221867)

For those whose stories never got told.

Contents

Introduction vii
1. A Dollar a Day 9
2. Shipping Out 17
3. Operation Torch 27
4. Algeria 36
5. Under Fire 43
6. Ridge by Ridge 49
7. Hill 772 56
8. The Long Patrol 61
9. Heading North 66
10. Sedjenane 72
11. Before the Push 76
12. Losing Commanders 81
13. Prisoners 86
14. Free of Axis Forces 89
15. Strawman at the Bordello 95
16. Invading Sicily 100
17. Troina 108
18. Two Medics 113
19. R and R 118
20. D-Day + 3 127
21. Vital Parts 132
22. Ashore in France 136
23. Operation Cobra 140
24. Taking Over C Company 144
25. Looking for the Enemy 148
26. Walking Fire 156
27. Finding B Company 163
28. Panic Is Contagious 167
29. Holding Our Ground 174
30. The Chase Begins 183
31. Liberation 190
32. Dinant 198
33. The Siegfried Line 206
34. The Journey Home 215
35. Epilogue 223
Maps 225

Introduction

Every combat situation is different, and even those in the same fight may not experience or remember it exactly the same way. This is Charles Scheffel's story, told with the hope that you can see World War II as it unfolded around one combat infantry officer.

I met Charlie a few years ago while recording oral histories for a World War II museum. In a brief taped interview, Charlie talked about his part in the war, a story at once unique and universal, as all good stories are.

The museum's archivist dutifully filed away the transcript to await future researchers, and I went on to do other things. But I couldn't get Charlie's personal combat experiences out of my mind. Finally, I called him at his home in San Antonio and he agreed to let me help tell his story.

During this long process, Charlie was incredibly patient and understanding. In addition to sitting through hours and hours of taped interviews and dozens of phone calls, he provided access to his memorabilia, introduced me to friends and members of the 9th Infantry Division, took me to reunions, annotated various books on the war, and reviewed the manuscript as it progressed.

Except for Charlie's immediate family and those persons more or less in the public domain, the names appearing in the book were changed or omitted, in some cases to spare embarrassment or discomfort to the persons involved or to surviving families. In other instances, we were not sure we pulled the names correctly from the distant past. Rather than get any wrong, it seemed prudent to leave them all out.

But long after names are forgotten, it will be what ordinary citizens accomplished in World War II that remains eternal. Countless numbers of them died, and millions more suffered grievous wounds and emotional scars in a conflict that spread like a bloody stain across the earth. Without question, today's world would be far different had the Axis powers prevailed.

The generation that achieved that victory over tyranny is leaving us now. It is already too late to save many of their stories. This book stemmed from the desire to save one more, to see the war through the eyes of one more person who was there.

Charlie Scheffel, a combat infantry officer, gave the prime of his youth to that momentous struggle. This is his story.

—*Barry Basden*

1
A Dollar a Day

Looking back on war is an old man's folly. I've known men who never talked about their wartime experiences or attended reunions until their final years. Similarly, my twilight thoughts now turn inward, back to the days of my youth and to the wonder of my survival in combat, while so many good men died around me.

My service as an infantry officer in the U.S. Army was set in motion long before I ever put on a uniform. My father arrived in America as a stowaway from Germany and, to earn his citizenship, enlisted in the Army during the Spanish-American War.

After his discharge, he roamed the West, mining for gold in Colorado and fishing for tuna off the California coast before settling in Oklahoma. It was 1918, and the curtain was coming down on the Great War that ravaged a generation in the stalemated trenches of Europe. The time had come to settle down, take a wife, and start a family. Nearing 40, my father courted and married Selma Amelia Ekdol, the 35-year-old spinster daughter of a Swedish immigrant.

My mother was a slightly plump, square-faced woman who wore her light brown hair pulled back in a severe bun. Her own mother had died early, leaving Mom, as the oldest of five children, to run her father's household before she was ten years old. She cooked and cleaned and in essence became mother to her brothers and sisters. The experience left her serious and steeled for future hardships.

When World War I ended, the country changed rapidly. Cars vied with the horse and buggy for the roadways. My dad opened a tire shop in Oklahoma City, but sold out within a few months and moved his pregnant wife to Enid, a small town a hundred miles north. He wanted a safe place to raise his family, a place quieter than the bustling city.

My parents moved into a one-story frame house with two bedrooms and a hand pump on the back steps for water. The living room was barely large enough to hold the upright piano my mother had played as a child and brought to the marriage as part of her dowry.

Still infatuated with the automobile, my father opened a filling station and established himself in the local business community. I was born in 1919, Charles Scheffel, Jr. By the time my brother Stanley came along in

1921, Dad was an officer in a small drilling company and active in the area's growing oil boom.

He invested in mineral rights, buying up all the leases he could afford, betting on striking it rich. He loved the exhilarating gamble of wildcatting for oil, and soon concentrated his efforts there. He came and went at odd hours, carrying his notes and leases in his coat pocket, doing paperwork on the run, his office the back seat of a Model T Ford.

Once in a while, he took me to the Elks Club, where he bowled, played cards, shot pool, and discussed the oil business. A tall, athletic man, Dad moved gracefully, and a smooth delivery made him one of the town's best bowlers. He came alive talking baseball or cars or the potential of a new oil field.

Some of my earliest memories are of riding with him out to his drilling rigs. Without restrictions on the spacing of derricks, scores of the wooden structures dotted the countryside.

Late one afternoon we drove out to a promising site. Several dozen men stood waiting to see if the well was going to come in that day. Clanking and grinding, the drill spun and the bit cut deep into the earth; the pump brought up mud and discharged it into a nearby slush pit.

Whiskey was common around oil rigs, despite Prohibition, and empty bottles and jars littered the area. A man talking to my father reached into his pocket and pulled out a coin.

"Here's a nickel, son," he said. "Go fill up one of those dead Indians with some of that slush water and let's see what we've got."

I ran to the pit and brought back a bottle full of dirty water. The man stuck his finger in the bottle, then brought it to his mouth and licked it. He smiled. "Sweet as sorghum."

The sweetness was a promising sign and drilling continued.

Suddenly, there was a roar and gas hissed from the well. Everyone moved back in case the pressure blew out the drill pipe. After a few minutes, the gas became a fountain of oil spewing out the top of the derrick. Catching the wind, it turned into a dark plume that coated the ground with a fine black spray. It was a real gusher and, with more oil strikes, our family prospered.

But something was wrong with my brother Stanley. By the time he was five, it was obvious his arms and legs weren't growing right. This was long before much was known about dwarfism. Doctors all over Oklahoma examined him without success. They said he was fortunate to avoid most of the major complications that often accompanied the condition.

We would make the best of it. Dad moved in with me, and Stanley moved into the other bedroom with Mom, a surefire birth control method of the day. There would be no more children in our house.

My father dressed well as he prospered, generally wearing a vest with a gold watch and chain. He bought a new Buick with a rumble seat where Stanley and I rode like princes, the wind blowing in our hair. Sitting in his rocking chair after work, Dad smoked his pipe and read the *Oil and Gas Journal* or *Literary Digest*. We had Shakespeare in the bookcase and a big Philco radio to listen to in the evening. Times were good.

In the summer of 1929, our family took off on an extravagant trip to California in a brand new four-door Studebaker President, a wonderful car that came with leather luggage custom-made to fit into its trunk. Standing before the majesty of the Grand Canyon, Dad draped his arm across my shoulder.

"Son," he said, "I want you to try to see all the national parks. Then you'll realize how lucky you are to be born in America."

In Los Angeles we met with a leading specialist in a last attempt to see if anything could be done to help Stanley. The doctor, like all before him, offered little encouragement, but being of some renown, he knew many Hollywood celebrities. After the examination, he picked up the phone and got Stanley an appointment at Hal Roach Studios.

Stanley auditioned for a part in an Our Gang movie, but when the talks turned serious, my parents settled for a tour of the studio instead. Too many oil deals brewing back in Oklahoma, and Mom was not about to move to Hollywood without my father and me just to get Stanley into the movies, an uncertain business at best.

The next day we took a sightseeing boat to Catalina Island out in the blue Pacific, my first ocean voyage. What a great vacation. We basked in its afterglow all the way back to Enid.

A few months later, everything changed. The Great Depression descended on America like some dreadful monster. With a flurry of margin calls, the stock market crashed under waves of panic selling. Commodity prices plummeted. Wheat was not worth harvesting. Oil dropped to twenty-five cents a barrel. By December, commerce and industry had sputtered to a halt.

New Year's Day arrived bleak and cold at our house. My father turned silent, shocked by his crumbling fortunes. He spent the next week away from home for long hours each day, trying to shore up his holdings. By week's end, exhausted and ill with a bad cold, he went to bed and stayed there.

On Saturday morning, January 11, 1930, I was down the street playing in the snow with some friends, when our next-door neighbor ran up and told me I needed to go home right then. By the time I got there, my father, age 50 and an old man in my childish eyes, was dead of pneumonia. Dad, always so strong and vital, would no longer be there to protect us. All of a sudden, we were alone in a world that seemed increasingly uncertain. I was scared.

But I need not have worried quite so much. My mother's coping skills served us well as she took charge. Although we bent under the weight of the Depression along with most other folks in Enid, we did not break. Mom sold the Studebaker. She took in sewing and made many of our clothes. In the backyard we grew peas, tomatoes, onions, corn, and other vegetables. A sturdy, tireless woman, Mom hauled pails of water to the kerosene stove and cooked and canned the harvest. I ate so much okra I still don't like it. In winter a quilting frame sat on the dining room table where she and her neighbors sewed quilts to sell at fairs and church sales.

Somehow, we managed. I never heard Mom complain about her burden as a single mother of two during those hard times. We had plenty to eat, and I never felt more deprived than my friends. Mom's grit and determination kept us stable and eased my fears enough to keep the Depression from stealing my childhood. It amazes me even now how strong she was.

Stanley, because of his physical limitations, devoted his time to school work, excelling in math and science. Eventually, he would become the head chemist for an oil company. After tiring of the lab, he successfully traded stocks and commodities.

But I preferred the outdoors, though my mother made sure I kept my grades up. She knew what I was capable of and didn't let me slide. She gave private lessons on her upright piano, and by the time I was 12, she decided I needed to learn to play.

That was a problem. I was far more interested in baseball and other sports than in practicing scales, so I made a deal with her. I would learn music if she would let me play something besides the piano. Knowing we had little money, I opened the Montgomery Ward catalog and picked the most expensive instrument I could find, a xylophone.

Mom looked at my choice and said, "Go play ball." She never brought it up again.

For seven summers after my dad died, I worked on my aunt's farm. "You'll learn a lot," Mom said. "It'll be good for you."

I worked in the fields for room and board and a dollar a day. The unemployment rate hit 25 percent in the depths of the Depression. A dollar was big money for a kid, when desperate men with families tramped the country looking for work.

Not having to feed a growing boy for a few months had to be a great help to my mother, but there was more to it than that. She was a wise woman and, with no father figure in the house, she felt an honest day's work away from home would make a man of me.

I felt good doing my part to help with our finances, though my resolve waned during the long summer days of hot, backbreaking work. But I grew up lean and hard, in great shape for sports. By my senior year in 1938, I was six-two and weighed 175 pounds. My ambition was to be the next Bill Tilden, and that spring I won the city tennis championship, charging the net aggressively to defeat a University of Oklahoma varsity player.

I also lettered in football and baseball, but basketball was my best sport. With fluid moves and a good two-handed set shot, I caught the eye of future Hall of Fame coach, Hank Iba, who offered me a full athletic scholarship to Oklahoma A&M.

I accepted at once. With the country still in the grip of the Depression, I couldn't go to college without help. A&M, now Oklahoma State, was in Stillwater, sixty miles east of Enid. I could come home regularly to see my family and my steady girl friend, Ruth, who stayed home and attended a local college.

It was time for me to start my life's journey away from my father's house. I felt excited to be leaving, but anxious about the unknown. As I packed, I noticed the large framed document above the bed that celebrated Dad's military service with the Kansas Volunteers. I had studied it many times, wondering about his life. I missed him and hoped he would have been proud of me.

In 1938, Oklahoma A&M, a Federal Land Grant College, required male freshmen and sophomores to take basic courses in the Reserve Officer Training Corps. Advanced ROTC was optional for upper classmen, and led to a second lieutenant's commission in the U.S. Army.

With my basketball scholarship, I had no intention of taking any more than the mandatory ROTC courses. My major was finance, and I planned to go into banking and marry Ruth as soon as I graduated. But there's an old saying: If you want to make God laugh, tell Him your plans.

I took basic ROTC three days a week. During the summers, I played semipro baseball for a dollar a day, the same pay I'd earned working on the farm, but a lot more fun. In the fall of 1940, Congress passed a new draft law requiring males eighteen or older to register for military service. By my junior year, the fighting had already started in Europe; Japan was in China, and talk of war spread across the campus.

ROTC actively recruited for the advanced course. If we signed up, we wouldn't have to register for the draft, but those who didn't might be drafted out of school.

With the Battle of Britain raging, some students went north and enlisted in the Royal Canadian Air Force, hoping to fly Spitfires against the Luftwaffe. That sounded romantic and patriotic, but I wore glasses for distance vision and could not pass the eye test for fighter pilots. Even so, I knew I had to do something. I was determined that my country would not go to war without me.

Concerned that his gung-ho athletes would volunteer for military service, Coach Iba called us into his office individually.

"Don't do anything stupid," he said when I told him I thought I'd take my chances in the draft lottery. "Go talk to Colonel Harper and sign up for advanced ROTC. That way you can graduate and go into the Army as a second lieutenant."

Colonel Harper was head of Military Science and a member of the athletic council, so I knew him well. I trotted over to his office where he gave me a sales talk. When he told me the Army would pay me 25 cents a day during advanced ROTC, I signed up. Then he reminded me that, as a future officer, I would have to buy my own uniform, shoes, and the Sam Browne leather belt officers wore at the time.

"I don't have any money to buy a uniform."

He smiled. "That's okay, Charlie. You can pay for your uniform with the 25 cents a day."

So I was still going to be broke. The Army was not dumb. I had just volunteered for the "Queen of Battle," the Infantry Corps.

I was a platoon leader in my junior year. In the summer of 1941, a hundred of us traveled under military orders to Camp Bullis near San Antonio for two weeks of field training.

We had a great time running around the countryside and playing soldier. Not very realistic, but a lot of fun. We chased armadillos through the tent area at night and shot at birds on the rifle range about as often as we aimed at the targets. With all the horsing around, only one of our six-man team qualified as an expert rifleman, though I managed to earn a sharpshooter's badge, the next highest rating.

One afternoon, the range control officer suddenly halted the firing. We gathered in a large circle behind the line and an old man about five foot four walked briskly into the middle of the circle. He wore the dress uniform of a lieutenant general, three stars on each shoulder. Hands on hips, he stared at us.

"You men should take your training a little more seriously," he said. "Next year many of you will be leading troops into battle and you'll wish you had."

I thought the old man had lost his marbles, but how right he turned out to be.

In my senior year, I became Cadet Major and commanded one of three ROTC battalions. We had a good basketball team that year and looked forward to playing several games along the eastern seaboard during Christmas vacation.

On Sunday afternoon, December 7, 1941, a shrill whistle halted practice, our final workout before leaving by train the next day for the East. Coach Iba hurried across the floor and gathered us around him. "The Japs just bombed Pearl Harbor," he said.

We were stunned. Most of us didn't even know where Pearl Harbor was. That evening was chaotic, the campus in an uproar as grim damage reports came out of Hawaii. The Jap bastards would pay for this sneak attack.

Some of us rushed over to the military department and learned we were now second lieutenants in the infantry. Later, a sergeant stopped by the dorm and said no, we weren't, but to stay on campus. The sergeant came around again the next morning and told us the Army wasn't going to activate us as lieutenants just then. We would take our Christmas basketball trip after all.

We played in New York's Madison Square Garden, Philadelphia, Baltimore, and other eastern cities. War news filled the papers, and arenas were half empty. People had much more on their minds than basketball.

When we returned to Oklahoma, the Army gave ROTC seniors a reprieve. Those of us scheduled to graduate in May would complete our degrees. We finished the basketball season as conference co-champions, losing in the first round of the NCAA playoffs to Kansas, a team we'd beaten earlier in the year.

This was no time for elaborate plans, so immediately after the Kansas loss, I called Ruth long distance. "Do you want to get married next week?"

She said yes.

I married Hetty Ruth Carnell in Enid on March 27, 1942. We honeymooned in a garage apartment we rented in Stillwater for a dollar a day. We had no time to go anywhere else.

The next week Colonel Harper called me to his office and introduced me to another colonel, a large, affable man from Army Headquarters in Washington.

"Charlie," the colonel said, "I'm recruiting for the Finance Corps. Your major is banking and finance and we need your help."

"I don't know anything about military finance."

"No problem. The Army's expanding so fast we've got only a few officers with any finance background at all. With your major, you'll move up fast. What do you say?"

A lot of things flashed through my mind. A surge of patriotism made me want to get the SOBs who had attacked us. I was also young and needed to prove myself as a man. How would I measure up in combat? Would I stand up to fear and do my duty? I would never know if I went to war as a finance officer.

"I'll take my chances with the infantry," I said finally.

But I didn't tell Ruth, afraid she wouldn't understand.

The ROTC students graduated in the middle of May 1942. On a bright, clear morning, I marched my battalion of 200 cadets across the windswept parade field, passing in review before various state and local dignitaries. Proud families sat near the reviewing stand.

That afternoon, 76 cadets became second lieutenants in the Infantry Corps. It was a moving time for all of us. The war was not going well, and everyone present knew that most of us would soon be in combat.

After the ceremony, I walked to where Ruth and my mother stood on either side of Stanley. They were smiling, but I could see fear and worry in their faces. I tried to reassure them, but I was scared myself, about to step off into an uncertain future.

Stanley looked up at me. "I'll get some maps," he said, "and follow along wherever you go. I'll read everything I can about where you are."

I hugged them all. "I love you," I said, which was the whole truth.

2
Shipping Out

In early June, I took the bus from Enid to Fort Sill to process into the U.S. Army. It took the doctors ten minutes to find me fit for active duty. I don't believe they turned down anybody that day who was breathing.

A second lieutenant now, I found myself on a bus again, headed east to Camp Robinson, near Little Rock, Arkansas. I knew this day would eventually arrive, but the uncertainty of what lay before me seemed almost unreal. Was I really going off to war?

I had been too nervous to eat breakfast and the swaying bus left me queasy. I sat up front and watched the road unfurl over the driver's shoulder, moving me toward something unknown, something that could kill or maim on a whim. How would I face up to that challenge? Behind me, the busload of new soldiers chattered noisily. They were nervous, too.

The bus dropped us at the train station in Oklahoma City, a madhouse of vigor and bustle. I picked up my ticket for Little Rock and pushed through the crowd to stand in line outside a phone booth. While I waited to call Ruth, a man in a business suit walked along the line, scalping tickets for berths in the Pullman sleeping car. America had been in the war for only six months, but the country was on the move. Recruitment and War Bond posters hung on the walls, and it was as if the Depression had never happened.

Soldiers, their families, businessmen, and defense workers packed the train, all on their way somewhere to do their part in the war. The collective energy on board revived my spirits.

Camp Robinson, covering almost 50,000 acres north of Little Rock, could train 20,000 men at a time. Assigned to the Replacement Training Center, I would teach new draftees basic military skills. The more educated might go to specialized branches, but most would remain in the infantry.

Being a platoon leader in a training company meant a lot of late nights and early mornings. I was responsible for turning forty recent civilians into soldiers in eight short weeks, and the recruits needed a lot of tending. After four years of ROTC training, I felt it was something I could do.

My accommodations on post were spartan. Each officer had a private hut, barely large enough for a cot and footlocker. I hung my clothes on nails sticking out of bare walls. Flimsy shutters closed over two small windows.

Most nights didn't cool off much from the pounding heat of long summer days, though I was usually so tired that sleep was rarely a problem.

Soon after I arrived, Ruth came by train to join me. I met her at the station and she looked radiant in a blue flowered dress, dark hair framing her delicate, smiling face. She had been the May Queen her last year in college, and I was proud to be seen with her.

We rented two rooms in an old house in Little Rock, sharing a bathroom down the hall with the owners, but I continued to spend most nights on post. On the rare nights I got into town, we cooked dinner on a hot plate that sat on top of the dresser.

The Army's allowances for quarters and separate rations increased my pay to $200 a month. One of the first things I did was set up monthly allotments for a $10,000 life insurance policy and a $25 War Bond. Everyone I knew bought bonds; we were financing our own war.

Ruth rode the bus out to the post most evenings when I couldn't get home. We usually ate dinner late at the small regimental club, but sometimes we went over to the main club to dine and dance to Big Band music. Laughing couples in a hurry to have a good time filled the smoky ballroom. Time was short for everybody.

Security was a major concern at Camp Robinson. Paranoid rumors floated around that enemy spies lurked everywhere, reporting on all our activities.

I returned to my hut late one evening to find a typewritten note under my pillow designating me the company's security officer. I was to report unusual or subversive activity in a weekly letter to the post office box of a dummy sporting goods company in Little Rock. Included were special stamps to put on the reports for authentication. I never detected anything suspicious, but I sent in my stamped activity report each week.

Most of our platoon's trainees came from the Chicago area. The Army quickly transferred the few with more than meager educations to the artillery, the medics, or other branches that could use their skills.

Getting right to it, we gave our trainees haircuts, took away their civilian clothes, and began turning them into GIs. They would become Government Issue, parts of the Army inventory like any other piece of equipment, sent to wherever they were most needed.

The recruits learned personal hygiene and how to march, follow orders, and take care of their equipment. We ran them to the various training sites around the camp and got them in shape to fight. We did side-straddle-hops, sit-ups, pushups, and a variety of other exercises for half an hour each morning during these uncertain days of 1942, when the war was not going well.

I led the platoon on 25-mile marches across rugged terrain, wearing steel helmets, full field packs, and carrying Model 1903 Springfield rifles. We practiced reading maps and using compasses while roaming the hills in a remote part of the camp north of the Arkansas River. Chiggers and mosquitoes ate us up. We sprinkled powdered sulfur inside our leggings and field shoes, but nothing stopped the bugs for long. Water moccasins and copperheads slithered through our tents at night and bit several men. But the men were growing tougher, becoming soldiers, and I liked my part in it.

The company commander knew I was a college athlete and put me in charge of close-combat training. I could see some sense to the bayonet, but not much. Why stick a guy in the stomach when you could shoot him? But it was Army equipment, so I taught the troops how to run through the course and poke a dummy with their bayonet-tipped rifles. If nothing else, it improved their agility and mental toughness.

Then came hand-to-hand combat. I had worked out with wrestlers at Oklahoma A&M, so I knew a little bit about how to take a man down. But I was skeptical. I had made up my mind long before that, if it ever came down to me and some other guy, I would go for my opponent's genitals. If I had anything in my hands, I'd hit him with it. I'd kick him, knee him, or club him where it hurt most. This hand-to-hand combat stuff was for guys in amateur wrestling or boxing, not real combat.

One warm afternoon, I held a demonstration on the trench knife, a vicious-looking weapon developed in World War I. The foot-long knife had a grooved blade and ridged brass knuckles built into the handle. It was heavy and cumbersome to carry on my pistol belt, but the Army's idea was that it could inflict serious damage on the enemy in close quarters.

I faced two hundred recruits sitting in wooden bleachers at the edge of a parade field and talked to them about the knife, holding it out in front of me. I had padded the blade with cotton, gauze, and tape, taking no chances that anyone would get cut during the demonstration. I figured I could make a takedown, either an arm or leg drag, and disarm a guy coming at me with a knife, but I wasn't sure I trusted anyone else to hold this weapon, even padded. I wanted to stay in control of the contest.

"I need a volunteer," I said.

A soldier halfway up the bleachers raised his hand. The kid was about five foot nine, a wiry 150 pounds, and 18 or 19 years old. I could tell he was athletic when he stepped easily down from the bleachers. Still, he was 5 inches shorter and a good 30 pounds lighter than I was. Besides, I was in good shape.

"Are you ready?"

The kid saluted. "Yes, sir."

I didn't know exactly what to do or how I would attack or defend, but I thought I'd better keep the brass knuckles with me. I didn't want him hurting me by mistake. I knew I wasn't going to hurt him.

I thought I'd give the kid a chance to be a good participant. "Do you want me to attack you and show you how to attack, or would you rather attack me?"

"I'll be the attacker," he said.

I crouched and held the knife toward him. "Okay, attack me," I said.

Next thing I knew, I was flat on my back. The kid had my hand, which still gripped the knife through the knuckles so that the padded blade was against my neck under my chin. I never saw his hand move. Now I was cutting my own throat.

He smiled at me, inches from my face. "Should we get up now?" he said.

All I knew was that I was flat on my ass and he had my hand so that the brass knuckle grip was pinching my fingers. "I believe so," I said.

I stood and saw all these recruits staring at me, waiting to see what would happen next. I paced before them, giving myself time to regain some composure. I decided to level with them.

"Listen," I said, "I was convinced before we started this demonstration that, if you get this close to the enemy and you still haven't shot him, you're in real trouble."

That was not Army doctrine. We were supposed to attack and kill the other guy with the knife. They sure didn't give us the thing to open a can of beans, although that would have been a much better use for it.

At that point, I didn't give a damn about Army doctrine, so I said, "Either shoot the enemy or get the hell out of his way."

Everybody laughed.

I kept the kid with me while the first sergeant marched the rest of the troops back to the company area. "How did you get me down so fast?"

"I was a wrestler in high school."

"Where?"

"Chicago."

"How good were you?"

"I was the city champion."

In September, I passed my overseas physical and got orders to report in early October to Camp Kilmer, New Jersey, an embarkation point for Europe. I picked up my authorized combat gear and went to the Post Exchange for items not in the Army's inventory. I bought a rubber air mattress, the best ten dollars I ever spent. Sturdy and inflatable with only a few strong breaths, the mattress would keep me up off a lot of cold, hard ground in the war zone.

Ruth made plans to stay with her folks in Enid while I was overseas, and I set up an allotment for her that left $27 a month for me. I didn't think I would need much where I was going.

The Army hierarchy expected Ruth to go away when I got shipment orders. The unstated attitude was that if we wanted you to have a wife, we would have issued you one.

To hell with that. We weren't about to part until we absolutely had to. When I found out our troop cars would be hooked onto a regular passenger train leaving for Memphis and points east, Ruth bought a ticket on the same train. A security violation for sure, but we didn't care.

We left in the afternoon and every time our military cars were switched to another train, Ruth changed with us. I went forward to sit with her through the long night. Early the next morning we arrived bleary-eyed in Washington, D.C.

We weren't scheduled to leave until late that afternoon and we spent the layover walking the National Mall, visiting the Capitol, and seeing as many of the monuments as we could. We took off our shoes and walked barefoot in the grass. Ruth never looked lovelier than that day.

"What are you looking at?" she said when she caught me staring at her.

"You. I want to remember everything about you."

She smiled a little, touched my cheek, and leaned closer to kiss me.

For dinner, we bought hot dogs from a street vendor. By the time our train chugged out of the city, we were numb with fatigue. We held hands and touched often, mostly without talking, watching the towns and countryside slide by our window as thoughts of separation filled our heads. Soon there would be no way of knowing anything for sure.

The train would drop its troop cars at New Brunswick, New Jersey, then go on to New York City while the Army trucked me over to Camp Kilmer. Surely, it would take at least a few days for me to process out and ship overseas. With that hope, we decided Ruth would wait for me at the Piccadilly Hotel in New York, where the A&M basketball team stayed on our Christmas tour the year before. There, we would spend our last precious moments together.

At New Brunswick, I kissed Ruth lightly, wanting to reassure her. She had never been out of the Midwest before.

"Okay, honey," I said. "Get a room at the Piccadilly and wait for me. I'll be there as quick as I can."

She nodded, tears shining in her eyes. I gave her another peck and stepped off the train.

As soon as the trucks dropped us at Camp Kilmer, things started to speed up. We got overseas shots and the rest of our combat gear that evening. Model 1903 Springfield rifles, the "oh-three," for enlisted men and the standard officer's sidearm, a Colt .45 automatic, for me.

Within three hours, our group of two hundred was completely outfitted and sealed into a holding area. We were ready to leave at a moment's notice for overseas shipment by surface vessel to a destination identified only by a number that told me nothing.

I didn't sleep that night, knowing I was only forty miles across the Hudson River from where Ruth waited at the Piccadilly.

After a predawn breakfast, we loaded up for the truck ride to a ferry landing on the New Jersey side of the river opposite Manhattan. I was the senior officer in my group, having been in the Army from my ROTC sign-up two years earlier. One of the first things I learned in the Army was that rank has its privileges, so I insisted on sitting up front with the truck driver. Before we got to the ferry, I slipped him two one-dollar bills.

"Keep one of these for yourself," I said. "Use the other dollar to send a telegram to Mrs. Charles Scheffel, in care of the Piccadilly Hotel."

The driver shook his head. "I can't do that, sir."

"Yes, you can," I said, not at all sure.

At the time, German submarines lurked off the coast, sinking ships as they exited New York Harbor. We were in a dangerous war zone and under tight security. Any mention of troop movements was a court-martial offense.

The truck jounced along toward the docks. There wasn't a lot of time and I had to be careful. I thought for several minutes and finally wrote on a slip of paper, "Honey, your husband can't make it. I love you. Charlie." I handed the note to the driver when I stepped from the truck.

We boarded ferries and pulled away from the landing with the morning sun in our faces. I stood at the rail, looking at the New York skyline and thinking of Ruth in a hotel a mile away. I found out later that she got my message and took a train back to Oklahoma to live with her parents.

Oil shimmered on the river as our ferries churned toward the New York piers. We moved slowly past the blackened hulk of a French luxury liner, the *Normandie*. Still lying on her side in the mud, she had burned and capsized several months before while being converted into a troop ship.

We pulled up to another massive liner, the *Queen Elizabeth*, a British Cunard liner, the largest afloat. She had been docked in America since the start of the war to keep the Germans from capturing her. Over three football fields long and as tall as a twelve-story building, she normally carried 2,200 passengers and a crew of 1,200. Her cruising speed was thirty knots.

She sported a fresh coat of battleship gray for her troop-carrying assignment. Laden with equipment, we trudged up the QE's slatted gangplanks with thousands of soldiers from the 29th and 34th Infantry Divisions and a large contingent of Army Air Corps personnel. The Navy crammed men into every available space on the ship's twelve decks.

A crew member handed boarding passes to the six officers in our group and directed us to what was the former second-class nursery on B deck, two levels below where the lifeboats hung. The nursery was a square cabin, ten feet on a side. Instead of children's cribs and playpens, bunk beds hung three tiers high on three walls. I staked out a lower bunk and looked out our one porthole, but could see only the pier next door.

Later that morning, three men, all about sixty years old and wearing civilian clothes, joined us to claim the remaining bunks. They were business executives on their way to England as the first overseas Red Cross representatives. That confirmed what I had already guessed about our destination.

We had lunch in the massive, two-story Grand Ballroom, which had been converted into an officers' mess. Even the food was elegant. There we would eat three meals a day. Thousands of enlisted men on board weren't so lucky. They ate in shifts in converted swimming pools. Operating twenty-four hours a day, the Navy could still provide the troops with only two meals daily.

After lunch, a naval officer took us on a tour around the deck. For defense, the ship had a few .50-caliber machine guns and a contraption on the stern that fired signal rockets trailing a thousand feet of wire to protect against low-flying aircraft. I doubted any of it would help much on the high seas.

My assignment would be to control a lifeboat station if we had to abandon ship. With my .45 and two clips of ammunition, I was supposed to maintain order in a 60-passenger lifeboat. The boats and other rafts would hold only 2,500 men. The rest of the 20,000 people on board would have to jump into the cold waters of the North Atlantic wearing life preservers. My job was to shoot anyone trying to board or threaten my loaded lifeboat, an eventuality doomed to end in tragedy. If forced to abandon the ship, I was sure we would all die.

At four in the afternoon, tugboats towed the QE away from the pier. I stood at my assigned lifeboat on the starboard side while we moved slowly downriver. As we passed the Statue of Liberty, I thought of Ruth. I wished somehow I could have redone our final kiss. I knew it would have to last me a long time.

A Navy blimp escorted us several miles into the Atlantic, serving as our lookout for enemy submarines. Then we were alone, cutting through the water at twice normal convoy speed, leaving a wake a mile long. Every ten minutes the ship changed course thirty degrees, zigzagging to throw off enemy submarines trying to get a bead on us.

That evening, the captain announced that our destination was an undisclosed British port. Peacetime passage from New York to Southampton for the *Queen Elizabeth* was six days. Our course, running further north, would take only five, even zigzagging.

Weather was good during most of the passage, no squalls, but clouds scudded by on the brisk wind that blew day and night. We wore our kapok life jackets at all times, and I spent a lot of time with one of my cabin mates on the main deck behind the rear smokestack. There, out of the wind and warmed by the stack, we talked of our fears and hopes and watched flying fish sail out of the water, their fins flashing silver in the wake.

One afternoon, a hundred yards to starboard, whales surfaced in the steel-gray water and blew air, oblivious to our passing ship. At the rail, I watched them until they disappeared in the swells. Wind whipped through my clothes and I breathed deeply in the salt air. The aching beauty and timeless immensity of the ocean constricted my throat and blurred my eyes. For a brief moment, the war did not exist. Then I felt the weight of destiny and my unknowable, uncertain future.

The ship ran without lights, her portholes closed and curtained; no smoking was allowed on deck at night. Nothing could be thrown overboard to leave a trail for the enemy.

One night, south of Iceland, with the temperature near freezing, the ship suddenly leaned over in a sharp left turn, much tighter than a normal zigzag. Without sideboards to hold us in, I rolled out of my bunk and onto the floor with the rest of the men on the high side of the ship.

The QE began to vibrate as general quarters blared from the speakers. A few seconds later, a loud banging started in the passageway outside our door. I stuck my head out and saw steel rivets popping loose as the ship strained through the turn. I ducked back inside and slammed the door.

The ship leaned into another ninety-degree turn and came upright, groaning and trembling as she picked up speed, running in a straight line to get away from whatever was out in the dark.

We sat in our life preservers, staring at each other, ready to move. After what seemed like a long time, the ship slowed noticeably, and a voice came through the speakers to tell us we had just outrun a German warship.

An ensign later told me that the QE's radar had spotted what they thought was a German battleship twenty miles away, steaming directly toward us. "We thought the boilers were going to blow for sure," he said. "The captain had her up to almost forty knots. The pressure gauges were pegged."

This meant the *Queen*, over three blocks long and weighing 80,000 tons, had plowed through the water at over forty miles an hour. No wonder rivets popped out of her skin. But the captain saved the day, and that was all that mattered.

The next morning dawned cold and gray. Without much sleep, I was on deck early. I could see a dark sliver off the bow that turned out to be Iceland. Soon, friendly aircraft appeared overhead. We turned south with fighter planes above us until two destroyers came out to escort us into port. We entered the sheltered coastal area of northwest Scotland and sailed past small fishing ports and farmland. We docked at Greenock, down the river from Glasgow.

We disembarked and immediately separated our six officers and two hundred enlisted men from the rest of the troops. I noticed that everybody in my group handled themselves well, moving with an athletic grace. Every man I talked to had been an athlete in high school or college. The Army obviously had something special in mind for us, but we still didn't know what.

A British sergeant made his way through the crowd and led us to a passenger train waiting on the quay. We loaded into several coaches, and the train pulled out without our knowing where we were going. For supper, we ate beans and franks, stew, and other combinations of canned C rations. The cities and countryside were dark.

At daybreak, we rolled into the outskirts of bombed-out Liverpool. The city looked desolate, almost uninhabitable; it was my first close-up view of what war can do. British lorries took us from the rail station in Lichfield to a depressing compound and dumped us onto a parade ground surrounded by dingy, two-story barracks that looked at least a hundred years old. Where was the rest of the American Army?

A British officer welcomed us to Whittington Barracks and pointed out two buildings for enlisted men and a third for officers.

Inside our quarters, sagging double bunks stood against drab walls. In the middle of the floor a coal-burning stove provided our only heat. Naked light bulbs hung from the ceiling. The place looked bleak and cold.

I dropped my gear by a bunk. The mattress consisted of three straw-filled cushions that were supposed to lie end to end. Try as I might, there seemed to be no way a person could sleep on these three "pally-asses," as they were called.

A British Tommy brought us two coarse woolen blankets each. He showed us how to set up our mattresses and took us out back to a building that housed the toilet and showers. After learning the Germans bombed almost every night, I was glad to see an underground air raid shelter at the rear of the barracks.

The next morning we walked to the Navy, Army, and Air Forces Institutes canteen, a sort of PX containing a post office, telegraph station, and even a pub. By picking from a list of code numbers that stood for standard phrases, I composed canned telegrams to let everyone know I was okay.

We picked up our British ration books so that we could buy personal items, and the local women's volunteer group served us hot chocolate, tea, and stout, a sort of warm beer. Because of the German blockade, their offerings were slim, but we appreciated their effort.

As the senior lieutenant by date of rank, I continued acting as commander of our company-sized unit. I tried to find out what was going on, but only the brigadier had any information about our assignment, and he was off training with his brigade and wouldn't be back for several days.

Left to ourselves, we did calisthenics and went on long marches to keep in shape. In the evenings, we hung around the NAAFI club and the Brits started calling us the American Group.

I wrote lots of letters home while I waited to see what happened next.

3
Operation Torch

I finally got an office call with the brigadier, the British equivalent of the American Army's lowest-ranking general. Wearing a tailored uniform, he was a dapper, sallow-faced man with a thin mustache.

"Sir, why are we here?"

"You don't know?" The brigadier spoke with a clipped, upper-class accent.

"No, sir, I don't."

"Well, you're attached to my brigade."

"We are? What are we?"

"You're a provisional company. You're here to learn our tactics and integrate with British forces. Our superiors want to see if we can work together in combat."

So this was some kind of experiment. "What do we do next?"

"Tomorrow you start training with us. But first you've got to turn in your American rifles."

The next day, we exchanged our Springfield rifles for the British Enfield, another weapon dating back to World War I. The Enfield fired a different caliber bullet than the Springfield, and if we were going to fight with the British, we had to use the same ammunition. The Enfield cocked itself when the bolt was pushed forward, unlike the Springfield, which cocked when the bolt was pulled back. The Enfield took some dexterity and a combination of handwork to slam the bolt forward. We spent a couple of days acquainting the men with it.

We drank and trained with our British comrades for three weeks. Most were tough professionals who had already fought the Germans in France, Belgium, and Norway.

During this time, we struggled with cultural differences, especially at meals. In the British mess, there was a lot of tradition. Even in the field, if not under fire, the Brits would set up tables, toast the King with a tot of whiskey, and sing dozens of verses of drinking songs like "Poor Little Sheep."

In the evenings I would go over to the NAAFI club and drink stout with those guys and try to find out how to stay alive in combat. As veterans, they seemed a bit amused at some of my questions, but I learned several things from them the American Army didn't teach.

The first thing they told me was to get myself a "bahtman."

"How do you spell it?" I said.

"B-A-T. Baht."

"What does a batman do?"

"You'd probably call him an orderly."

"You have to be a colonel in the American Army to have an orderly, so that won't work."

"Charlie, do you want to stay alive?"

"Yes."

"Then get yourself a batman."

"What does a batman do?"

"Well, first he needs to stay alive. Survival's the name of the game in combat. Your batman's first job when he comes under fire is to dig himself a slit trench. He's got to get his head down to keep from getting killed. He's no use to you dead. Then he digs a slit trench for you. Because, Charlie, if you're an officer in command and you come under fire, you're going to be so damn busy figuring out how to get out of the mess you're in, you'll never have time to dig your own slit. Next, your batman digs both slits deeper, making them foxholes. Then he starts making his own foxhole large enough so that two men can get in it."

At that time, the U.S. army taught one-man foxholes, but the Brits said, "If you want your men to stay alive, Charlie, have them dig two-man foxholes. Then they can support each other."

I came to believe the British were right. In a foxhole, two men back-to-back can cover 360 degrees, and they can spell each other, taking turns sleeping and watching for the enemy. Two men in the same hole can provide each other emotional support and help overcome the natural fear we all faced. So I decided our company would have two-man foxholes.

I knew I was going to get myself a batman. I told the other officers about it and we selected six good enlisted men to be our runners, which platoon leaders and company commanders would normally have anyway. These troops would be our batmen.

I also learned what a rifle squad was supposed to do when fired on. If they didn't do something quick, they'd get shot up. The British training exercise for their squads taught them to react automatically.

They put the men in an attack line, and a sergeant would yell, "You're under fire!" The squad would hit the ground and establish a base of fire with their Bren gun, a rapid-fire weapon similar to our Browning automatic rifle. Two or three riflemen would lay down covering fire while the rest of the squad flanked the enemy.

The worst thing a soldier can do in combat is curl up in a ball and freeze. That little drill gave a soldier something to do besides panic when he came under fire, and I incorporated the tactic into our group.

The third thing I learned was crack and thump.

One night over beer, I asked a British company commander what he was doing in training the next day.

"Crack and thump," he said.

"What's crack and thump?"

"Come with us tomorrow. We'll show you."

The next day he took me out on the firing range and handed me a sound-powered telephone.

"There are a lot of foxholes down range," he said. "Walk out exactly a thousand feet and get in one."

It was a damp, misty morning and a weak sun lit the day through a gray haze. I walked out on the range, counting my steps and stringing wire behind me. At a thousand feet, I jumped into a foxhole and scrunched down, not knowing what to expect.

A voice crackled through the phone. "Listen," it said.

The next thing I heard was a shot, then another. I rang up the phone real fast.

"Did you hear anything, Charlie?"

"Yeah, I heard you SOBs shooting at me!"

"Well, listen again," he said. "Carefully."

This time I heard two sounds: a sharp crack over my head and the sound of the gun firing.

"Do that again," I said.

I heard another crack followed by the shot.

"You're getting it, aren't you, Charlie? The difference between the crack of the bullet and the thump of the shot you're hearing is a thousand feet. That's what a thousand feet sounds like."

I remembered from science classes that sound travels a thousand some odd feet a second. At two thousand feet per second, the supersonic bullet was getting to me twice as fast. Though I didn't know the term then, what I was hearing was a little sonic boom—the crack of the bullet parting the air—and then thump, the sound of the gun firing.

So I started counting. *Crack!* "A thousand one." Thump. With a little practice at different distances, I could tell how far away the gun was. If I heard "crack-bang" or just "bang," the shooter was right on top of me.

The British taught crack and thump to all their men. They would place them in foxholes at various distances and fire different friendly and enemy weapons over them so they learned the sound each weapon made. By counting from the sound of the crack, they knew the approximate distance they were from the enemy. I followed their example and trained my men on the technique.

During our time at Whittington Barracks, I rode the train into London one weekend. Bricks and debris lined the streets of the cities along the way. The Battle of Britain was long over, but waves of German bombers still crossed the Channel.

As I rolled past the devastation, I thought of my father in the Spanish-American War and my uncles in World War I. I hoped I would measure up.

In London, barrage balloons hovered over the city, and there was rubble everywhere. As we pulled into an underground station, children were playing on the platform around piles of blankets, suitcases, and stacked boxes. People obviously lived down here, people who had nothing at all to do with the ongoing struggle; they just happened to be in the way.

I finally understood that war was not a contest played according to strict rules by willing participants. There was nothing noble or uplifting about it. War was a dirty, deadly business that would destroy anything and anybody in its path without a thought.

Despite the hardships, the English showed a great deal of stamina and grit. The destruction seemed to bring them closer together and they somehow coped.

Amid the ruins, I saw posters and banners that read, "Dig for Victory." Below a pub's broken window, someone had stenciled "Take Courage."

Whole sections of the city were without electricity, heat, or water, but lorries appeared in the streets with food and something hot to drink. One truck was apparently a mobile laundry; the sign on its side read, "National Emergency Washing Service." From tables in front of their wrecked stores, shopkeepers sold whatever goods they could salvage. A grim determination to prevail had settled over England.

Back at Whittington Barracks, I felt increasingly separated from my life in America. School and athletics seemed far away and I readied myself for the upcoming reality of combat. By mid-October, I had orders to assume command of Company C, Provisional Replacement Group. At last we knew who we were, but we still had no mission. Evening conversations at the NAAFI turned serious.

In early November, the adjutant handed me a sealed package with orders to give each man a pamphlet after we left England. Under no circumstances was I to open the package before then.

The next day we loaded onto British lorries and moved to Liverpool with the British brigade. We transferred our gear to the *Scythia*, a converted World War I-era liner, and sailed north out of the Irish Sea. My company was the only American unit on board.

Wearing American uniforms, but equipped with British winter gear, rifles, and shoes, we looked like some kind of hybrid soldiers, cast off by America but not yet a part of the British army.

Everybody had an idea about our destination and soldiers will gamble on anything, so we formed a pool. I threw in a couple pounds on Narvik, Norway, because of the winter clothing.

One guy thought we were going to Canada to protect against invasion by Germans lurking off the coast in U-boats. A few bet on Murmansk in the USSR, which seemed too far away to me. The supply lines would be too long and treacherous. Several thought we were going back to Dieppe, France, where a raid had met with disaster only a couple months before. Others thought maybe Dunkirk again.

Meanwhile, the *Scythia* sailed west, toward America. After a couple of days, the brigadier gave me permission to open our orders. Nobody won the pool. It would be North Africa, as part of Operation Torch, the largest Allied invasion of the war to date, and already underway. The British had been fighting the Italians and Germans in Egypt and Libya for two years. Now, Allied forces were attacking at Casablanca, Oran, and Algiers to try to keep the Axis forces from reaching Tunis and Bizerte, their evacuation ports.

Our convoy would be in the second wave. First, we sailed almost halfway back across the Atlantic. Then we circled south of the Azores and east again to the Strait of Gibraltar. The strait was only twenty miles wide and we drilled constantly on how to abandon ship in case German U-boats hit us.

But we sailed through the strait unnoticed late one night. We saw the lights of Morocco on the right and Spain on the left, the first lights I'd seen since leaving America. Gibraltar itself was blacked out, its moonlit hulk looming on the horizon.

The captain announced over the loudspeaker that we would stand offshore as a ready reserve for the invasion forces, and I went below to pack for combat, not knowing what to expect. The quartermaster issued each officer a small bottle of Scotch. I thought about storing mine in my bedroll, which I wouldn't carry with me, but slipped it into my jacket pocket instead.

Sometime after midnight, our orders changed and we sailed toward Algiers. We were going in. U-boats attacked us at the entrance to the harbor, and a sudden explosion off the port side lit the sky. Our ship clung to an illusion of safety in the middle of her escorts and moved steadily toward shore. A destroyer, siren whooping, cut across our wake. Our escorts dropped depth charges off their sterns and fired them two at a time from Y-guns that catapulted the charges in different directions.

Some exploded within a few hundred yards of our ship, throwing up waterspouts higher than our mast. Another ship exploded, setting fire to the sea. Geysers erupted around us like giant fists punching up from the bottom of the sea; they were an awesome sight.

I grabbed my musette bag and hurried down to be with my men. They occupied the ship's empty swimming pool several decks below, just behind the number one hold. The pool, fifty feet wide and ten feet deep, was stacked to the top with bunks. Personal gear draped over the bunks clanked and swayed with the ship's movement.

The men were antsy. I walked around the pool, chatting with them, telling them to stay ready. As nervous and excited as I felt, I'm not sure I had any calming effect at all. I hadn't a clue what awaited us. I was near the ladder at the edge of the pool when a sudden loud explosion jolted everyone out of whatever thoughts they were having. The ship groaned and shuddered. The lights flickered, dimmed, and went out.

I pulled a flashlight from my musette bag and snapped it on. The ship started to list heavily to one side, creaking. "Prepare to abandon ship!" blared over the loudspeakers.

All the practice drills we'd held paid off. There was no panic as we climbed out of the pool and moved up the ladders to our assigned station, a lifeboat on the rear starboard side. With three thousand troops on board the *Scythia*, almost four times its normal civilian passenger load, we hadn't nearly enough lifeboats. The Navy had added some little rafts, but they looked almost homemade, like mattresses with ropes around them. The idea was to slide these things down a chute into the water where folks were supposed to grab on to them.

As we crouched on deck, the noise of the battle increased and I began to feel helpless. Our fate was in the hands of the Navy and an enemy we couldn't engage. As infantrymen, we could do little to protect ourselves, so we cringed at our assigned station while the battle raged.

Aircraft dove at the ship, raking it with machine gun and cannon fire. We ducked and cinched up our life preservers, ready to jump into the water. A machine gun mount above me began firing. Antiaircraft tracers from our escorts ripped into the sky, exploding in orange fireballs that illuminated bombers droning overhead. A German fighter, on fire, its engine screaming, spun across and exploded astern. The noise was deafening. Bullets clanged off the ironworks, chirping and buzzing around the deck.

We cowered under the lifeboats and against the bulkheads. I felt naked and wanted off this deathtrap.

Then, just as suddenly, the planes were gone. After ten minutes of relative quiet, word came over the PA system to stand fast at all positions. The order to abandon ship was rescinded. A torpedo had hit us near the bow, but sealing the compartments had stopped the flooding and stabilized the ship.

Enemy aircraft attacked the convoy sporadically all night. Tracers and shells burst in the sky, creating a deadly display of light and color. I wanted desperately to get into a hole somewhere on land.

My company clerk took a bullet in the leg and fell near me. We took him to the ship's infirmary and placed him on an operating table. The medics were treating two other wounded men, one with a huge gash across the side of his head. We watched the doc calmly sew a raw flap of skin back in place.

Then he turned to my clerk, who looked pale and sweaty. The doctor asked him where he was hit, and he pointed to the inside of his right calf, where blood seeped through his legging. When a corpsman turned his foot, the kid winced and I saw the nose of a small caliber bullet sticking out of his calf. The doc laid him back on the table, cut off his trousers and started to work.

I left when they told me it was a clean penetration and not severe. My first wounded man. He must have been evacuated to England, because I never saw him again. He was the only man I had who could type.

At daybreak, the ship made a right turn and sailed toward shore, listing at twenty degrees. We limped through the breakwater under small-arms fire, but the shooting stopped by the time the ship docked at the empty wharf.

We grabbed as much gear as we could carry and moved out of the harbor area on the double in case of another air attack. I had no map and no specific orders for my company except to clear the area west of the dock and engage any opposition we encountered. I think the Brits just wanted us out of their hair.

We moved up an inclined road parallel to where our ship sat listing at anchor. Bombers must have been on the way, because our ack-ack started up again. Fragments from shells exploding overhead sounded like hail on the rooftops. I picked up a jagged piece an inch long. Its heat blistered my fingers and I dropped it quickly. I never picked up another shell fragment.

I didn't want to get into combat in town, fighting from building to building. My British friends at Whittington had warned me that urban street fighting could be full of vicious surprises, so I wanted to move to open spaces.

Algiers was a good-sized town of ancient, whitewashed houses fronting narrow streets that intersected at odd angles. Nobody was around to tell me what to do, so I did what I thought best and got the hell out of there. A little range of mountains encircled the city and up there was where I wanted to be. As our antiaircraft guns continued firing, I moved the company up a slope and followed trolley lines to higher ground. Bombs exploded in the harbor, but we didn't get fired on and never saw any civilians.

A couple of miles into the hills, we came to a tunnel. We secured both ends and waited inside where I felt reasonably safe from stray bombs. We had food for three days and plenty of ammunition. By then maybe I could figure out what to do next.

Algiers was bombed nightly. From the safety of our tunnel, we watched the searchlights and antiaircraft fire lace the sky with light trails. After two days, we foraged out and made contact with locals who provided plenty of wine and bread. We never saw anybody hostile. Except for his planes, the enemy seemed to have vanished.

On the third afternoon, I ran into an American patrol led by a lieutenant from the 39th Infantry Regiment of the 9th Division. They had captured the airport at Maison Blanc so RAF Spitfires could move over from Gibraltar. The lieutenant told me the 1st Infantry Division was also in the area. Except for a few scattered pockets of Italian troops, who surrendered immediately, they hadn't run into any resistance. That was comforting.

That evening we hooked up with the brigade again. They had been in an intermittent battle with the French Foreign Legion. One day they'd shoot at each other, and the next day they'd drink wine together. In the first chaotic days of the invasion, the Vichy French didn't know whether to fight with us or against us.

The British assigned my company all the crappy jobs—night patrols, digging for mines with bayonets, pulling guard duty to keep the locals from stealing everything we had. I think we got these shit details because we were rookies, and the Brits didn't much trust us. Now that we were in the war zone for real, nobody seemed to take any interest in us, and they avoided us as if they didn't want to be caught near us when a firefight broke out.

That got old fast. After a few days, I arranged an office call with the brigadier. I walked in, saluted, and came right to the point. "Sir, this is not working out for me and my men."

"What do you want to do, son?"

"I'd like to rejoin the American Army."

The brigadier looked at me steadily for a moment. "Take off," he said. Just like that, no orders, nothing. The cooperative experiment dreamed up by desk jockeys somewhere was over.

I saluted the brigadier and went over to the 39th Regimental Headquarters to see how we could join them. The adjutant made some calls and told me to bring half the men and officers back to the 39th and send the other half to the 1st Infantry Division with my executive officer.

I ran back to the company and split it in half. The XO and his half left with an officer from the 1st Division. The rest of us joined the 39th Regimental Combat Team, to be assigned wherever needed. The next morning, I reported to 1st Battalion, Company A, bivouacked in tents near the Maison Blanc Airport.

I handed off the personnel records I'd carried around for my bastard provisional company and took the rest of the day off, happy to be back in the American Army.

4
Algeria

Three months had passed since our troop ship limped into North Africa and I joined the 9th Division. Strung out along the Mediterranean coast of Algeria, 1st Battalion waited with the rest of the 39th Regiment for supporting artillery, still languishing in Morocco more than 500 rugged miles to the west.

In Tunisia, the war raged against the retreating Germans, but we couldn't face Rommel's tanks without our big guns. The units trying that at Kasserine Pass suffered a devastating defeat.

I was now a B Company rifle platoon leader, charged with securing strategic sites around Philippeville from saboteurs and thieves. A good-sized town with rail service and a major highway, Philippeville lay snuggled in a natural harbor where three or four Liberty ships unloaded supplies almost daily.

Since German planes sometimes raided from Sicily or Sardinia, we tethered cigar-shaped barrage balloons over the ships and docks. These balloons, measuring fifteen feet across and thirty to fifty feet long, protected against low-level attacks.

One night after a heavy windstorm, the Air Corps called to say German paratroopers were landing on their base near Constantine, forty miles south. We sent troops in full combat gear racing off to fight the invaders, but it turned out to be a false alarm.

What the Air Corps had seen were several of our barrage balloons that had broken loose during the storm. Dragging along in the dark, they must have scared the hell out of the airmen. I couldn't blame them. We were all new to the war, and we were jittery.

The French had a garrison up the hill from Philippeville's main business district. French troops normally housed there were off fighting the Germans, so my company moved in.

We officers had our own villa, with a large patio overlooking the bay on the rear side of the garrison, a great place to relax at the end of the day. The enlisted barracks was in a walled compound, where the men rigged up an outdoor shower in the courtyard.

A couple hundred feet away, on the other side of the ancient stone wall, stood a four-story dormitory that housed young women. From their upstairs windows, they started watching the soldiers take showers. After a while it became a ritual. The men would stroll out to the shower naked, putting on a show while the women pointed and made comments about talent and equipment. To cut down on potential problems, the battalion put the women's building off limits.

Not that it mattered much to the men. Several whorehouses lined the waterfront and most bistros attracted their share of independent prostitutes. Our soldiers kept them plenty busy, drinking and carousing being their favorite off-duty pastime.

After local hoodlums roughed up several soldiers, the British, French, and American units formed joint patrols to police the hot spots. I commanded this patrol several times. Our job was to close the bistros and whorehouses at dark and make sure no blackout violations helped German bombers find us.

A lot of the madams running the houses were French. Most spoke English and, since prostitution was legal in France, they knew well how to cater to their clientele.

We walked into a building one night and the madam met us at the door. She was older, her face a little saggy and wilted around the edges, which heavy makeup couldn't hide.

"Are all the soldiers out?"

The madam nodded. "Yes," she said around a lit cigarette.

Then we heard a muffled noise inside the building. "Let's see," I said.

We walked down a semidark hallway, the madam trailing behind. We stopped at a room where we heard grunts and bed noises through the locked door. Our British Tommy popped the knob with his rifle butt and the door opened.

Inside the tiny room, a small bed jiggled and squeaked as a soldier pumped away at the woman beneath him, her legs gripping his waist. The soldier's pants were down around his shoes. He hadn't even bothered to take off his shirt, which had a 1st Infantry Division patch on it.

"I'll be through in a minute," he said, not missing a beat.

I stepped out of the room and pulled the door closed. There were no 1st Division units around Philippeville. This guy had to be AWOL. The 1st was fighting in Tunisia, and even if he was a support troop, his unit was a hell of a lot closer to the war zone than where he was right now.

We let the guy finish and he walked out of the room a few minutes later buckling his belt. One of our jobs was to turn AWOL soldiers over to the military police, because we couldn't process them. Didn't even want to.

I looked at my AWOL soldier. He was just a kid and I knew supply trucks passed through here almost around the clock on their way to the front. "Do you know how to get back to your unit?"

"Yes, sir."

"I tell you what," I said. "You get your ass back up to your outfit and I won't do anything about finding you here."

The soldier saluted and took off.

The next day we had beach patrol duty. It was a lark, and we didn't do much of anything except enjoy the day. About noon, one of my men pointed to a convoy of ships sailing down the coast.

I scanned the sea with my field glasses and spotted five cargo ships steaming east three or four miles offshore. They were probably on their way to resupply Malta, a strategic island outpost a few hundred miles east of us. The convoy was the first I'd seen except for those that came into our port, usually escorted by British warships.

As I watched the ships crawl across the horizon, one of them exploded. Almost before the muffled sound of the explosion reached us, another blew up, and after a few seconds, another. In a matter of minutes, all five ships went down and there wasn't a damn thing we could do about it. Apparently, U-boats had been following them. There were no other ships or planes in sight.

We had no way to get to them and never saw any debris. My binoculars weren't good enough to detect lifeboats, but I never heard of any survivors.

We continued to pull guard duty at nearby installations and patrol the town and surrounding areas. I liked to ride along on supply runs to our battalion headquarters in Bougie, located on the coastal highway west of Philippeville. We'd pick up supplies, mostly cigarettes, and I'd get to see what was going on at headquarters and talk to a few friends, a pleasant way to screw off for a few hours.

One morning, I laid a Thompson submachine gun in the back of a jeep, jumped into the front beside my driver, and we headed down the coast road. We weren't pulling our quarter-ton trailer, and we planned to throw whatever supplies we picked up into the back seat.

It was a great day for a joyride. The sun spread a soft yellow glow across the countryside. The road swerved inland through a shady wooded area, then back along the coast. The Mediterranean on our right was a deep, rich blue beneath the cloudless sky.

In Bougie we spent an hour trying to learn available war news. We picked up cigarettes, a week-old newspaper, and a few odds and ends. Then we headed back around the coast.

Close to Djidjelli, we drove through a grove of cork trees growing almost to the edge of the water. I heard monkeys chattering in the trees near the road. This would be a good place to test the submachine gun. "Stop here a minute."

The driver pulled the jeep off the road. I could smell the sea. There was no traffic, no civilians anywhere. We were three hundred miles from the fighting in Tunisia.

I walked fifty yards off the road to where monkeys sat chattering in the trees, sunlight filtering across them. They stopped and watched me. The Thompson was still in the back of the jeep. Okay. Charlie, you're in Africa. Time to hunt some game.

I walked to the road and asked the driver if he wanted to see me shoot a monkey. I grabbed the Thompson and we walked a few yards into the forest before I spotted a large male squatting in a tree. There I was, in Africa with a weapon, thinking I was some big-game hunter. I lifted the Thompson and let loose a good burst, the barrel rising as the gun kicked against my shoulder.

Screaming and jabbering erupted around us. The monkey I had aimed at disappeared into the forest. I hadn't hit anything that I could see. Big-game hunter, my ass.

My driver snickered. "Good thing that monkey ain't a German."

"Yeah, we'd both be dead."

Far behind the front lines, we had mail call at the end of each duty day. Men gathered round and a clerk called the names of those who had letters or packages. After months of not hearing my name, I quit showing up. It was too painful to go day after day without a letter. I had been on the move so much there was no telling when I might get mail. It was probably still going to the Brits.

One day the company clerk called. "Lieutenant, you've got several bags of mail down here."

Finally. "Send it up."

I dumped the bags on the patio floor and sorted the mail into piles by date and sender. I read Ruth's letters first. Many were several pages long and I lingered over them, catching up on her life since I'd been gone. I sniffed at the pages, longing for her scent, but they had come too far.

Ruth had returned safely to Enid and was working as a secretary for the high school. There was no hint in her letters that she was being sexually harassed. She didn't tell me about that until after the war.

But some things she wrote puzzled me, such as, "I'm really enjoying the magazine."

Next, I read the letters from my mother. She tried to be upbeat and positive, but I could feel the worry and tension behind her words. She couldn't put aside the fact that her son was in a war zone.

I had several packages—cookies, a dried-up chocolate cake, and some cigars. I never smoked, but I chewed tobacco while playing semipro baseball. That stopped the night before we got married. I was courting Ruth on the couch at her house and she said, "Honey, you've got to quit chewing that filthy tobacco."

I didn't chew much anyhow, but she didn't like tobacco kisses so I promised I wouldn't use it any more. But I craved it again when I got overseas, and I kidded Ruth in my letters that I missed chewing tobacco almost as much as I missed her, trying to keep it light. So she started sending cigars, and I had several boxes in this mailbag. It would be nice to smoke one every now and then, if only to keep away mosquitoes and flies.

The Army furnished smokes in our rations, little packs of four or five cigarettes. Guys who didn't smoke traded them on the local economy, even for sex, so they were a valuable commodity as we settled into the routine of living like support troops.

I had been writing my brother more candid letters than I wrote to Ruth and my mother. I told him I'd seen some action at sea, that the Germans had torpedoed us. As an officer, I censored my own letters, so I took a more liberal interpretation of censorship than I did with my men. I might tell Stanley if we saw combat, but I couldn't mention locations or what ship I was on or how many men we'd lost or the names of soldiers wounded or killed.

The newspapers stateside regularly reported the progress of the Allied Forces soon after military actions, and my brother was sharp. He had a world map and tried to keep track as I moved from place to place. The fourth letter from Stanley read, "Dear Charlie. I figured out from your mail that you are not in the middle of combat. I think you might be somewhere in Algeria."

Exactly right. It felt good to have him following along. I didn't feel so alone.

Then one of his letters read, "*Reader's Digest* is offering a lifetime subscription to any serviceman for the cost of a 25-dollar war bond, so I have sent in a subscription. Momma and Ruth are fine. I'm getting along okay and enjoying my work at the refinery. Be careful. Love, Stanley. P.S. I put the subscription in Ruth's name."

A nice gesture but, boy, he sure didn't have much faith in me getting out of this war alive.

My wife enjoyed *Reader's Digest* for over fifty years. I have no idea how much postage she spent on their millionaire contests, but she entered hundreds of times.

"Honey," she'd say, "You're the expert. If we win this million dollars, should we take a lump sum or lifetime installments?"

"Oh, let's just take it all now and blow it."

During the last year of her life, when she was so sick, I sat by her bed and read her the latest copy of the magazine. Then I'd try to get her involved in the millionaire contest to get her mind off how bad she was feeling.

Finally, one day she said, "Honey, you fill it out for me. I don't need a million dollars anymore."

A few weeks after she died, I notified the magazine's subscription office and they connected me to someone who remembered the lifetime subscriptions. I told the man my story and how much we enjoyed their magazine all those years. I asked him how much it would cost to keep the subscription.

"Mr. Scheffel," he said, "we'll just transfer that lifetime subscription to your name. You don't owe us anything."

There are some nice people. That magazine has given me priceless memories. Each time I open it, I feel blessed, thankful for my brother's gift, and thankful for the wonderful years I got to spend with Ruth.

In late February 1943, I transferred to the Setif area southwest of Philippeville and rejoined Company A. We still didn't have our artillery with us and continued to guard communication lines, bridges, and the railroad between Algiers and Constantine. While the German army fought for its life, the Allies feared saboteurs or paratroopers might create havoc behind the lines.

My platoon guarded the railway station in Setif near the company headquarters. This was a major rail line, vital to moving supplies and equipment eastward into the combat zone, running from Oran in western Algeria to Bizerte and Tunis on the northeastern tip of Africa. Setif had several sets of tracks and a small switching yard for assembling trains.

General Eisenhower traveled often from his headquarters in Algiers to Constantine and other areas close to the Tunisian front to get first-hand information on the war, particularly when things weren't going well.

Not long after the debacle around Kasserine Pass that cost General Fredendall his command, a dust-caked dispatch rider motorcycled in from Algiers with orders for us to make preparations to accommodate a British army female arriving that night. The only British female important enough for such elaborate advance notice had to be Kay Summersby, General Eisenhower's personal driver and companion.

Summersby began working for the general in England during the summer of 1942 and their relationship quickly became controversial. Vulgar jokes floated around the American Army about Ike and his attractive driver, who had modeled in London before her military enlistment.

41

The British, on the other hand, were not inclined to joke about it. By now, eight months later, many Brits resented that an American general worked and traveled in such close contact with one of their women. It was unseemly. Coarse rumors circulated about how their army had furnished Eisenhower a British girl to sleep with. Wasn't it enough that the overpaid and oversexed Americans had already seduced half the women in England? Did Ike have to shove it in their faces, too? Bloody Yanks.

British officers I served with had said, "Where's your wife, Charlie? Want us to assign you a girl, too?"

So we expected Kay Summersby that night. We cordoned off a waiting room and cleaned up a place for her to sleep.

One of our lieutenants, a first sergeant before the war and several years older than the rest of us, considered himself quite the ladies' man. A French woman lived with him in the officers' apartment building in downtown Setif, but as we prepared for our guest, he couldn't help boasting, "I think I'll come over here tonight and get me some of Ike's gal."

"Yeah," I said, "and go straight to the stockade. You better keep your hands to yourself."

The lieutenant wouldn't have a chance if he bothered Kay Summersby and he knew it. He was just running his mouth.

Summersby arrived alone in the general's staff car, a khaki-colored cloth covering his four stars on the front plate. She was in her mid-thirties, dark hair, a lot better looking than the pictures taken of her during the period.

Charming and engaging, she had dinner with us at a local restaurant and seemed genuinely interested in hearing about my training with the British army.

She left early the next morning for the forward headquarters in Constantine. It had been a pleasure and we all thought Ike was a lucky man. She was good company, no doubt a good driver, and probably a good lover, too. Or maybe she just held the old man's hand. Maybe he just wanted to have a woman around his office. I've heard different opinions about their relationship, and I think historians might be treating Eisenhower kindly, but that's okay with me. Ike's sex life didn't have a hell of a lot to do with his combat abilities unless it helped clear his mind.

Later, at the joint battle group school I attended after fighting in southern Tunisia, several British officers still complained that Ike had a British woman but Alexander and Montgomery didn't have American ones.

Young men, no matter the circumstances, are full of hormones and interested in sex, even if they have to make it up.

5

Under Fire

The Afrika Korps was on the run again after their fleeting victory at Kasserine Pass, and the 39th Regiment was ordered into southern Tunisia. We trucked to Camp Constantine and then east to Tebessa, a supply depot with miles and miles of stacked equipment and supplies to support the fighting.

We stopped one evening on a ridge in sparse, rugged country at the northern edge of the Sahara Desert. A few hundred feet high, the ridge overlooked a tangled maze of canyons and dry creek beds, or wadis, as they were called. In the fading light, we saw a line of hills maybe four miles across the valley. They would be our next objective, but tomorrow we would rest and wait for units strung out behind us to catch up.

The sun was almost down and it was getting cold again when I walked through the platoon and warned the men to spread out, dig in, and not light fires. I posted guards along the crest and walked back to my area, satisfied with our security. Later, the cooks brought up canisters of hot food from somewhere behind us, and we had canned meat, peas, cookies, and coffee for supper.

The next day, without movement orders, we lazed around, enjoying the warmth of the morning sun. The cooks sent up another hot meal, this time powdered eggs.

The chaplain held church services on the backside of the ridge. I made the rounds of our defensive positions and stopped by the service. As we got closer to the front and the possibility of dying became real, more men turned to religion. It was comforting to stand in a group of GIs and recite the Lord's Prayer together. That's when my soldiers looked most like what they were, a bunch of young kids.

After church, I sat leaning against a tree and started a letter to Ruth, wishing more of her mail would catch up with me.

A hundred feet away, a soldier stood in the bed of a quartermaster truck, working on a .50-caliber machine gun fastened to a ring mount behind the cab.

I finished my letter and was walking back to my command post when I heard the sound of an aircraft engine. I looked back and saw a plane standing on its left wing as it banked around toward the ridge. It was a German fighter, black crosses on its wingtips, tan and brown desert camouflage paint in sharp contrast against the blue sky. The plane completed its turn, flipped level and swooped down on us. Lights flashed on its wings and bullets tore through our bivouac area, kicking up little fountains of dust. Soldiers scattered.

I hit the dirt as the plane roared over almost low enough for me to touch its gray belly. It passed directly over the quartermaster truck.

Miraculously, the soldier in the truck bed hadn't been hit. He bounced up and stepped into the ring mount. Coolly, he swung the machine gun around and held the trigger down in a long burst, spitting out red tracers that arced up and chewed into the German fighter as it climbed away from him.

The kid had it on him all the way. He probably never would have hit the plane if it had been flying across his line of fire, but there was no deflection to adjust for and the plane started smoking, its engine sputtering as it banked left.

Climbing slowly, the plane struggled up and suddenly the canopy flew open. The plane banked again and the pilot tumbled out. His parachute blossomed as the plane nosed over and crashed out of sight. We heard the explosion and saw black smoke rising against the sky.

I watched the pilot float down, thinking he was lucky he bailed out. Most of my soldiers were still in their holes. Many wouldn't come out until someone told them to. Probably good advice, but I stood and watched the pilot hit the ground. I checked a few landmarks and thought I could find where he landed, which was closer to our side of the valley than to his own.

After making sure we had no wounded soldiers, I decided to go get him. I knew how to make a litter with two rifles and a coat so that four men could carry a wounded man. I was still wearing a combat field jacket over my coveralls, so I rounded up four guys to come with me in case the pilot was hurt.

We walked down off the crest into no man's land. I oriented myself and looked back to make sure I could return to the same place. In less than half an hour, we walked to where I thought the pilot had landed. The ground looked disturbed, like something had been dragged over it. The trail led to a little wadi a hundred feet away.

We crept forward, using what cover we had, weapons at the ready. The pilot lay on his back inside the wadi. He looked about twenty-five, definitely German, with a Luftwaffe patch sewn over the right breast pocket of his dirty flight suit: an eagle, wings spread, holding a swastika in its talons. A parachute lay crumpled beside him. He still wore his canvas flight helmet, goggles pushed up, the lower half of his face smudged with oil. He watched us silently as we approached.

He didn't seem to have any wounds, no bleeding that I could see.

"Where are you hurt? Are you okay?"

No reply, no reaction at all.

I knew he had to be hurt or he would have run. I grabbed his arm. Nothing. But when I moved his left leg, he winced.

I took off my jacket, buttoned it, and a couple of the soldiers ran their rifles from the bottom up through the sleeves. We laid it next to him, sat him up, and got him on it. The four guys lifted him and we started back.

With the pilot on our makeshift litter, we had to stay in the dry streambeds as much as possible, avoiding the steeper and rougher, but more direct route back to our lines. After an hour of wandering vaguely west, tired and increasingly frustrated, we came to the foot of a rocky slope. We scrambled up the side, the four soldiers cursing and grunting as they dragged and pushed the litter up the hill. The pilot never said a word.

At the top of the slope, I heard the sudden shriek of incoming artillery fire. We hunkered down as the rounds screamed over, topped the ridge where my troops were, and exploded somewhere farther west.

For several minutes, shells roared overhead, the last one exploding near enough to shake the earth. I looked at the four men I had brought with me on this fool's errand. They pressed themselves into the ground, trying to disappear. I hunkered lower. Was I going to get us all killed?

The pilot didn't flinch or change his expression as another round tore over, closer still, making ten or so altogether. The bastard never moved. I'd had it.

"Goddamn Germans!" I yelled. "We're trying to save one of you sonsabitches and your asshole friends are trying to kill us all. What the fuck's the matter with you people?"

I got close to his face and yelled every curse word I could think of— about him, about his mother, and about his sorry-ass country. Rage and adrenaline rushed through me. Exhilarated, I leaned even closer, squeezing the rifle in my hands.

"Fuck Hitler and fuck you, too!" I screamed into his face, spraying flecks of spit on him.

The pilot looked at me without speaking, waiting. I stared into his eyes for what seemed like a long time. He never moved or took his eyes off mine. Finally, the rage drained out of me and I backed away.

I noticed then that the firing had stopped, for no reason I could see. We struggled on, taking no more artillery fire as we climbed exhausted back up the ridge to our bivouac area.

"Set him down in the shade of the truck and call for a litter jeep," I said, glad I would soon be rid of my prisoner.

Several men walked over to take a good look at the pilot, the first live German they'd seen up close. As we stared at him, he lifted himself on his elbows and looked around.

His eyes narrowed, the first hint of emotion he'd shown. He looked right at me and, in perfect English, said, "You Americans shoot very well."

The litter jeep pulled up. Two medics got out, transferred the prisoner to a real stretcher, and strapped it to the jeep. They drove slowly down the hill, heading for the nearest aid station. The pilot would be treated and turned over to intelligence for questioning.

What a smart guy he was. If he had said anything to me, anything at all during the shelling, I might have said, "Men, let's go. Somebody else can take care of this guy."

Or I might have just shot him. I like to think not. I want to think I'd have tried to get him back no matter what, but I'll never know for sure.

After the middle of March 1943, our regiment moved through Gafsa to the oasis at El Guettar.

I still carried all the gear issued to me. A Brit gave me good advice when he first saw my gas mask.

"Let me tell you something about gas masks, Charlie," he said. "The first dead Germans you come across, see if they have gas masks. If they do, keep yours. If they don't, get rid of it."

Since I hadn't seen any dead Germans, I still had my mask with me the night we dug in at El Guettar. It was a big place, covering a hundred acres or so, with palm trees, springs, and canals cutting through it.

We thought we would have a quiet night, but German planes came over about midnight and bombed hell out of us. They seemed to know exactly where we were, and after huddling in our holes and taking casualties, we couldn't wait to get out of there.

We left on foot the next morning. My platoon led the battalion on a twenty-mile march across the desert toward another group of hills. Before noon, I came upon my first dead German. He had been there a few days, killed by a bullet to the chest. Fly-covered, swollen and black-faced, he exuded a putrid, sweetish stench, but he didn't have a gas mask. It was time to get rid of ours.

I had my platoon bury their masks so no one would find them. Abandoned equipment violated Army regulations, but if lost due to enemy action, it was expendable. I looked at my trench knife with its ridiculous brass knuckle handle and remembered the kid at Camp Robinson who had taken me down with it still in my hand. Time to get rid of it, too.

I kept my whistle, a regular metal coach's whistle attached to a chain hooked onto my belt. In ROTC, besides arm and voice signals, I had learned whistle commands. One whistle meant charge, two stop, three disperse. Basic stuff.

In England, a major asked, "Charlie, what's that thing for? You got a dog?"

"This is a command whistle," I said. "You can give orders when you can't be heard or seen."

The Brit shook his head. "You'll learn," he said, and walked away.

We hadn't engaged any German infantry, so we kept advancing, always walking toward higher ground. In early afternoon, we stopped in front of a hill a mile and a half away. Somehow, my platoon was still in the lead, and the company commander, who didn't know any more about combat than I did, walked up and said, "Okay, move out with your platoon and take that hill." Just like in the movies.

We loaded up and moved across open ground toward the hill. Giving hand signals and yelling directions, I positioned a squad on my right, one on my left, and one behind. That's the way the book said do it and, by God, that's how I would do it.

At the base of a long rise, we came under small-arms fire and hit the ground. My first real combat. The only automatic weapon we had was a BAR, a Browning automatic rifle. No machine-gun support, no mortars, no artillery. Just my platoon and our rifles against whatever was up there. The firing stopped. We couldn't see anything or anybody.

My men crawled and scrambled for better cover. "Pass the word," I yelled. "When you hear my whistle, we'll attack."

With the men spread out and ready, I blew the whistle and stood up. Bullets cracked over my head and thudded into the dirt around me. I hit the ground. My men didn't move, and that was it for the whistle.

I lay there for several minutes trying to calm myself and figure out what to do. Fortunately, the unevenness of the ground gave us a little protection, and the Germans didn't seem to have mortars.

Come on, Charlie. Think. Do something. Then I remembered. Set up a base of fire and start flanking, the basic British squad drill.

I ordered one squad to crawl off to the right in a flanking movement. Now I was beginning to think. The enemy can't be everywhere, at least not in the desert. They can't just hold the high ground and hope nobody comes up on their rear.

I turned so I could see my BAR man. "When I give you the sign, start firing at the crest of that hill, particularly on the right where our flanking attack is going to be."

47

Then I had to get the other two squads in action, "If you see anything," I said, "I want you to fire. Don't waste ammo, but fire when you see good targets. Even if you don't, fire up the hill every so often anyway."

So I established a base of fire and the BAR started firing, a heavy, thumping sound. This was the first time these guys had fired their weapons in anger. I looked around and saw four or five men hunkered down, not firing.

"Private," I yelled, "fire your weapon!"

One kid squeezed the trigger and then the others started shooting. We fired up the hill for several minutes, each man firing two or three clips of ammunition. I don't know what they saw, but at least the enemy troops were hearing a hell of a lot of bullets cracking overhead and some gun thumps in front of them.

Then I saw some men on the hilltop bouncing from position to position. The BAR opened up on them, and the Germans quit firing. They were leaving! It was time to charge the hill. I stood up and yelled, "Let's go!"

When the guys saw me on my feet, they moved forward. Nobody shot at us. We raced to the top and poured fire down the back side of the ridge until the retreating Germans were out of sight. I felt like yelling. We had captured our first hill.

That night I threw away the whistle.

6
Ridge by Ridge

Now and then, the BBC skipped in on the company radio, or we picked up Axis Sally, the sultry, English-speaking woman broadcasting propaganda on the German network. She told us more about the big picture than we got from our own sources. Knowing what was going on in other war zones boosted my morale when our situation wasn't going well.

My map case was stuffed with maps, and when I heard any major war news, I marked a large map of Europe and North Africa to show the men where the local front was advancing and what was happening in Russia.

On March 27, 1943, my first wedding anniversary, I took out Ruth's picture and wished I was back in Enid. My maps showed the only thing we had in common at the moment was that we were both on the same parallel, 36 degrees north.

Later that cold morning, I was at the head of my platoon as it led the battalion across the desert. We wore overcoats over wool winter uniforms and long underwear, our objective a ragged line of hills to the southeast.

I kept thinking what a shitty place to spend an anniversary. With my second lieutenant's pay of $150 a month, I could buy this entire wasteland if I could find the owner. Then I would tell everyone to get the hell off my land.

I stopped the platoon every hour for five or ten minutes, another trick I learned from the British, who actually called it a tea break. Their theory was that officers cannot push themselves and their men too hard or no one will be effective. So unless they were in a firefight, they took a break every hour and brewed up some tea.

Stopping gave the men an opportunity to adjust their packs, take care of their feet, urinate, and take a sip of water. But the most important benefit was that laggards had a chance to catch up. They knew the other men were off their feet, an incentive to keep up so they could rest at the next break.

This allowed me to keep my unit closer together. Combat is a hell of a mess to begin with, and I was all for anything that made my unit more effective for the day's mission.

We had been moving for a week without rest. By noon, the temperature had risen sixty degrees to almost a hundred and we had those damn overcoats, so we stopped and broke out rations. Normally we ate two meals a day, but the men needed the extra break. Carrying the overcoats, we itched and sweated in our wool uniforms and long johns as we trudged toward higher ground. The men bitched about everything all afternoon.

That evening, we found our objective deserted, a lucky break at the end of a crappy day. To the south, across a broad, desolate valley, a mountain range rose a couple thousand feet. No doubt, Germans and Italians were on those ridges.

Soaked with perspiration, the platoon dug in and huddled in two-man foxholes as the temperature dropped quickly. After shivering for an hour, I got the men out of their holes to dig until they worked up some body heat. That warmed us for a while, then we'd climb out and do it again. When daylight came, the area looked like an Oklahoma prairie-dog town. I counted five holes I had dug myself.

What a first anniversary. At least we weren't fired on during the night, and for that, I was grateful.

Ridges, one after another, ran down off the mountain range before us. It would be nice to get radio communications up there so we could bring forward our artillery. That meant going at it ridge by ridge, more or less isolated. We didn't have enough sense to do anything else. The division was under pressure to root the Germans off the crests, and orders came down for our company to make a big push.

This would be a coordinated attack, two platoons abreast and a third following in reserve. The heavy weapons platoon would follow with light mortars and machine guns to lay down covering fire.

At the signal, I led my platoon into a sloping wadi, our objective a hazy ridge in the distance. I thought about Germans dug in up there, waiting. It was going to be a long war if we had to face a new hill every day. Or it might be very short if I were unlucky.

We walked a couple of miles into the sunlit valley. Being at the front of the attack, even with another platoon beside us, gave me the strange feeling that our guys were the only ones fighting the war. I had the urge to run.

We moved steadily forward. The real danger was now, three hundred yards from the top. Here, we could be hit by small-arms fire from the crest and by mortar shells lobbed from behind the hill.

I moved the platoon into a T-column, squads to my right and left and another behind me, and spread the men out in case we got shelled. Please let there be nobody up there. Let them be gone.

A machine gun suddenly opened up on us. We were pinned down that quickly, with no way to maneuver. I could hear screaming and moaning, but we couldn't move to help anyone or even return fire.

Bullets poured down on us. I rolled into a slight fold, not quite deep enough to protect my head or my butt. I wanted to hear friendly fire from the platoon on my right, to know at least one flank was protected, but I couldn't hear any firing except from the Germans.

"Stay still and dig in," I yelled. "I'm here. I'm okay." I wanted the men to know they still had a lieutenant because most of them couldn't see me. I didn't want them to panic and run away.

I didn't have a trench shovel, and even if I had, I wouldn't have been able to use it without getting hit. I reached in my pants and pulled out a pocketknife. I loosened the ground and pushed dirt and rocks behind me and to the side. After an hour of tunneling forward like a mole, I'd dug myself into a slit trench deep enough to get my ass below the surface. At least now, I might survive long enough to figure out what to do. I couldn't communicate with anybody behind us. I hoped that someone back there had seen what happened and had the guts to help us, but I had the sinking feeling we were on our own.

By mid-afternoon, still under sporadic small-arms fire, I had dug my trench a little deeper, just hanging on. We had certainly ceased to be any kind of threat.

As we offered fewer targets for the enemy, their firing died down, but I knew they hadn't withdrawn. I couldn't hear anything except artillery crumps in the distance and wounded men crying. After it was quiet for a while, a kid ten yards away called to me.

"Lieutenant, I think they've gone."

"Stay where you are," I yelled. "We haven't pushed anybody off that ridge."

He quieted down and I kept digging to improve my position. About four o'clock he yelled again. "Lieutenant! They've all gone. There's nobody up there."

He was trying to be encouraging, but he didn't know anything. I hadn't even seen the enemy yet. They were shooting from hidden positions above us, and I wasn't about to look for them. If I could see them, I was liable to get shot.

"Keep your goddamn ass down," I called in my best command voice, trying to put some authority into it. Finally, the kid shut up.

By this time, I had to pee, so I did, right where I lay. Pissing my pants was the least of my worries.

Another hour went by without our taking fire. The sun would set soon, so I yelled to the men, "Stay where you are. I'll get you guys out when it gets dark."

We weren't in a minefield, and I didn't see any problem if we let it get dark enough. I believed everyone understood what we were going to do. Artillery shells shrieked over and exploded somewhere behind us, but we didn't take any more fire from the hilltop while we waited for the time to pass.

A helmet has a certain camouflaged look on the ground and I eased my head up enough to peek around. I looked to my right in time to see this damned kid stand up. Before I could say anything, he was shot and fell without a sound. My head went down fast. I wouldn't be any good to anybody dead. The kid was dead, though, because he never made a sound.

My men hunkered down after that. When it got dark, those of us who could move crawled out of our holes and started down the slope. I had to trust that the Germans would take care of our wounded. There was nothing anybody could do for the dead.

Neither side threw up flares, and we got back to the line of departure without losing anyone else. We were the last platoon back. I had lost seven men.

The battalion was in chaos, shelled by the artillery we'd heard all day. Three rifle companies lay mixed together in a ravine that looked like a filthy alley, with empty ration cartons, ammo boxes, and five-gallon water cans scattered amid tangles of communication wire. Over thirty men were dead or wounded.

I had no idea where my company commander was. I hadn't seen him for a couple of days, and in fact, never saw him again. Noncoms and a couple other lieutenants were trying to keep things organized. The walking wounded I brought back added to the confusion for the harassed medics, and it was after midnight before I got my men taken care of and settled.

While we struggled for control, it occurred to me that tactically it might be worse for an army if soldiers got seriously injured instead of killed. Taking care of the wounded uses lots of resources, and men screaming in pain is not good for morale.

Pinned in the ravine, we had become a lost battalion. We kept digging in. The enemy held the high ground, and continued to shell us with harassing fire. They'd lob a few in every so often to get our attention, but they couldn't shell us continually or they'd run out of ammunition. So they paced themselves. After a while, we could predict when they were about to start up again. Trying to hold our own, we set up mortars and a machine gun to keep enemy troops from coming down the slope.

The battalion hadn't moved for days except for little probing attacks like the ones I'd made. We took casualties every day, and the area kept getting filthier. Our wool uniforms and long underwear smelled bad enough when clean. Now, after unwashed weeks in the field, we stunk horribly. Being under sporadic fire, we couldn't bury our garbage or dig latrines. The lack of hygiene attracted all sorts of vermin and insects. We could hear lizards and rats rattling empty C-ration cans at night. I never took my shoes off at night, because scorpions would crawl in them. Besides, I wanted to be ready in case I had to move quickly.

Flies would swarm anything we opened to eat. I ate more than a few, along with the sand and grit blown in by the almost constant wind. Most of us had diarrhea.

If I crawled out of my hole during a lull to take a crap, flies would cover my butt. No use wasting energy brushing them away. Men who had to go during a bombardment usually just messed their pants, or at best, in the bottom of their holes and shoveled it out later. Raw crotches, jock itch, and foot fungus were common.

One day I sat at the edge of my foxhole with another second lieutenant, a platoon leader from a different company. I was bitching about my company commander to this other lieutenant. I'll call him Kelly, though that was not his name.

"I don't blame him," said Kelly.

"What do you mean?"

"I mean I'm not going to do this shit anymore. I can't take it. I'm not this kind of person."

"Come on," I said. "I don't like it either, but here I am."

"Well, I'm going to drop back and quit."

"Don't be stupid. That can get you court-martialed."

He didn't say much more as I tried to encourage him. Then I let it go. The guy was pissing me off.

Kelly disappeared later that day. Someone told me he just walked away. I never saw him again in combat.

Two weeks later, after the Germans retreated north toward Bizerte, I got orders to report to division headquarters at Gafsa and passed through the 39th Regiment where I ran into Kelly, wearing the silver bars of a first lieutenant.

The army was not free with promotions during those early days of the war. They always seemed to have first lieutenants, captains, or majors to fill the slots that might otherwise go to junior officers.

I couldn't believe it. After quitting his post as an infantry officer, this guy had been promoted instead of punished, while I fought up and down the miserable wadis of Tunisia and was still only a second lieutenant.

I stared at him. "What are you doing, Kelly?"

"I'm working in S-4 as a transportation officer."

"I see." That's all I could say. This bastard was running trucks and vehicles, a shirker with a cushy job in the rear.

When I saw the other platoon leaders, I said, "Fellows, if you want to get promoted, just tell them you've had combat up to here. It's a sure way to a promotion and a job off the line."

But I had my own worries and didn't think much more about Kelly. At least he was honest. He didn't want to fight and he didn't think he was capable. Who knows, maybe he was the finest transportation officer the regiment ever had. If so, he was in the right spot. But I still thought he deserved punishment, not reward.

Years after the war, sometime in the early 1960s, I went to a 9th Division reunion in the Midwest. Over a thousand people attended, including General Westmoreland, an artillery officer and battalion commander in World War II, who later became the controversial commander of U.S. forces in Vietnam.

Before lunch one day, a friend I had served with, his two teenage sons, a couple of other retired officers, and Westmoreland stood in a hallway, chatting and reminiscing.

Past our little group, an officer in uniform walked toward us with rows of ribbons on his chest and a 9th Division patch on his right sleeve, denoting the unit he'd served with in combat. It was Kelly, wearing the silver leaves of a lieutenant colonel.

I felt an angry flush. He walked up and before he could say anything or shake hands with anyone, I said, "Kelly, you're still a son of a bitch."

He turned and walked off.

After a silent moment, somebody said, "Charlie, you really insulted the man."

"I'm sorry. It just came out." Then I told them the story.

After lunch, I looked for Kelly to apologize, but he had already left the convention. I never saw him again. It's something I've regretted, one of those things I wish I hadn't done. I had no idea I was still angry.

War separates us from our illusions. Combat strips men to the quick, as it did Kelly and a lot of others. Stay in it long enough and it'll take everything you've got. It just broke Kelly in a hurry. I'm sure he was a good transportation officer. And I'm sure that after the war he did well in his various assignments. Otherwise, he wouldn't have made lieutenant colonel.

But he must have had a hole deep inside from quitting the battlefield, and maybe he stayed in the army to prove himself, ashamed that fear got the best of him back in Tunisia. I know I wish I'd shown more compassion that day at the reunion.

Military psychologists treating combat fatigue in North Africa found one common trait. Many men who broke under the strain of war had lived with anxiety close to the surface of their lives long before they got into combat. Those soldiers were the first to break; the battle fatigue they suffered was a natural result of who they already were.

But by the time we got into the Sedjenane Valley in northern Tunisia, guys who couldn't hack it had pretty much disappeared. Most of them, like Kelly, went to the rear and filled in wherever the Army needed them. It was a tragedy that we lost so many combat infantry officers that way, but the war was a crucible. There was no place to hide, and we became who we really were.

7
Hill 772

The night after Kelly disappeared, the battalion commander sent a runner for me. I stumbled around in the dark until I found his command post, a hole dug behind a large boulder. His intelligence officer, a captain, spread a map and we studied it by flashlight under a blanket, their faces grimy and haggard in the dim light.

The enemy had shelled us most of the day and I was tired and irritable. "What's up? This fucking map is not the right scale."

"The shelling we're taking is too accurate," said the colonel, poking at the map impatiently. "There's got to be an observation post on Hill 772. It overlooks this whole area. Regiment thinks there's a bunch of Italians up there."

We had been running into Italians for almost two weeks. They didn't have much fight left in them and usually gave up when they saw Americans. Over two hundred Italians had surrendered to my company a few days before, walking out of the hills one morning with their hands up, subdued, worn out, and hungry.

"We're taking too damn much fire," the colonel said. "You know the ground better than anybody. I want you to go up there tonight and capture that hill."

I thought about the sorry mess the battalion was in and figured it couldn't be much worse out on my own than being pinned down in this ditch.

"Okay," I said. "How easy is this going to be?"

"Should be no problem. They're Italians. Just go up there and scare them out."

I picked up ammunition and grenades from some of the wounded and hand-picked a dozen men to go with me, including a corporal who spoke Italian, and a BAR man. We might need extra firepower if things went bad.

It was a windy, moonlit night. About 2300 hours, we picked our way through the other companies and checked passwords and countersigns with the outposts, making sure they knew we would be coming back in the dark. Then we walked out of the ravine and into the valley, headed southwest in a flanking movement around Hill 772. I could hear artillery rumbling in the distance and now and then glimpsed flashes of explosions over the horizon. To the south, arid mountains meandered a few miles before flattening out at the edge of the desert.

We found an old goat trail and followed it single file up the backside of the hill. Finally, we reached the bottom of a steeper slope, almost a cliff, about seventy-five feet high. We pulled ourselves up, holding onto the tough desert vegetation and whatever handholds we could find in the rocks.

It was a rugged climb, and I counted on no enemy soldiers being on the rear of the hill. The wind blowing down from the crest would make it hard for anyone up there to hear us.

At the top of the cliff, the ground leveled out again and we crawled up until I thought I could make out the rim of the hill in the pale moonlight. I hoped the wind masked any noise we made in the rocks. We crept a few more yards and I saw a sandbagged fortification on the ridgeline about fifty feet above.

This was close enough. So far, we hadn't heard anybody, but I didn't want to get into a firefight. If Italians were up there, we would try to talk them into surrendering.

As quietly as possible, I spread the men out to either side. I kept my BAR man next to me and sent the Italian-speaking corporal way over to the left in case he drew fire when he yelled for them to surrender. We were about to capture some Italians.

Ten minutes later, we were ready. The corporal shouted up the hill in Italian that we had them surrounded, to put down their weapons and come out with their hands up.

Thirty feet in front of me, a man stood up from a position below the crest I hadn't seen, scaring the hell out of me.

"*Ya?*" he said. He damn sure didn't sound Italian.

I didn't say anything and my corporal didn't yell anything else, either. We pressed into the rocks as low as we could get.

Machine guns and rifles opened up, spitting fire, pouring bullets over our heads. Greenish white tracers arced down the slope behind us. I don't think the Germans realized that we were only a few yards from their position. Even if they'd seen us, their machine gun barrels were propped on sandbags and they probably couldn't lower them enough to hit us.

But then hand grenades, the kind with handles we called potato mashers, began looping over the sandbags. Most clattered in the rocks beyond us, but a few exploded close by.

I could faintly hear some of my men moaning and crying. No screaming, but I could tell we were taking casualties. Still, I didn't think the enemy had figured out how many of us were out here or exactly where we were.

Gunfire flashed from the parapet for several minutes. We didn't shoot back. All we could do, lying on top of the ground, was to press ourselves in among the rocks as low as possible. I had no idea how many of my men were hit, but there was nothing I could do about it.

The German firing slacked off, but I could still smell cordite as the wind brought gun smoke down over us. One of my men threw a grenade up the hill and the German machine guns opened up on us again. More explosions went off.

I looked up and saw a grenade coming right at me, sputtering, sparks flying off it like a lit firecracker. The grenade landed a foot in front of me. I covered the sides of my face with both arms, my hands pressing my helmet tightly as I ducked my head into the ground, expecting to die.

The grenade exploded just in front and to the right of my head, most of the fragments slicing through the air above me. My ears rang and my right hand started stinging and hurting. I felt a wet raw spot on my index finger where the fingernail had been torn off. The sling on my rifle was hanging loose, severed below the front swivel. Lucky. I was shaking, but alive.

We lay there, waiting it out, pressing ourselves into the ground to get away from bullets sparking and whistling off the rocks. I thought we were going to die, but we didn't fire back and eventually things quieted down. I looked up the hill and saw a dark figure stand up in his trench. After a moment, he climbed out and shuffled down the slope directly toward me.

With the wind covering any noise I made, I picked up my rifle, slipped the safety off, and brought it to my shoulder. If he kept coming, I was going to have to shoot him or he would walk right into me. And when I fired, I would be the next to die because the flash of my weapon would pinpoint my location.

The German sidestepped down the steep slope, dislodging pebbles and dirt. When he got halfway to me, I started squeezing the trigger so I wouldn't jerk the aim off him. I didn't know my rifle very well, because I didn't fire it much, so I squeezed slowly as he approached, not knowing when it would go off.

The German stopped three yards from me, and I quit squeezing. He stood for a moment, holding a short-stock Schmeisser machine pistol, looking down the slope beyond where I lay with my rifle aimed at his chest. Then he turned around and climbed back up the hill and into his defensive position. He never knew how close we both came to dying. I took a couple of deep breaths and flipped the safety back on.

We didn't take any more fire from the top of the ridge, but I knew we had to get away before daylight. I passed the word for the men to crawl to my position. Fortunately, the wind was still blowing off the crest, the only noise I could hear. Five guys made it over to me, all of them wounded.

The worst was a man with half his jaw shot off. I wrapped a bandage around his wound to stem the bleeding. I couldn't do anything about the missing men. My job was to save what was left of the patrol. We left eight men on the hill, including a volunteer corporal we'd picked up from another company. He was found dead, shot through the head, some days later.

We had to get out of there or we would all die. I was afraid the Germans might shoot flares over us. I had never been under enemy flares, but the British trained me on what to do. When a flare goes off it's hard to pick up anything except movement, because it's so bright and there's too much to see all at once. Anything moving stands out, otherwise it's just rocks or bushes or crevasses or blown up trees.

"We're going down single file," I said. "If a flare goes up, don't run. Just freeze. Just stop."

We crawled a hundred yards and up went a brilliant white flare, not directly over us, but close enough to expose us until it dropped behind the hill. I felt naked and vulnerable in the changing shadows as it descended slowly. But we stayed still, becoming part of the stark landscape, and nobody shot at us.

As soon as the flare went out, I stood and nothing happened. We moved as fast as we could, not running because a couple of men limped badly. Two more flares went up, catching us on our feet, but the men froze and we weren't fired on.

I didn't think the wounded could make it down the cliff we had climbed up, so we felt our way over to the right until I found a spot where we could get down a little easier. But this put us in front of another company's defense line. Afraid their guards would shoot if they heard us, I halted the men behind a rock outcropping and yelled across the ravine, "This is Lieutenant Scheffel, A Company, coming in from a patrol. Don't shoot."

But they did, the bullets whining and buzzing off the rocks in the darkness around us.

"Stop firing! Give me the password. I know the countersign."

They answered by shooting at us again. I'd left eight men up on Hill 772. That was bad enough; I wasn't ready to lose any more. "Okay, we'll stay here until daylight. Then we're coming in."

We toughed it out for the rest of that long cold night, all of us wounded and shivering in the rocks. I was most worried about the kid shot in the jaw. He sat up so he wouldn't choke, and his face made a sucking noise with every breath, but he never whimpered. That soldier had guts.

When it got light enough, I stood up, stiff and cold. "We're coming in."

Fifty yards up the opposite embankment a guard waved us across. We straggled down, glad to be alive, and moved into the ravine where our troops were dug in. Someone else would have to clear the Germans off Hill 772.

8
The Long Patrol

I hadn't seen my company commander since I got back from Hill 772. He kept fading away on us, which put me in charge of his company and pissed me off. One morning, the battalion commander walked into our area and headed straight for me.

Pointing to a distant ridgeline, he said, "I want you to find a way across that range. It shouldn't take over three days."

The hills shimmered like a mirage in the heat, ten hard miles, maybe more, from where we stood. "Sir, it'll take me two days just to get out there and back."

I was fast losing respect for the man. A career officer, about 35, he had transferred from the quartermaster corps and didn't seem to have much of a clue about the infantry.

"Regiment needs it quick," he said.

No wonder he was up here with me. If he were back in his command post, his boss could prod him for results. How the hell could he coordinate his battalion up here at one of his companies?

"Yes, sir," I said. "If the Germans don't object too much."

I thought the old man was crazy. Following his orders, I'd already left most of one patrol on Hill 772 for the enemy or graves registration to pick up. Now I was to take another patrol out to see what the Germans were doing in those hills? What kind of outfit had I gotten myself into? Did this old man know anything? What happened if I ran into trouble out there? This patrol scared the hell out of me.

But I got twelve men together. "We're moving fast," I said. "Don't carry any ammunition except what's on your web belts."

To move faster, the enlisted men loaded up with light combat packs and one blanket. I tucked my raincoat into the back of my belt next to my first aid kit. I took my rifle and my .45, enough rations for three days, a canteen of water, and some halazone pills to treat polluted water.

We took off across the rocky ground and trudged through dry wadis—those streambeds and ravines coming off the mountains in odd ways that could get us lost. We watched for mines and trip wires, careful not to expose ourselves too much to the high ground. We saw no signs of the enemy the first day and stopped after only five miles. I set out pickets and tried to sleep under my raincoat in a cold slit trench.

We left next day after the sun was up, hoping we didn't stumble into a minefield or an ambush. About midmorning, we came to a junction where another wadi angled sharply in from behind us on the left. We couldn't keep going until I knew what was up there. I spread the patrol out on both sides of the junction and took two men a few feet up the wadi where we crouched behind a large boulder. In the eerie quiet, I scanned ahead for cover. The narrow streambed was dry and fairly flat, with a few small rocks scattered about, but nothing much to hide behind.

"Stay alert," I said and stepped from behind the boulder. I walked up the middle of the streambed carrying my rifle in front of me, trying to look like just another enlisted man to anyone who might be watching.

I strained to see trip wires or other signs of mines. The Germans had one mine we called the "Bouncing Betty," a small cylinder loaded with steel fragments, ball bearings, or nails. When buried, the only part visible was the triggering device, three prongs the size of matchsticks. If stepped on, the mine popped out of the ground and exploded at groin level, leaving horrible, maiming wounds.

After a few minutes, I glanced up and saw movement ahead. Fifty yards from me, two bodies lay side-by-side in the streambed. One of them moved again and I slipped the safety off my rifle. As I got closer, I saw they were Bedouins, a nomadic people who roamed the countryside trying to stay out of the way of the war. They wore sandals and typical loose-fitting sacks made of coarse cloth. No sign of any weapons.

I walked up to them, wondering why they were lying on a battlefield in the midday sun. Then I saw dried blood on their clothes and on the ground around them. There was nothing German or American about either, but I asked, "Do you speak English?"

One man lifted himself slightly and shook his head. Blood soaked the bottom half of his dirty clothes. The man beside him stared at me from beneath a forearm shielding his eyes. His other hand clutched at a wound in his side. The sun beat down from the cloudless sky, and I doubted these two would survive the day.

Their mouths were parched and cracked so I laid down my rifle and took out my canteen. The man nearest me smiled, recognizing I was trying to help him.

I held his head up and, as he drank, he brought his right hand up onto his chest and pointed back over his head with his thumb, trying to tell me something.

I tilted my head a little and scanned peripherally up the creek bank behind us. In the rocks, a hundred feet up the slope, I saw two Germans sitting behind a machine gun pointed right at me.

I'm dead, I said to myself, but I willed my body to stay still. Don't panic, I thought. They haven't shot you yet.

Taking my time, I gave the other man a drink. I screwed the cap on the canteen, picked up my rifle, and stood, wondering when the machine gun was going to open up on me.

I forced myself to look only at the nomads and nodded to let them know there was nothing more I could do. Goodbye. The nomad who had warned me nodded slightly.

I started back to where my men were, still looking at the ground for mines. Several yards from the nomads, one foot already lifted, I started to step off a little embankment when I saw three black prongs sticking out of the ground. If I had stepped straight, I would have landed right on the mine.

I stood shaking, scared shitless. Whatever you do now, Charlie, don't panic, don't run, or that machine gun will open up on you.

I didn't move for a few seconds, wondering if the mine next to my foot was going to go off. Then I looked around and saw not just one Bouncing Betty, but a bunch of them. Not all together, but every five yards or so. I'd walked right through this minefield without seeing a damn thing on my way up the wadi.

The Germans could have shot me at any time. I don't know why they didn't. If they had recognized me as an officer, they would have picked me off, for sure. Maybe they thought I was walking point, and they waited to see who else showed up. Or maybe they wanted to see me set off a mine.

I wiped my hand across my grimy face and tried to plan the quickest way out of the minefield. I took a deep breath and moved ahead, scanning the ground as I walked slowly and carefully away from the machine gun. Twenty yards. Thirty more, and still alive.

I saw one of my men on his belly peeking around the side of the boulder. I kept moving slowly. About fifty feet from the boulder, I yelled, "I'm coming in!" and sprinted toward the rock, zigzagging.

I took several steps before the German machine gun opened up and bullets thudded into the ground around me. I slid in behind the boulder without getting hit.

We hunkered down while the Germans peppered the whole area. Bullets cracked past us, kicked up dust, and screamed off the rocks. I knew we had to move before they called in mortars. We retreated around a bend so the Germans couldn't fire straight down the wadi at us, but one of my men, a corporal, got hit in the leg and couldn't walk. Blood seeped through his right pant leg above the knee. We got a compress on him, rigged up a litter, and retreated another quarter mile. The guys carrying him switched off, but it was a struggle in the rough terrain.

After a while, I changed directions in case the Germans tried to flank us. The sides of the new wadi got steeper until we rounded a bend and ran into a solid wall. We were in a box canyon. If counterattacked here, we were done for. The men waited for me to think of something.

I wasn't certain we could scramble out of the wadi alone, much less carrying a wounded man. Finally, I walked over to the corporal. "You know we're in a bad situation here," I said.

He nodded.

"I'll be frank," I said. "I don't know what to do with you. We can't get you up this wall. We'll be lucky if any of us get out. I can do several things." I was only thinking aloud by this time.

The corporal looked at me, waiting.

"I can stay with you and send my men up the hill," I said. "Or I can leave you and take the rest of the men out."

The corporal knew I didn't know where the hell I was. And he knew there was a good chance nobody would find him, not even the Germans.

It was a terrible choice. "Do you want my .45 to defend yourself?" Unspoken was that, if no one came, he could commit suicide.

A lanky, quiet man, he had been in my platoon for two months. He knew me and I thought I knew him. Looking straight at me, he said, "I don't need your .45. Get the men out of here."

We moved the corporal into the shade of an overhang. I thought about leaving my canteen with him, but it was almost empty and I didn't even do that. We looked at each other in one clear moment of truth before I moved out of his line of sight. As the rest of us climbed out, it occurred to me that I was leaving a part of myself in that canyon. I would never be the same again.

At the top of the cliff, I took a careful compass bearing and tried to burn the surrounding landmarks into my mind before we struck off across country. By late afternoon, we were out of water when we came to a slight depression. At the bottom was a stagnant pool covered with a vile, stinking scum, flies all over it and in the air.

"I'm not drinking that shit," someone said.

"You might never see any more," I said, pushing aside the scum. I filled my canteen half full. The directions for halazone said one tablet for each canteen full of water. I dropped in two. It was the dirtiest water I ever drank.

We walked several more hard miles and it was almost dark before we ran across some of our troops and got back to the battalion. I told them I had abandoned one of my men, an admission I almost choked on. I showed the

S–3 operations officer where I thought I'd left the corporal, but it was impossible to go out until the next day. Looking for someone at night would only get more guys lost or shot.

Two days later, I asked about the corporal. They'd found him the next morning and sent him to the evacuation point.

Thank you, God.

9

Heading North

It had been days since we'd seen another American unit. I think the whole battalion was lost on the northern edge of the desert, as if we had no unified command at all. My next patrol made a sweep to the south without enemy contact. On our way back the second night, I saw a campfire on a hillside. Normally the only lights were stars, which shone luminous and bright in the dark Tunisian sky. We had to check it out.

Creeping closer, we heard voices speaking French. We stayed in cover and identified ourselves as Americans. French Senegalese troops waved us in and shook hands. They could have been stragglers from a big camel caravan we'd seen days earlier, or they might have been deserters. They seemed unconcerned about being in a war zone.

We drank wine offered us, while a man sat at the edge of the fire turning a half-roasted animal on a spit. I saw no officers, only a sergeant who didn't speak English. None of us spoke French, and my few words of Latin were no help.

By hand signals and sound effects, I asked the sergeant what they were cooking. I thought maybe sheep, so I said, "Baa, baa?"

He shook his head.

"Moo, moo, moo?"

No again. Finally, he put his hands up to his ears and said, "Eehaw, ee-haw."

Smelling vaguely sweet, the donkey's fat crackled and dripped into the fire. Two men carved chunks of the meat with vicious-looking knives and we ate a few bites, but I didn't feel secure. We thanked them and left shortly thereafter, arriving back at our own lines at dawn.

Other American units, somewhere north of our battalion, started taking enough of the fight to the Germans to relieve the pressure on us. We heard faint sounds of battle, and the artillery bombardment on our position slackened as the enemy shifted to meet new attacks. We certainly weren't causing them much trouble.

We left the ravine where we'd been pinned and moved onto higher ground at the edge of Djebel Berda, a range of desert mountains running east. In our new position, we could see for miles across a long flat plain.

That afternoon a German panzer unit moved up the valley, fifty or sixty tanks spread out in ragged skirmish lines, one group behind the other. All of a sudden, several tanks burst into flames, black smoke rising off the desert floor. Some big guns were firing down the valley at them. It must have been almost point-blank, because in a matter of minutes a dozen or more tanks were knocked out. They had driven right into an ambush. The tanks fired a few rounds but mostly they dodged erratically. Finally, the survivors scrambled the other way, dust billowing behind them.

Less than half an hour later, a small formation of Stuka dive-bombers flew past us. Their attack sirens screamed as they dove and disappeared behind the ridge to our left. Bomb explosions crumped in the distance. The tank killers were now catching hell.

The next morning we heard more planes above us. I got out my field glasses and saw the lovely curved wings of Spitfires high in the sky. This was the first time I'd seen the RAF in that area. Happy hunting, guys.

The Spits circled, waiting, and then twelve Stukas flew over in groups of three, cruising well below the Spitfires. As the Stukas dove on the artillery sites again, the Spits peeled off and fell in behind. They caught up quickly and fired at close range into the dive-bombers.

The lead Stuka exploded. Several more burst into smoke and flames as they hurtled toward the ground. We couldn't see where they crashed but we had good seats for the whole aerial battle and watched the rest of the Stukas scatter wildly. One banked toward us and I thought he was going to drop his bomb right on us, but he slid past at a forty-five degree angle, heading back east, trying to get the hell out of there.

A Spitfire caught up and pumped machine gun fire into him. After a long burst, the Stuka exploded in a giant fireball over the German lines and our whole battalion jumped out of our holes and yelled like we were at a football game. Every one of the Stukas went down. It was crazy and exhilarating, cheering at the death of our enemy.

By the end of the week, the Germans had melted away to the north in a fighting retreat toward Bizerte and Tunis, their escape ports. Their days in North Africa were numbered.

When I received orders to go back to II Corps Headquarters near Gafsa, I came off the ridge and picked up a jeep and driver at the 39th Regiment. On the way west, we passed incinerated tanks that had been pushed off the cratered road. Other wrecked vehicles pockmarked the landscape like huge burned toads. I knew they were part of the armored unit I'd seen from the ridge a few days earlier.

Soon we came across a black soldier standing by a sign for an artillery unit. We pulled over and he saluted me.

I returned his salute. "Are you quartermaster?" I had heard rumors of blacks in quartermaster supply and other support outfits.

"No, sir," he said. "Field arty." He pointed at the sign. "That's my unit."

This surprised me. I'd never heard of blacks in combat. "You're in artillery? A Negro?"

"Yes, sir."

"Were you the guys firing at those tanks that came up the valley the other day?"

"Yes, sir. That was us."

"I'd like to meet your battery."

He pointed to the left and told me I couldn't miss it. While the driver waited with the jeep, I walked a hundred yards off the road and, topping a small rise, I saw the long barrels of several 155mm artillery pieces sticking above the ground. I shook hands with two black soldiers.

"Where's your battery commander?"

After a few moments, a white captain about my age came out of a gun pit and introduced himself as the commander.

I thanked him for their work and pointed to where we were when his unit had blown up all the tanks. I told him that if the Germans had gotten up the valley past us, we'd have been cut off. Then their attached infantry would have come up in personnel carriers and slaughtered or captured us.

"This is the first Negro combat unit in theater," the captain said.

"Can I meet one of your gun crews?"

We walked to an emplacement where the captain turned me over to the crew chief, a black sergeant, in charge of a Long Tom, a weapon with a barrel over seven meters long.

The massive gun and its carriage had been dug deep into the pit. I sighted along the top of its barrel straight down the valley. From this stable platform, the monster could fire a six-inch shell almost fifteen miles with great accuracy. No wonder the Long Toms had knocked out all those tanks. Empty ration packs and the debris of recent firing lay around the gun. A hint of burned cordite lingered in the air.

A long trench led away from the pit. Down in the trench, on an empty ration case, sat a black kid with a can of paint and a small brush. On some 155mm shells he had written, "Hitler count yo men."

By this time, several soldiers had gathered around. I shook hands with every one of them. "As a white guy from Oklahoma, I want you guys to know you can fight with me anytime."

Back on the road to Gafsa, I thought about how good those artillerymen were. The 9th Division had no assigned black troops and the scuttlebutt among the men was that blacks—or niggers, as the men called them—couldn't fight.

"They don't have any guts," they'd say. "They can't take what we're taking."

But playing ball against blacks in college had taught me they could be just as good at their jobs as whites. If the war lasted long enough, somewhere down the line we would have them in the 9th. The division was losing too many men too fast.

We drove through the barren countryside and past the scraggly palm trees at the El Guettar oasis. As our jeep approached Gafsa, I knew we were finally out of danger when an MP flagged us down and wanted to charge me for not being shaved. He relented only after I told him I lost my gear fighting the Germans and would shave that night as soon as I found a razor.

We had entered the chickenshit zone.

The day after I reported into the regiment, the adjutant told me I'd been promoted to first lieutenant.

"That's the good news," he said. "The bad news is we've got to send an officer to the British battle school. You've had experience with the Brits, so you're it."

The idea was for British and American armies to familiarize themselves with each other's tactics. I'd already trained with the British and knew how they operated, so I didn't understand why he didn't send someone else. But I didn't say any of this. I saluted, packed my gear, and hitched a ride north to the school, located halfway up to the coast.

The British trained their soldiers as close as possible to the battlefield. Occasionally, German airplanes flew over, and we were within range of harassing artillery fire. Most of our exercises were simulated, but some involved operational missions, although my class never came under enemy fire. We went out on combat patrols and then critiqued them in a kind of show-and-tell.

We made one mock attack a hundred yards behind a rolling artillery barrage. As we advanced, I hoped a short round didn't fall on us, but the exercise provided a powerful lesson. Anybody out in front of us on the receiving end of those thunderous explosions would have had their heads down, unable to shoot at us while we closed on their positions.

The school lasted a week. I had been lucky in the fighting around El Guettar, making mistakes under fire and still surviving. So I took lots of notes and paid closer attention than I had in England. I had seen first hand that what they were teaching me could save lives.

One night, after a fruitless patrol to engage the Germans, a small group of junior officers got together in a large tent. Six of us sat on the ground drinking local wine and bullshitting. I was the only American. We had no electricity, no fire, only one small kerosene lamp that spread a dim glow, the light dying before it reached the corners of the tent.

We sat there giving coarse opinions on the war. We cursed the enemy and we cursed Roosevelt for not sending enough supplies to the Brits. I cursed British food, which consisted primarily of tinned bully beef and inedible biscuits. We gave everybody hell—Patton, Eisenhower, Churchill, Montgomery, Alexander—we didn't miss anybody except ourselves. We were the only good guys in the war, serving at the mercy of fools.

As we talked, it became obvious that these officers still thought they would never make it home. They thought the war would not get better, because it wasn't getting any better for them at that particular moment, and hadn't since 1939, when they first got into it. They felt the Germans dominated the air space over Africa and the Mediterranean. Their vehicles couldn't move at all in the daytime without Stukas or Messerschmitts attacking them.

But to the south, where I had been, the Allies had already started to gain control of the air. I saw more and more Allied planes overhead in southern Tunisia.

So I said, "I think we've got air superiority now, and I think we whipped the Germans down where I came from."

But the Brits, sitting at the tail end of their supply lines, felt beaten by their long struggle with the enemy.

I tried to cheer them up. "From what I hear," I said, "the Russians are doing better on their front, and it looks like we're starting to turn the war in the Pacific. And I can tell you folks that when I left the States, American factories were producing everything we need. It's only a matter of getting it to us."

We'd been drinking and talking for two hours when the entrance spread open. A trim, uniformed man stepped into the dim light, closed the flaps, and stood just inside the tent.

The other men got up and saluted. I was in an American combat uniform; I didn't have to salute this guy. A lieutenant nudged me with his foot. I stood, looked closer, and recognized General Alexander from pictures I'd seen. As commander of the British 18th Army Group, he reported directly to General Eisenhower. I saluted smartly.

The general said, "You're an American?"

"Yes, sir. Oklahoma."

"I've been to Fort Sill," he said, and made a slight motion with his hand. "Sit down, gentlemen."

We offered him a drink. Sitting cross-legged before us, in a tent close enough to the enemy to get hit by their artillery, General Alexander took a small swig from our bottle and looked at each of the young officers gathered around him.

"Gentlemen," he said, "I've been standing outside your tent for several minutes, and I've heard you lace into the entire Allied command. I can understand it. I was a young officer myself at one time." Then he looked at me and said, "Young man, you're really the only optimistic one in this group."

And he sat and discussed the war with us. He stayed for half an hour, an extraordinary time for a general to stop and talk with a bunch of junior officers. That's what makes a good general, I think. Listening and having experienced what we were dealing with.

The general stood. "I want you to remember this," he said. "If you other men think it's bad on this side, and the American lieutenant here thinks it's getting better, then it is getting better on our side. Gentlemen, the Boche are beginning to lose this war. If you think it's bad on our side, just be glad you're not on theirs."

I never forgot what General Alexander told us that night. I gave my men the same pep talk during hard combat later, when some of them doubted the outcome of a battle or the war. "Well, look," I'd say. "If you think it's bad over here, look how much more artillery we're firing at them than they are firing at us. Look at how many more airplanes we've got."

So I had great respect for Alexander and he turned out to be, I think, one of the better generals of the war. Maybe my meeting him had something to do with that opinion. Every general made mistakes during the war. Every commander, every platoon leader—we all made mistakes. But General Alexander inspired me, and I know I was a better officer for having met him.

10
Sedjenane

After battle school, I caught truck rides north to the 9th Division's rear area and started walking in the afternoon rain up the line to the 39th Regiment. The roads were supposed to be clear of German mines, but I avoided any road big enough to drive on, taking goat trails through the drab gray underbrush instead. An occasional sprinkling of wildflowers provided the only color.

Huddled in my raincoat, I spent a cold, wet night sheltered under a scrawny pine. From midnight till dawn, the sky to the southeast lit up with the largest night artillery barrage I'd ever seen. I slept little, thankful the explosions were miles away.

Tired, muddy, and frazzled, I walked into the headquarters tent late the next morning to process back into the regiment. The commander, a colonel I'd never seen before, strode up to me. He wore shiny boots and a .45 in a polished leather holster on his hip. In his left hand was a lit cigarette in a long ebony holder.

"Welcome to the 39th," he said. "Where are you coming from?"

"Sir, I'm with 1st Battalion. I just finished the British battle school."

"Well, I'm sure you'll put what you've learned to good use." The colonel stuck the cigarette holder in his mouth at a jaunty angle.

"Yes, sir." And where did you come from, you pompous ass?

A week later, the colonel was relieved of his command after nearly being captured close to the front with classified documents.

I followed our telephone wire up to 1st Battalion's rear command post. The commander was not there, so I walked on until I found the forward CP, a small, L-shaped bunker. Inside sat the operations officer, a captain.

"Where's the old man?" I asked. "Hanging out at the companies?"

"He's probably up with A Company. That's where you're going. They're short of officers."

It was not unusual for companies to have fewer than their five authorized lieutenants. Sometimes a platoon leader found himself the only surviving officer and would assume command, appointing experienced sergeants as platoon leaders.

I found A Company occupying forward positions on Hill 295. The battalion commander was not there either, but the company commander, another lieutenant, told me to take over 2nd Platoon.

"They're off to the left," he said, pointing down the sloping ridge. "When you get squared away, you're going to have to secure that small crest directly to the east, in front of Hill 432."

The platoon sergeant was glad to have me take over. The platoon wasn't at full strength, but I recognized most of the men from my time with them in Algeria. They would do okay.

Hill 432 loomed before us, a stony mass with a long flat top, known locally as Little Ainchouna. On our maps, we gave the hills different names—Cadillac, Ford, Tuna—anything that would not be meaningful to the enemy, because Hill 432 was on their maps, too. The Sedjenane River was our left boundary to the north, with a smaller river limiting our area on the right. Facing us was a jagged spine of high ridges and peaks running between the two rivers. The map showed no roads, no manmade landmarks at all. Our objective was a ridge a mile east of our position.

Thick brush, five feet high, covered the rough terrain for several hundred yards in front of us. After we checked our gear, I formed my half-strength squads into a column and led the platoon into the bush. I moved in a crouch, but every few minutes I looked over the top of the thicket to gauge how far we had come. A quick glance only. I didn't want a sniper to shoot me in the head. At six foot three, I made a nice target.

It was a hard slog, the ground muddy, the undergrowth tangled and almost impenetrable. After an hour, we came to open, level ground covered with knee-high grass. I stopped the column to let stragglers catch up.

I took off my helmet and mopped the sweat off my face and scanned the field with my binoculars. The afternoon was muggy and we were beat, our uniforms soaked. I saw more of the same thicket on our flanks and decided I wanted no part of it. Maybe the enemy didn't know we were moving, so I would risk crossing in the open. Small decisions, a part of combat everyday. Some turned out okay and were forgotten; others could kill or change lives forever, with rarely any way to tell beforehand which it would be.

I scattered the men in a skirmish line to the right and left. We moved out of the brush and into the soggy field, walking steadily, rifles at the ready. After two hundred yards, the screech of an incoming artillery round filled the air. We dropped on our bellies for what little protection the open field offered.

But instead of exploding and sending steel fragments slicing through us, the shell plopped harmlessly into the wet ground somewhere behind and to the right. Several more rounds screamed over and plopped into the spongy ground, also without exploding.

These had to be armor-piercing rounds. They needed to hit a hard surface to detonate, and this soft ground was saving our ass. I stood up.

"They're duds," I yelled. "Let's move it."

I took off in a fast walk across the field. If we could get into the thicket, we would be in pretty good shape, out of view of any observers. When the men saw me advancing, they got up and moved forward. Nothing encourages an infantry officer more than men who will follow his orders in combat. Right then, I felt a surge of confidence in this platoon.

A dozen more rounds whined over us and landed in the area where the first shells struck. Only one exploded. The artillery observer must have taken off, because we stayed in plain sight until we entered thick undergrowth again. We moved cautiously toward our ridgeline objective, but took the crest without any trouble. The Germans had bugged out.

The 39th Regiment moved forward without opposition. The Germans pulled back along the main road from Sedjenane Station toward Jefna, ten miles away. They made their stand on two strategic hills overlooking the valley, and anything moving toward Jefna drew their artillery fire.

Spread thin across a wide front, the 9th Division regrouped for a flanking attack to force the Germans off the hills. While we waited for the big push, my platoon conducted combat and reconnaissance patrols in the thick brush along the edges of the valley. Our mission was to gauge enemy strength and look for infiltrators.

During this lull, I visited a friend, another platoon leader in 1st Battalion. I found him about ten o'clock one morning on the forward slope of a hill, several hundred yards to the right of my platoon. He sat looking down the valley through his field glasses, his back against the tree, knees up, feet spread.

A few random shells had sailed over the battalion's positions earlier, so I sat ten feet away in a bit of cover. I never wanted to get too close to another guy in a combat zone, because if something hit one of us, maybe the other would survive.

"What do you see?"

"Nothing," he said. "I'm watching that road coming up the valley."

We sat in a grove of twenty-foot pines without much underbrush, the hill sloping at a moderate angle toward the dusty plain. I took a look through my glasses, but couldn't see anything moving.

Suddenly, with a piercing shriek, a high-velocity artillery round hit five yards in front of the lieutenant and burrowed into the ground. It came out again to rest a yard in front of his spread feet. The shell, over a foot long and four or five inches wide, had a red nose and yellow markings on its side, obviously another armor-piercing round. As dust settled over us, I sat shaking, frozen in place, my heart pounding.

"Don't move!" I said, afraid he might set off the round, but my friend had already scrabbled backwards to stand against the tree. He jumped sideways quicker than I thought possible, and we got the hell out of there.

Over the next few days, the regiment relieved British units in the area. Their liaison officers oriented our troops to the situation on the ground, pointing out peculiarities of the land and where the enemy held dug-in positions. One afternoon, at the edge of a small clearing, I ran into a British officer who was leading a reconnaissance patrol of several Americans.

The Brit had a French Goumier soldier with him. Goums were dark-skinned Moroccans who had been fighting for the French since before the First World War. I'd seen them before, most recently coming across the desert with camels in southern Tunisia.

This Goum was impressive physically, standing about six foot six. He had on a French helmet, unstrapped, and pushed back off his weathered face. He wore a loose, gray-striped tunic over his pants and shirt. Made from what looked like an old mattress cover, the tunic hung well below his knees. Strapped across his massive shoulders was an Enfield rifle. Suspenders held up a belt of canvas ammunition pouches. A leather pouch big enough to hold a grapefruit dangled from his waist.

As the Brit and I stood talking, the Goum pulled a whetstone from somewhere beneath his tunic, walked off to one side, and began sharpening a long dagger.

The Brit saw me watching the Goum. "My bodyguard," he said. "Do you have any gold teeth?"

I pulled back my upper lip to show him a large gold filling on the right side.

"Well," he said, "don't smile too much around a Goum."

"Why not?"

The Brit said something in French to the Goum, who walked over, grinned at me, and opened his pouch. He reached in and pulled out a handful of gold teeth.

"A Goum searches every corpse he comes across," said the Brit. "He makes field extractions with his knife or the butt of a rifle. So don't ever let one see your gold tooth. He's liable to pop you in the mouth while you're asleep if he thinks he can get away with it."

I hoped the Goum's pouch was full of German teeth only.

11
Before the Push

During the last half of April 1943, as the regiment waited for the Allies to begin their great push to rid Africa of the enemy, our scouting missions continued. They kept the men busy and the Germans from infiltrating our lines for a surprise attack.

Late one evening, I got orders to make a short patrol in front of my platoon before daybreak. I bedded down in my hole at dark, hoping to get some extra sleep. I was constantly fatigued and never seemed to catch up. A couple of hours before dawn, my eyes gritty and swollen, I left the platoon's forward positions with one of my runners after double-checking the sign and countersign with outposted sentries.

We moved into the darkness and pushed through the underbrush, trying to make as little noise as possible. We covered a mile without speaking, the only sounds our labored breathing and the crunch of our shoes against hardscrabble. In the pale moonlight, we didn't stumble too much and avoided walking off a cliff.

As we approached a small rise, a helmeted German suddenly stood up from behind a bush five feet in front of me. His hands were over his head, but I was so startled I almost shot him anyway.

I pointed my rifle at his chest. He looked maybe thirty years old, and made no trouble as we frisked him. He had no weapon. Apparently, he'd had enough of the war.

I decided not to go any farther away from our lines in the dark with a prisoner. The next German who popped up might not be so ready to surrender.

"*Raus*," I said to the PW, and moved my rifle slightly in the direction I wanted him to go. Halfway back to our point of departure, I began to worry that our troops might not recognize us in the dark. They were already jittery, having heard stories of enemy soldiers infiltrating Allied positions. I also didn't want to take a chance on someone forgetting the password or countersign.

"Hold up," I said. "We'll stay here until daybreak."

The temperature was down to 40 degrees or below, the coldest part of the night, and standing still while the cold seeped through us didn't seem to make much sense either. I moved us into a small gully, pulled out my .45, and laid the German down on his side in as smooth an area as I could find.

"Lie down behind him, front to back," I said to my runner. "Keep your rifle behind you."

After he settled in against the German, I lay down with my back pressed into the prisoner, holding the .45 in front of me. It worked fine. When my front side got cold, I switched positions with my runner to warm up our cold sides. The German never moved, either too scared or so exhausted that he slept. At dawn we got inside our perimeter without a problem, and I sent the German to the rear. That's as close as I came to sleeping with the enemy.

The company moved out the next morning with orders to get to the base of Hill 432 by nightfall. The Germans were using the ridges to direct artillery fire onto the road and dominated the valley all the way to Sedjenane Station. Until we moved the enemy off the hilltop, our supplies couldn't get to us.

We had advanced less than a mile through dense brush, gullies, and small ridges, when we ran into enemy mortar and rifle fire. For the rest of the day the company dug in and exchanged sporadic small-arms fire with Germans across the valley. By late afternoon, we were short of water and ammunition. I found my CO and volunteered to go back for supplies.

I left an hour before dusk. The battalion was spread all over the high ground behind us, and it was after dark before I found the rear CP. The S-4 supply section had fifteen small mules loaded with water cans, field rations, and ammunition. They seemed more like large burros than the American mules I was familiar with. Their high, outsized loads looked too heavy for them. Each was led by an enlisted man from the battalion's headquarters company. My job was to take the first mule, which had two water cans tied onto the packsaddle, and lead the caravan back to the front.

After giving the men brief instructions on handling the mules, I led off. Fifteen mules and a bunch of new muleskinners did not give me a great deal of confidence. Using only short lead ropes and halters, we didn't have much control over the animals and their massive racks of supplies. My mule wanted to go down a little path to the right instead of up the trail I had used. Since it was in the general direction I needed to go, I went along with the mule.

We made a lot of noise as loads shifted and clanged along the rugged trail. A misty rain soon soaked us and made the path slippery and uncertain. My mule picked his way and I hoped the trail eventually led back to the company. As we struggled along, the night seemed to amplify small sounds, despite the light rain.

I worried that we were too far to the right. If we wandered into an open area, the enemy could hit us by firing at our noise. Finally, we came to a left turn that led up a slight rise. With some relief, we changed course, but I didn't recognize the valley on my right or high ground on the other side. Nothing seemed familiar.

Sometime after midnight, as we advanced up a ridge, I realized I didn't know where the hell I was. The mules didn't know either. They just plodded along the path of least resistance. I sure didn't want to walk all these supplies into enemy hands, or worse, into a firefight at point-blank range.

I stopped the column and passed the word that we were lost. No use beating around the bush about it. We would stay here with the mules until daybreak.

It was still raining and miserable. The mules, with their top-heavy loads, made lots of noise. Every time one shifted, something clattered. I looked back at the column and saw mules standing, warm and sweaty. Some men had hunkered down, squatting or sitting, getting colder by the minute.

Bone-weary, I worried that, if I fell asleep, my lead mule might take off, so I needed to lay him down. Standing slightly up slope from me, he seemed small enough. I knelt at his right side, reached under, grabbed front and rear legs on the side opposite me, and jerked. The mule fell with a grunt and a rattle of water cans and harness. I scrambled on top of him and began to pet him as if he were a dog. After a few moments, he lay still. Then I eased my body between his legs and snuggled close to his belly to warm up. I was comfortable enough, but I couldn't sleep. The Germans were no farther away than the next hill, and we would come under fire at first light if we didn't move quickly.

At daybreak I recognized the mountain on my right flank. We'd circled our own positions in the dark and were now low on the forward slope in front of the company, between our troops and Germans a few hundred yards across the valley.

A heavy fog hung in the bottom of the valley, and clouds clung to the tops of Big and Little Ainchouna. Between the fog and the clouds, we had a clear view of the slope across from us. That meant the enemy could see us, too.

I scrambled up, tugged my reluctant mule onto his feet, and started up the hill, leading the column almost straight up the slope to where I thought our own troops were. With my back to the enemy, I felt the skin on my neck crawl, expecting small arms or mortars to open up on us at every step. But as big a target as we made, nobody shot at us. After struggling up two hundred feet, we ran into our troops outposted on the crest.

We moved the mules to the rear and unloaded, and one soldier said we scared the hell out of him. He thought the whole German army was coming up the hill. Apparently, our noise scared the Germans, too. If they'd held their forward positions, they could have picked us off easily. Sometimes luck is all that saves you.

I ate a can of cold C-ration hash for breakfast. The day stayed overcast and cool, and I doubted we were going anywhere. I needed sleep, but I hadn't met all my troops, so I toured our firing positions instead. Dug in at the top of a slope in a stand of stunted, scraggly trees, we couldn't see thirty feet in the misty fog that clung to the hills.

I crawled from hole to hole until I found a rifleman I'd never seen before, a pimply-faced teenager, crouched in a one-man foxhole, obviously new and scared. That was my fault. I should have ensured the sergeants made the men dig two-man foxholes so they could protect each other.

I scrunched as low as I could and introduced myself. The kid seemed uncomfortable with an officer lying next to his foxhole. I asked him where he was from and how old he was, trying to gauge his frame of mind.

I kept glancing toward the German lines to be sure the fog wasn't clearing to expose me even more. Sometimes it could disappear in a few seconds. Sure enough, as I was looking, the fog started to lift. I touched the new man on the shoulder.

"You want to watch now," I said. "The Germans are just across the way there."

The fog continued to lift and we saw three Germans on the forward slope get out of their holes and begin setting up a machine gun. We watched them work hard, digging the gun in solid, orienting it to face us.

I eased my Springfield into a firing position and looked at my new troop. "What are you going to do?" I said.

"I don't know."

"What should you do?"

"I guess I should start shooting."

"Well," I said, "why aren't you shooting then, soldier?"

He stared at me. "Sir, if I shoot at them, they'll shoot back."

"Look," I said, "are you going to wait for them to get set up?" I kept my eye on the Germans because I was going to unload my rifle at them if they started to get behind their weapon. I thought maybe some of my other guys could see them, too, but I wasn't sure. The scrub brush around us, some of it twice my height, was hard to crawl through, tough to fight in.

My replacement soldier continued to stare across the little gully, watching the enemy hard at work right in front of us.

"Do you know what's going to happen if you don't start shooting?" I poked him on the shoulder. "They're going to pick you off. What are you going to do now?"

"I guess I'm going to start shooting, sir." He raised his rifle, squeezed one off, and a German with his back to us crumpled.

"You got him!" I said.

"I did! I did!" He unloaded the whole clip at the other two Germans as they ran up the hill. Then soldiers near us opened fire, kicking up dirt around the Germans until they disappeared over the ridge.

The new kid would do okay.

12
Losing Commanders

The Americans had only been fighting in Africa since Operation Torch in November 1942—not quite six months. The Brits, on the other hand, had been at it for over two and a half years, chasing the Axis forces in running battles all the way from Egypt. Now our forces were joined. Now our huge battle groups, comprising several divisions and supporting units, had the enemy pinned in the mountainous corner of northeast Tunisia, their last stronghold on the continent. In a great coordinated effort, we would now destroy them or push them into the sea. Not that it would be easy.

My platoon advanced without opposition to the line of departure for the next day's attack and took up positions on a densely wooded hill the Germans had recently held. They left us a lot of garbage and piles of excrement. I don't think the *Wehrmacht* ever dug latrines.

I set up two-man outposts to guard against infiltrators. The rest of us holed up close together and stayed awake most of the night, straining to see movement in the darkness.

The main attack began at dawn. French African troops were somewhere on our left flank and a sister battalion of the 39th regiment on the right. The regiment's front stretched five miles or more, impossible to cover completely. The Germans fell back to prepared defensive positions: elaborate dugouts with connecting trenches, barbed wire perimeters, protective minefields, and interlocking fields of fire. Many of these well-stocked fortifications even had power generators. Their sturdy red communications wire tied everything together.

The attack made erratic progress; some units forged ahead while others bogged down and fell behind. I couldn't see anything beyond our platoon, but the immense shelling and gunfire around us told me we weren't fighting alone. Somewhere to my right, mines exploded and men screamed. As we walked through heavy brush, MP-42 machine guns opened up in front of us and three men went down. I couldn't see the German gunners. They must have heard us or saw the brush move as we walked through it. Firing blindly down from the high ground, they raked the undergrowth while we cringed with nothing to shoot at.

Bullets snicked through the bushes, clipping twigs and leaves a foot over my head. The platoon was scattered. I crawled to the left, gathered several men, and tried to flank the enemy, but we never found the machine-gun nest. By the time we got to where I thought it should be, the firing had stopped. We kept moving.

The platoon took more casualties, but not all our losses were to enemy fire. Some men got separated and lost in the thick brush. The dead were left where they fell; we could do nothing for them anyway. Graves registration units, somewhere behind us, would catch up and take care of them later.

The most wrenching part of the day was having to leave wounded men who couldn't walk out. It took at least two men to carry a wounded soldier any distance, men I couldn't spare. We stabilized the wounded with tourniquets, sulfa powder to guard against gangrene, and a promise that reserve units would be along soon. I could only hope the troops following behind would find our wounded and get them back to an aid station, but the Sedjenane was not a good place to get hurt. A lot of men died before they got any real help.

By the end of the day, I counted only twenty-one men with me—half a platoon. I had no idea where my CO and the rest of the company were. When we advanced onto slightly higher ground at the edge of a large field, I decided we would stay put.

Isolated, we spent a tense night watching and waiting. The morning dawned cold and damp, with heavy fog. Then it began to drizzle, normal weather for the infantry. I contacted two other platoons by radio, both with sergeants in charge. None of us knew what to do next. After a couple of hours, my company commander still hadn't come forward, so I walked back to find out what was going on.

Half a mile south of my platoon, I found the battalion commander with three of his staff and two officers I'd never seen before. They stood in front of a large rock outcropping studying a situation map. It was still misting; the high area where we stood was wrapped in a low cloudbank. I didn't like standing in the open in fog that could lift at any moment, so I quickly briefed the group on what was happening at my forward position.

The battalion commander stabbed the map with his finger. "Okay, Scheffel," he said, "you take your company straight ahead across this area and secure the top of Little Ainchouna here."

Now I was the designated company commander? The map showed only a few contour lines and elevations, with no colors to show vegetation or other details. The colonel was pointing to where I had just come from, but there was no indication on his map of the large open area facing my platoon.

After getting poor orders from this lieutenant colonel more than once back in El Guettar, I'd vowed to question any missions that didn't make sense to me.

"Colonel," I said, "I don't have a clue where the rest of the company is. I haven't seen my commander in two days."

"Well, I haven't either, so you're it." The colonel looked at his watch. You've got two hours to reform the company. H-hour is 1400."

I pointed at the map. "Sir, there's no way I can take my men across there. It's open area and the Germans will have it zeroed in with mortars and artillery."

The colonel looked at me steadily. "You will assemble the company and commence the attack at 1400 hours," he said, and turned to discuss objectives for his other companies.

I stood still, not trusting myself to speak, afraid I would say something rash in front of his staff. Besides, arguing out here in the open was crazy, so I walked to the sheltered side of a large boulder and waited to see what other great ideas this bunch came up with. I thought about the stupidity of attacking into the teeth of the enemy over open ground and made up my mind I would swing to the left once the attack started.

A few minutes later, another lieutenant walked around to my side of the boulder. He faced the same problem: how to advance his men across open ground without getting them slaughtered. As we sat discussing it, I noticed patches of sunlight and shadows on the ground around us. The fog was lifting.

Before I could move, there was a sharp whistle and explosion on the other side of the boulder. Fragments buzzed through the air and clanged off the rocks. We huddled on the shuddering ground against the backside of our boulder while more shells burst in a pattern moving away from us. Then the shelling was over as quickly as it had begun.

We heard terrible screaming and ran to find everyone on the ground. A shell had hit in front of the command group, its fragments slicing through the men. Some enlisted soldiers nearby ran up to help.

Blood was everywhere. The executive officer, a major, died instantly, half his face ripped off. A captain, probably reporting in to take over a company, was also dead. The battalion commander, hit in the chest, lay on his back, choking in his own blood. We raised him and tried to stop the bleeding, but he died within minutes. The rest stayed down, but they were alive.

I grabbed a soldier by the arm. "Get back to the command post. Tell them we need help up here."

After a few minutes, a captain ran up with two medics. While the medics worked on the wounded, we discussed how to proceed.

"I'm the ranking officer," said the captain. "I'm assuming command of 1st Battalion. I'll send someone to pick up the wounded as soon as I get back to the CP."

"Who's going to take over the forward CP?" I said. "There's no one left."

"You do it, Scheffel." He turned to the other lieutenant. "You get back to your men."

The lieutenant left and I looked around at the mess. No staff, not even one of my own men with me. "There's nothing left here to command," I said. "I can put the forward CP up front with my platoon. Anybody needs me can find me there."

My new battalion commander agreed, and I returned forward. I never saw that captain again.

I sent two runners out to try to find other platoons, but before they got back, the Germans launched an attack across the open ground I'd argued against crossing. To hell with finding the rest of the company. My immediate concern became the survival of my men.

Well dug in, we had a good view of the Germans as they walked toward us in a skirmish line. Halfway across the open ground, they broke into a run, coming straight at us, firing their weapons. Muzzles flashed and bullets snapped around us. My men screamed curses and poured rifle and BAR fire back at the suicide charge, scoring hits that jerked the bodies of the enemy soldiers and knocked them down. The Germans took a terrible beating before they ran back toward cover. They left their dead and wounded on the field. It was as crazy as the rest of the day. After the battle, we heard moaning and cries for help in front of us, but by nightfall the field was silent.

Our sector remained in a state of confusion. I still had no idea where my company commander was, or where we were in relation to other units. Communications at our position were sporadic. The battalion must have set up another forward CP, but I don't know how much command and control they were able to establish. I didn't hear from them all afternoon.

We dug deeper and hunkered down, expecting another attack, but it didn't come. Next day it rained again. When we moved through the killing field, the puddles were tinged pink, and we counted over thirty enemy dead.

Another captain showed up to take over the company, which was okay with me. Over the next few days, the regiment advanced against a series of hills, trying to outflank the enemy in a sweeping maneuver to the north. But the Germans retreated onto higher ground and directed harassing artillery fire toward the lower hills we occupied. I stopped my platoon whenever we reached our objective, whether it was before noon or late in the day. As we dug in on one ridge, we heard heavy rifle and machine gun fire to the south. The enemy didn't attack us, but nobody had to tell the men to keep their weapons clean.

I made sure that newer troops paired with seasoned men who had learned a lot since those first days of combat in southern Tunisia. Instinctively, they knew where to dig in so there were no blind spots in our field of fire. They felt more secure in two-man foxholes and groused when we posted them singly as early warning outposts several yards down a ridge.

We didn't move for two days as the regiment tried to figure out what to do next. I sent out patrols, but their forays were mostly uneventful. I let them roam wherever they wanted in case they stumbled onto a hut or a cache of supplies. One patrol brought back canned sardines the Germans had abandoned.

There was no mail in or out. We hadn't had a hot meal for days, and we lived on what we scrounged and on cold rations left over from the mule-train delivery. The country was too rugged for the kitchen trucks to bring up hot food.

I also had another worry in the field. Without a cup of hot coffee every morning, I had trouble with constipation. More than one cup and I was apt to be crapping all day, not an easy thing to accomplish on the move, wearing long underwear stiff with impregnated chemicals and filth. Also, the slick brown toilet paper the army issued us didn't lend itself to a quick cleanup.

Though we stayed in the same filthy clothes, we tried our best to keep our feet in good shape. Healthy feet were particularly vital to an infantryman. I carried an extra pair of socks in the webbing of my helmet liner to keep them dry. While we waited for orders, I holed up to change my socks and air my feet, and it suddenly occurred to me that the date was 27 April 1943. I'd been married for one year and one month.

I reached in my pants pocket and pulled out a ragged emergency D-ration chocolate bar. Celebrating, I ate it slowly and thought of Ruth, wondering what she was doing right then.

13
Prisoners

With little rest, we chased the Germans from ridge to ridge toward Bizerte. Late one afternoon, the company crossed a rocky crest and dug into defensive positions on the forward slope that overlooked a wide, barren valley. We had outrun our supply lines and had orders to hold at the edge of some evergreen woods.

After we settled in, I walked along the ridge to visit another platoon leader, a friend I'd known since Algeria. We sat in the shade off by ourselves, looking out over the plain. Almost a mile away a road cut diagonally across in front of us. It led to Mateur, which was still in German hands. I glanced across the plain and saw what looked like a truck moving toward us along the road, kicking up dust.

"That can't be ours," I said. I took a closer look with my field glasses and saw that it was towing something. The truck pulled off the road and stopped on the far side of a small bridge. Men got out and bustled around the rear of the truck.

"Germans," I said. "They're pulling an artillery piece."

I picked up my rifle and fumbled with the rear sight. To shoot that far, I would have to raise it. Aiming over the front sight through the raised rear sight would bring the barrel up so that the round would arc in a rainbow trajectory toward the distant target.

Firing a rifle at long range is generally not effective and can disclose the soldier's position, bringing enemy fire down on him. It's a matter of self-preservation. Nevertheless, I raised the rear sight until it looked about right.

The tow truck started turning around to go back down the road.

"Let's see if these sights are any good." I lay in a prone position, drew a bead, held my breath, and squeezed off a round.

"He's down!" yelled my friend.

Incredibly, at more than half a mile, I had hit one of the Germans. The rest ran to catch the truck as it drove away, leaving the gun sitting there. Those soldiers were obviously support troops, not infantrymen; my silent kill had scared them off. They never heard the crack of the bullet because it hit the guy, and I know they didn't hear the muzzle thump, not that far away. If they did, it would have sounded like somebody stepping on a stick.

"Charlie, you're the crack shot in the Army."

"No," I said, "that German was just unlucky."

The next morning we received orders to consolidate our positions. Down the slope to my platoon's immediate front was a large area covered with brush and trees. Over the top of these trees, we could see the far-off wreckage of German field guns and vehicles still smoldering on the plain where our artillery had destroyed them the day before.

Of immediate concern was the possibility of enemy soldiers sneaking up through the thickets on the hillside. I sent patrols to comb the area for signs of infiltration, and about midafternoon, one of the three-man patrols came back with twelve prisoners. My corporal said they had walked up the hill toward him with their hands up, shouting "*Kamerad, Kamerad!*"

I crawled out of my hole and looked them over. They were young enlisted men, filthy, scared, and hungry—certainly not elite SS soldiers. They seemed beaten and glad to be out of the war. We scrounged around and found them a few rations, which they gobbled down.

It was standard procedure to get PWs to the rear as soon as possible. But with enemy soldiers in the nearby woods and less than half a platoon, I couldn't spare a bunch of guys to escort the prisoners. One soldier with an automatic rifle and a full clip would have to do. I didn't think they had enough fight left in them to give us trouble, anyway.

After the Germans finished eating, I called my BAR man over. "Take these prisoners back to battalion and drop them off."

The BAR man, a private not yet twenty, looked at me kind of funny, but I didn't think anything about it. He had the weapon needed to get the job done, and I had plenty of other things on my mind.

"You're it," I said.

"Yes, sir." He put a fresh clip in the weapon, swung it around, and motioned the prisoners to move up the hill behind us. They climbed over the ridge and dropped out of sight.

Less than ten minutes later, I was debriefing the soldiers from the patrol, trying to find out what else they'd seen, when I heard the unmistakable deep thumping racket of a BAR firing a long slow burst.

Normally, a good BAR gunner will squeeze off only three or four rounds at a time so that the weapon's aim doesn't jump off what he's shooting at. This was different. This sounded like a full magazine.

I started toward the hilltop, motioning to a couple of men to come with me. As we reached the crest, I heard three more bursts, this time shorter ones. We picked up the pace, but before we got far, my BAR man came walking toward us through the trees and brush.

"What the hell happened?" I said, afraid I already knew.

The kid looked at me, the BAR cradled in his arms, its barrel slanting across his body. "They all tried to get away, sir," he said quietly. "I had to shoot them. They would have escaped."

Rage almost lifted me off my feet. My right hand floated down and touched the leather flap of the .45 holster on my hip.

"I'm Jewish, Lieutenant," he said.

That stopped me. "And you just shot them? What the fuck's the matter with you?"

"Those bastards killed my parents and a whole lot of other people, way before Pearl Harbor. I want to kill every fucking one of them."

When he told me his story, I understood his hatred and the why of what he had done. We'd already heard about concentration camps in Europe. This kid was sent to America to live with relatives in the mid-1930s, after it was clear what Hitler had in mind for Jews. He never heard from his parents again.

There was nothing I could do to change what had happened. I didn't even send anyone back to check on the prisoners. I already knew they were dead, because I'd heard him reload his BAR and make sure.

The kid had no accent or obvious Jewish name, and it never registered on me what I was doing when I assigned him to take the Germans back. It was just a job that needed doing, and I didn't think much about it. Big mistake.

"You know, shooting prisoners can be a two-way street," I said, aware I had come real close to killing an American soldier. I took a step toward the kid and poked my finger at him. "This will not ever happen again. You got that?"

We never spoke of the incident after that day, and I found out later the kid died fighting in the hedgerows of Normandy after the D-Day invasion.

14
Free of Axis Forces

Sitting in the hills northwest of Mateur, the company got word that an armored division had flanked the enemy and captured the city. The rout was on, and the Allies would now try to cut off the Afrika Korps before it reached Bizerte and Tunis to escape.

We trudged down the slopes the next afternoon, happy to see our kitchen truck waiting for us. The truck carried our field ranges and staples such as salt, sugar, and coffee, along with the officers' bedrolls. After the enlisted men went through the chow line, the cooks set up a table and served the officers, a small privilege of rank that gave us a chance to discuss and compare notes on our situation.

We climbed on vehicles and rode north. Most of the 9th Division chased the Germans through a narrow gap between two large lakes. Our battalion, as a rear guard, stayed on the south shore, happy to be out of battles with a desperate enemy.

Instead, we rested and caught up on our sleep. One evening we scrounged a few bottles of wine from a nearby farmhouse and watched artillery flashes light the sky across the lake. The sound of explosions kept me sober, thinking of Americans caught in the barrage.

The distant shelling stopped the next morning, bringing sudden quiet. It was early May, and the plains of Mateur bloomed fiery red and orange with poppies as far as the eye could see. Men climbed out of their foxholes, bedazzled. The poppies at Flanders Field couldn't be any better than this.

Suddenly a private jumped up and began pacing, waving his arms across the expanse of flowers.

"I've had all this combat shit I can take!" he screamed. "I'm not fighting another fucking minute!"

Someone said, "And just how the fuck are you going to do that?"

"Yeah," said another soldier, "tell us your secret. How are you going to stay out of combat and not go to the stockade?"

"Just wait and see."

I'd heard enough. "Shut up," I said, walking toward the kid. "You're not going to do a damn thing, so just shut the fuck up. Don't think I won't remember this."

Although I spoke directly to my reluctant soldier, I meant it for all of them. Not as a direct threat, but I wanted everyone in the platoon to know we were all soldiers in the same war. Quitting was not an option.

Two days later, several tanks stopped by, and a captain told us the battalion was now attached to the 1st Armored Division. As we rumbled east, streams of Allied aircraft flew over on their way to attack the retreating Germans. Give them hell, guys.

The tankers let us off near the coast, and I watched our planes drop tons of bombs on ships trying to rescue the Afrika Korps, which began surrendering by the thousands. Later that day the British captured Tunis. It was almost over.

Assigned to guard a section of the main Tunis-Bizerte highway, we straddled the road, set up outposts, and sent out patrols to watch for infiltrators who might try to mine the road or blow it up. Late the next afternoon, one of my sergeants found an abandoned German motorcycle with a sidecar. He convinced me he had owned a motorcycle back in New York.

"Hop in, sir. Let's go for a ride."

The sergeant smeared a handful of mud across the black swastika on the sidecar. I grabbed a Tommy gun and jumped in.

"Okay," I said. "Let's go to Bizerte."

The sergeant gunned the motorcycle and we roared out of the bivouac area, churning up dust. When we wheeled onto the highway, not another person or vehicle was in sight. I guessed friendly troops had already moved east, and this road was not being used in the chase.

We headed north with Lake Bizerte on our immediate left. We came to a small village of low mud huts and narrow side streets that meandered a ways, then played out. We slowed and I lifted the Thompson, but we didn't see a soul.

After clearing the village, we zoomed on toward Bizerte. Even without cheering crowds, I felt like a conquering hero, the wind roaring in my ears under my helmet and whipping through my uniform. The sergeant leaned forward, grinning.

Near the south bank of the ship channel that emptied Lake Bizerte into the Mediterranean, we entered a small built-up area and turned into a plaza along the waterfront. I expected to see American troops, but the plaza was empty and eerily quiet.

I stared across the channel to the docks but saw no movement there, either. This didn't make sense, and I got a bad feeling sitting there in a German motorcycle.

Just as I started to tell the driver to turn around, a bullet slammed into the ground ten feet to our right. I heard a crack as another zipped past, fired from across the channel. The sergeant turned the cycle and we roared the other way, skidding around the corner to get out of the line of fire.

We made the return trip a lot quicker, but I had plenty of time to think about the stupid thing I had done. Safely back at the bivouac area, we opened a bottle of local wine and took several swigs to calm our frazzled nerves.

At daybreak, our platoon's outpost on the main road sent a runner to tell me that an American officer in a staff car wanted to see the officer in charge. I climbed out of my hole and went to the road where a major told me a large column of Germans was coming north under surrender conditions. They were moving into open confinement in a dry lake bed.

"Let them pass," he said.

"Yes, sir." I saluted and went back to tell everyone.

About midmorning, a long column of vehicles came up the road. In the lead, moving at walking speed, was a German command car flying a large white flag on its front fender. Strung out behind must have been fifty thousand German soldiers, most walking, some riding in all sorts of vehicles. What a sight. We were looking at the beaten remnants of the Afrika Korps.

The prisoners I had seen before preferred to surrender to Americans. They feared British reprisals, not only for bombing England, but also for the savage combat waged for years across North Africa. Now here they were, as far as the eye could see.

At first, we stood at the ready, but after an hour we realized this was a beaten bunch, subdued, glad to be finished with the war. Short of rations, I ordered my men not to give the PWs food or water, but every so often one of our guys would toss out a package of cigarettes or a D-ration chocolate bar.

At noon, I went back to my foxhole and opened a can of C-ration meat and beans. As I sat spooning the pasty stuff into my mouth, I noticed the leather case containing my mediocre six-power field glasses, not nearly as good as the fine optics of German binoculars.

When I got back to the road, I looked for a prisoner carrying binoculars. Soon an open staff car rolled slowly toward us. In the back seat sat three officers, one with field glasses hanging around his neck. I had one of my men pull the car out of the column. He motioned the officers to get out and walk up the bare embankment to where I stood.

I held up my hand and stopped them ten feet away. The man with the binoculars appeared to be the ranking officer in the group. He was a trim, aristocratic man, maybe fifty, wearing a neatly tailored uniform and a peaked dress hat with a polished bill. Spiffy, probably a full colonel. He looked at me as if he knew I was only a lowly lieutenant.

I motioned for him to take the strap over his head and hand the glasses to me.

He hesitated a moment, staring at me without expression. Then he reached up and lifted the strap over his head. In one sweeping movement, he swung the glasses in a vicious arc and slammed them into the ground, smashing the lenses. He flipped the end of the strap toward me.

"They are yours," he said in clipped English.

None of my men said a word, waiting to see what I would do. I was pissed, but I kept my composure and didn't react. I stared at the arrogant bastard who was so proud no American officer would have the pleasure of using his fine equipment. Then I laughed.

"Well," I said, "you sure as hell won't need them where you're going."

Two days later, when the British cut off the final escape route to the Cap Bon Peninsula, Germans again surrendered in droves. On 13 May 1943, the German high command formally surrendered, and General Alexander issued a message to all troops that North Africa was free of Axis forces.

We were unprepared for the number of prisoners at the end of hostilities. What do you do with over 200,000 enemy soldiers you didn't expect to capture? We put them in large pens with no food or supplies. Before long, Allied forces were on half rations, the rest going to feed our prisoners while we figured out what to do with them.

Wrecked and sunken ships littered the Bizerte harbor and blocked resupply. The only ports open were at Algiers and Oran and around on the Atlantic side of Morocco. To ease the situation, most of the 1st and 9th Divisions moved back into the desert somewhere south of Oran, Algeria.

Our battalion, down to half strength, stayed in Tunisia as part of a rear guard, camping in pup tents along the coast ten miles west of Bizerte. We played ball, swam in the Mediterranean, wrote letters, and generally lazed around.

One morning we got our first supply of bazookas for the heavy-weapons platoons. The battalion commander told me, "Charlie, get yourself a bazooka and take the battalion out and show them how to use it."

I had heard about bazookas back in ROTC and knew they were supposed to knock out tanks, but I had never seen one. "I don't know anything about it," I said.

"Well, nobody else does either, so you're the training officer for this weapon."

We marched 400 soldiers to the beach and sat them down a short distance from a wrecked Italian tank I was going to aim at. If I missed the tank, the round would go out to sea.

I explained the weapon to the men. The bazooka was basically a shoulder-mounted launch tube almost five feet long that fired a two-foot-long rocket. It had a leaf sight that flipped up in front with ranges marked on it. A latch kept the missile from falling out of the tube if you tipped it. There was a shoulder rest and two grips for aiming. The trigger was on the rear grip. I held the weapon as I talked, studying it, learning as I went along.

"Okay, men," I said finally, "you're about to see what a bazooka can do to that tank."

My platoon sergeant broke open a case of ammunition and pulled out a round. "Where should I stand?" he said.

"Just don't stand anywhere behind me. Go ahead and load it." He shoved the round into the tube and moved to the side.

One of the other officers said, "I think you're supposed to have a gas mask on when you pull the trigger." We had thrown away our gas masks long ago. Besides, a guy shouldn't have to wear a gas mask to use this thing in combat.

We were a hundred yards from the tank. I raised the leaf sight pretty high to allow for the round to drop a good bit, sighted down the barrel, and pulled the trigger. The projectile shot out of the tube and cleared the tank by forty or fifty feet.

That got a big laugh. "Hey, Lieutenant, you missed it."

At least the weapon didn't throw debris in my face. We wouldn't need gas masks to shoot bazookas. I lowered the rear sight. "Load it again."

I pulled the trigger and this time the projectile took off on a serpentine path, as if it had no tail fins, not coming anywhere close to the tank.

That got another big laugh, and someone yelled, "Boy, that would be great on the Fourth of July, Lieutenant."

I began to feel skeptical, but if this was a combat weapon, then somebody ought to be able to use it. "Put in another round."

By this time the sergeant was a little scared about what was going on. He loaded the bazooka again and said, "Wait until I get behind the jeep."

He knelt with the jeep between him and me and I pulled the trigger. An explosive flash engulfed me. I thought my head had been blown off. Nothing came out the front end, but the propellant had torn open the tube and shot up past my helmet. I couldn't hear anything but a loud ringing in my head. I smelled burning powder and dropped the weapon, wondering where I was hit.

Nobody laughed this time. My sergeant ran over. "You should have seen the fire and smoke coming up next to your head."

"This demonstration is over," I said. "You men go for a swim." I laid the bazooka in the jeep and we drove back to battalion HQ.

"How'd it go?" the commander asked.

I showed him the scorched hole in the top of the bazooka tube. "I'm going over to talk to the ordnance guys," I said.

The ordnance officer, a colonel in his forties, knew his business. He explained what had happened, and taught an ignorant young lieutenant some basic ordnance facts. The bazooka ammunition had been sitting in one spot for eight months in some supply dump. Powder that sits for months in one place without climate control will pack itself down, liable to explode when fired.

I gladly went back to being a plain old platoon leader.

We still had German prisoners confined behind concertina wire fifteen miles from our encampment. The English didn't have enough food or supplies for PWs, so most would go to the United States or Canada. I got orders for my platoon to take a trainload of them to Oran for transport to America. We marched 700 prisoners under loose guard to the railhead and loaded them into "forty and eight" boxcars—meaning they held forty men or eight horses.

I boarded my platoon into a vintage 1890s passenger coach at the end of the train. We squared our gear away and tried to get comfortable for the five-day trip across the top of Africa. As we chugged slowly out of the station behind an ancient narrow-gauge steam engine, I felt a bit overwhelmed by the number of prisoners on board and sent for the ranking German officer, a full colonel who spoke good English.

"Colonel," I said, "there are 700 of you people and there's me and twenty men with one machine gun and our personal weapons. They'll put you on a ship at Oran and send you back to the States. If you won't try to escape, or cause us any trouble, I'll stop every time we come to fresh water, and let your men take a break, bathe, take a leak, or whatever. Is it a deal?"

"Agreed." We shook hands.

We were quite a sight for the locals along the way, a few Americans surrounded by Germans we'd fought so bitterly against, watching each other wash up.

15
Strawman at the Bordello

I delivered my prisoners at Oran and found out the 9th Division was encamped south of Sidi-bel-Abbes near Magenta, a small, isolated oasis. The division was trying to stay hidden from German spies and sympathizers while it restocked with troops and supplies for the next invasion.

We headed for the bivouac area, catching rides on supply trucks, grinding along through increasing heat, the dusty landscape becoming more desolate and barren as we made our way south. The sun burned down from an empty blue sky, waves of heat shimmering in front of distant hills.

At noon on the second day, we reached a gigantic tent city at the edge of the Sahara Desert, a forlorn place to bed down the division. The temperature was over a hundred, with none of the sea breezes that cooled Oran. The Germans would never find us here.

Shortly after I arrived, an epidemic of diarrhea broke out, caused by contaminated drinking water. Some men had to be evacuated back to the hospital at Oran. As one of the most senior lieutenants, I became S-3, plans and operations officer, of the 1st Battalion, normally a major's slot.

I was determined to make the best of my opportunity, and during the last days of May 1943, I trained the battalion on what I'd learned from the Brits. I doubt if Brigadier General Stroh, the 9th Division's assistant commander, knew who Lieutenant Scheffel was, but one morning he watched me demonstrate the British battle drill for squads. That afternoon I was ordered to report to his office.

"I've heard about the stuff you're doing with the companies in 1st Battalion," he said. "I want you to teach this to your whole regiment."

That became my full-time job for the next week. I went over why two-man foxholes work best, how to maneuver an infantry squad under fire, what a batman is—all the important little things the Brits had taught me, stuff that helped keep me alive.

The men of the 9th Division did not take well to living isolated in tents at the edge of the desert with nothing to do but drill. Thirty miles to the north lay Sidi-bel-Abbes, an ancient walled city of some 50,000 civilians. With the city and its pleasures so near, discipline in the division broke down. Soldiers, needing release after their war experiences, went AWOL, hitchhiking and walking toward civilization through the heat and dust at all hours of the day and night.

A French Foreign Legion headquarters was in the city, but their troops were still back in Tunisia, where they fought with the Allies after the French changed sides. With the Legionnaires gone, the prostitutes of Sidi-bel-Abbes hadn't seen soldiers for months. Young American GIs by the hundreds, safe for the moment from intense combat and happy to be alive, streamed into the city with their back pay, looking for good times. The ladies were pleased to oblige.

At company short-arm inspections, soldiers had their genitals inspected for signs of venereal diseases, and soon doctors were treating more and more cases, some with symptoms they'd never seen before. It wasn't long before we had an epidemic.

On any given morning, a company commander might walk into his orderly room and have a conversation something like:

"First Sergeant, what's the strength today?"

"Well, sir, we've only got 160 men; we need forty replacements to get up to full strength."

"I know that. What's the strength level?"

"Sir, forty men are here in the camp with diarrhea or VD, forty are AWOL, walking to Sidi-bel-Abbes, forty are already there, drunk and whoring around, and the rest are walking back here."

One afternoon the regimental commander sent for me. When I walked into the colonel's sweltering tent, a couple of combat surgeons were already there, as well as a lieutenant named Bob, whom I'd met before, and a battalion surgeon who was a major. None of us knew why we'd been summoned. We waited, sweating in the 115-degree heat, flies buzzing around us.

After several minutes, the colonel came in through the open tent flap and walked straight to the major.

"I want you to take a two-and-a-half-ton truck right now and go to Oran. Get a load of that new miracle medicine that just arrived. I think it's called penicillin, and I want a truckload of it."

Oran was over a hundred miles from where we stood. The major saluted and walked out. The colonel turned to me and Bob.

"Can you two look at a naked woman without going crazy?"

"Barely," I said.

"If Charlie's in bad shape, I'm in worse," said Bob.

"You'll be fine," the colonel said. "I want you to set up a whorehouse. Charlie, you go collect money from every company. Right now. Then you and Bob go to Sidi-bel-Abbes and get started. We're going to run our own house."

I walked around to every company commander in the 39th, most of whom I knew. Each had a slush fund for beer busts, softball equipment, or whatever. Recreation stuff. It was the company commander's fund, carried in a safe on the kitchen truck.

"What do you want two hundred dollars for, Charlie?"

"The colonel said we're going to have our own whorehouse."

"Is it going to be for officers, too?"

"Nope. Just enlisted men. Officers ought to have more sense than to fool around with that stuff."

I collected three thousand dollars, put it in a musette bag, and Bob and I drove into Sidi-bel-Abbes. The whorehouses were on the downtown plaza, all legal and running wide open. The French government had nothing against them, especially with a Foreign Legion headquarters nearby.

Several houses for enlisted men were located on three sides of the plaza. But on the east side, in a nice, five-story hotel, the French officers had their own luxurious bordello, served by two dozen of the prettiest girls in town. That was the house the 39th Regiment took over. With the Foreign Legion still in Tunisia, it was easy. Bob and I walked into the lobby with the money, met the madam, settled on a price, and it was done.

On the way back to camp, I asked our driver how we should set up the operation. I thought he might know some pitfalls to look out for.

"You know, sir, there are a lot of other outfits around here. The 1st Division, the 47th Regiment, and some others. We ought to have cards for our guys, so nobody else can get into our house."

We had little red cards made at a shop in town. Each card was numbered and had a unique picture of a cart without a horse on it, printed from a plate we then confiscated.

Transportation was the next problem. We unloaded the battalion's kitchen trucks—field ranges, water cans, everything. Those trucks became our shuttle from Magenta to Sidi-bel-Abbes. Instead of the men going AWOL, we were going to transport them in an orderly fashion.

The regiment had 1,200 men in it, and we had transportation for 400 at a time. The round trip to Sidi-bel-Abbes took two hours, so we decided we would make three shuttle trips a day. That left each group a couple of hours to mess around town.

With so few women working in the house, we had a logistical problem, even though the madam assured us that any one of her girls could easily take care of ten or twelve guys a day. Bob and I, as young married men, figured ten or fifteen minutes of sexual activity should be enough for fellows who hadn't been around women for a long time. Still, four hundred men were too many for the time allotted.

In the end, we set up a rationing system that allowed only a hundred men from each shift to get laid. We called company formations, counted the men into groups of four, and had them draw straws. The soldier in each group who drew the long straw got the ticket. Since I held the straws, one of my nicknames, among many, was "Strawman."

A lively secondary market developed. Many tickets were sold, traded, or given to friends before being collected at the door of our house.

We set up a prophylaxis station in a room off the hotel lobby. One of our doctors inspected the ladies daily for venereal diseases and gave penicillin shots to any he found infected. Every man got a pro kit, a small package with a condom and some salve that was supposed to prevent most everything a man could get from sexual intercourse. If the kit failed, we poked him with penicillin, too.

Military policemen rolled out concertina wire, guarded the place against intruders from other units, and kept our drunks and rowdies in line. They rousted soldiers out of rooms when they overstayed their fifteen minutes and generally kept overall order.

The madam collected the tickets and groped each soldier for signs of an erection before she allowed him up to the girls. A man better have his flag raised or he went to the end of the line and watched his buddies ascend the stairs.

Bob was in charge at the house, while I ran things in the bivouac area. Romantic it was not, but it ran smoothly. The army long ago figured out how to handle large groups of soldiers efficiently, and we were no exception.

Our venereal disease rate went down. The penicillin did the job, or so the doctors told me. And the men believed in it. This had nothing to do with combat directly, but indirectly it was most important. It got men ready to fight.

After a couple of weeks, the regimental commander summoned me again. Three civilians were waiting with the colonel when I got there.

"Lieutenant Scheffel, these gentlemen are from the Red Cross in London. They're down here to find out what you're doing to corrupt the morals of American servicemen fighting in North Africa." The colonel couldn't quite suppress a smile. "Explain what you've been doing, Lieutenant."

Even though mail was censored during the war, word had somehow gotten back to the States that American military services were operating houses of prostitution. Now the Red Cross was here to investigate. One gentleman had been an executive with a steel company, another with Heinz, and the third was a former businessman. All were in their 60s or 70s, doing their patriotic duty as Red Cross bigwigs, sent on this important mission to find out how an Army lieutenant was corrupting the morals of American boys.

So I told them. When I finished, the fellow from Heinz looked at me and said, "That's an incredible story, Lieutenant."

"Yes, sir, it is. But if you'd been in my shoes, or the colonel's here, what would you have done?"

"Same as you did, Lieutenant. Forget this visit." And they walked out of the tent.

The operation lasted another few days before the 9th Division went back to Bizerte, Tunisia, the jumping off point for the invasion of Sicily.

As we left for combat again, I mailed a red whorehouse ticket to Ruth and said I'd tell her about it later. When I saw her again, almost two years later, I told her the story of how I came to run a whorehouse.

"Did you just run it?"

"Yes, I just ran it."

A few years ago, I offered the ticket to the museum at Brooke Army Medical Center in San Antonio, but the director refused it.

"We're a little concerned about putting anything to do with sexual activity in the museum," he said.

16
Invading Sicily

One morning, General Patton showed up in his staff car with a motorcycle escort and an entourage that included General Eddy, 9th Division commander. Patton, by this time commanding the Seventh Army, came to give us one of his famous pep talks.

Changes he mandated for the thousands of officers under him grated on many of us. We were fined if caught not wearing a tie or leggings, not being freshly shaved, or for violating a host of other chickenshit rules. Combat, the desert, water shortages—nothing made any difference to the man, nor mitigated any of his bizarre rules.

So by the time he arrived at our bivouac near the ruined port at Bizerte, I already had my opinion of him. I sat on the beach with the rest of the officers of the 39th Infantry Regiment and looked up at Patton strutting on the flat bed of a tank carrier, resplendent in his tailored uniform, shellacked helmet liner, shiny boots, and bright belt buckle. He wore an ivory-handled revolver strapped on his hip. General Eddy, slightly pudgy, wearing glasses and looking like a small-town banker, stood a couple paces behind Patton to his left.

Patton began an amazingly bellicose and agitated tirade about what we were going to do to the enemy when we got to Sicily. Then he said, "And gentlemen, when we land on the beaches of Sicily, there will be no prisoners taken."

I sat stunned in the first row of officers, not ten feet away from this pompous man. His words made my skin crawl. Nobody said anything for a long moment.

General Eddy stepped forward and tugged gently at Patton's shirtsleeve. "General," he said so softly I could barely hear him, "you might want to rethink your last statement."

Patton looked out over the group of officers sitting on the sand before him. Then he wagged his hand toward us. "Forget what I just said."

Well, you don't forget those things.

On the night of July 10, 1943, we trudged on board several large landing craft the Navy used to transport infantry troops. These LCIs were about 150 feet long with a bow instead of a flat ramp in front. In addition to the crew, they could transport almost two hundred combat soldiers and their gear.

Laden with equipment, we loaded via stepped ramps lowered from each side of the vessel. The convoy eased out of port bound for Sicily, snaking its way around the sunken wrecks still littering the Bizerte harbor.

Two days later, at the small port of Licata on Sicily's southern coast, the 39th Regiment landed without being fired on. It was a hot day and the ship was full, running aground on a sandbar many yards off the beach. I waded ashore in water up to my shoulders with two of my shorter troops hanging off my arms so they wouldn't go under. With all the gear we were carrying, there was no way we could swim, but somehow we got ashore without anyone drowning.

After pausing long enough to get the companies and platoons organized, we started west along the coast. I was still the S-3 plans and operations officer for 1st Battalion. The next day, as we approached a small town along the coast, I went out on an advance reconnaissance patrol.

Back at the battalion, before I could give my assessment, the commander told me to plan for the companies to attack the town. I guess, as a major, he was anxious to perform well in a lieutenant colonel's slot.

"That town's not a threat," I said. "We ought to let whoever's in there starve to death."

The major pushed back his helmet. "I said I want the companies to take the town."

"Sir, am I your plans and operations officer?"

"Yes."

"Then let me do the plans and operations."

He looked at me, startled. After a moment, he said, "Do it your way."

From then on, I did all the planning on how to move the troops. The major would give me the objective for the day. Then I would go to the companies and tell them what we were going to do, how we would advance, and which company would lead the attack.

The next morning, with my duties settled, I made another recon patrol. The day was muggy, hot, and dusty. We were parked at the side of the road when a lieutenant colonel from the 82d Airborne Division walked up with a half-dozen soldiers. They looked like they'd been on the move for a while.

Some U.S. ships had mistakenly fired on the division's planes as they flew over on their way to the drop zone, shooting down several and scattering the formation. As a result, the paratroops had been dropped almost everywhere except where they should have been.

Sweating through his uniform, the colonel seemed to be in a hurry. He pulled a large map out of a case strapped over his shoulder, spread it on the jeep's hood, and asked me to show him where the 39th was.

"I don't know exactly, sir. I'm the S-3 with 1st Battalion."

He slammed his hand on the map. "What are your orders?"

"Sir, we're supposed to advance along this coastal road as far and as fast as we can."

"Okay," the colonel said. "Hold on." He grabbed a man with a radio on his back and they walked ten feet off the road. After talking for a few minutes with someone I assumed was on one of the ships sitting off the coast, the colonel walked back to the map and grease-penciled a line from our location to Palermo on the northern coast. Left of the line he wrote "Provisional Corps."

He turned back to me. "You're now under my command."

"Sir, what am I supposed to do? It's just me and my driver here. What do I tell 1st Battalion? We came ashore without artillery. Are we going to get any?"

"No," he said, looking at the jeep and then back at me. Abruptly, he stuffed the map into his case. He rubbed his hand across his mouth and said, "Continue as you were."

The colonel and his men walked east away from us, back toward where I'd left the battalion earlier that morning. I never saw him again. Part of the chaos of battle.

Most of the Germans in Sicily stayed in the eastern half of the country, fighting a running battle back toward Messina, where they hoped to cross the narrow strait to the toe of Italy. That left the central and western portion of Sicily defended largely by Italians, who seemed to have little stomach for combat. Back in Tunisia, they often surrendered in large groups without fighting.

So we didn't expect much trouble as we continued west on the gray, dusty road along the southern coast, passing orchards and vineyards scattered among the rugged hills. About midmorning one day, I was in my customary S-3 position, scouting ahead of the companies in an open jeep with the windshield down.

"There's a jeep coming up behind us," said my driver.

We pulled over and the other jeep stopped. A young naval officer got out and walked toward us. I stepped out to meet him. He was a lieutenant, junior grade, a young guy about my age.

"I'm looking for the operations officer," he said.

"Well, you found him." We shook hands.

"I thought you were supposed to be a major."

"Nope, I'm your man. What can I do for you?"

"I'm here to support you."

"The Navy? With what?"

"I've got two cruisers standing off shore."

I looked out to sea. It was empty, no ships anywhere. I looked again with my field glasses. "Where are they? I don't see anything."

"They're about ten miles out. You can't see them."

"What can they do?"

"I can control their fire. Would you like to see it?"

"Yeah," I said. "I'd like to know what kind of support I've got."

"What would you like me to shoot at?"

"Have you ever done this before?"

He shook his head. "Not for real."

Oh, boy. I didn't know what was ahead of us, and I sure didn't want him firing anywhere toward the battalion back down the road. He would have to fire over our heads, and I could only hope he didn't call this thing down on top of us. With more than a few doubts, I said, "Okay. Fire one round up that hill. Show me what you can do."

The lieutenant called one of his ships on the radio and we ducked behind our jeep. A few minutes later, a shell roared over us and exploded halfway up the hill, gouging a huge hole in the hillside, powerful enough to have vaporized us if it had fallen short.

"Fine," I said. "You stick around. You're going to be a great help."

The battalion moved slightly inland to Agrigento, a town of pale stucco buildings. High on a hilltop ridge east of the town stood a roofless, stone-columned structure. As our convoy approached, we took sporadic small-arms fire and bailed out of our vehicles. I put my glasses on the town. No white flags anywhere, but I didn't see smoke from weapons being fired in the windows either.

I heard a couple more shots and scanned the hillside overlooking the town. The fire had to be coming from somewhere near the stone building on the hill. I sent word back along the convoy for the Navy officer to come forward.

He crouched behind the jeep next to me. "What do you need?"

"You see that big structure on top of that hill? Let's knock that thing down."

"Can't," he said.

"Why the hell not? That's where they're firing from." As if on cue, we heard several more pops from shots being fired some distance from us.

"My map says it's a Greek temple, historical, same as the Acropolis in Athens. We can't destroy it."

My map didn't show anything like that. I scanned down the slope in front of the temple and saw nothing but olive groves, vineyards, and what looked like almond trees. I knew we had to do something or we'd be here all day. If they were Italians, it shouldn't take too much to get them to surrender.

"I still need to see what you can do," I said. "Why don't you give me some time on target?" I pointed to a spot below the structure, about fifteen hundred feet up the slope. "Fire all your weapons at that open space halfway down the hill from the temple."

"Okay. It'll take me a couple of minutes to get the ships where they can do that."

He got on the horn, and we waited while the ships maneuvered to bring their big guns to bear on the target. These were only light cruisers, but each had about fifteen six-inch guns and several five-inchers, so they could unleash considerable destruction.

The lieutenant got off the radio. "They're on the way," he said.

We waited with mouths open to save our eardrums and chinstraps unhooked to keep our helmets from snapping our necks when the concussion waves hit. After several seconds, a roar sounding like all the freight trains in the world passed overhead and crashed into the hillside. The blasts shook and lifted us off the ground. Columns of smoke and debris rose into the cloudless sky, and the small-arms fire stopped.

I scanned the town again. Sheets and white cloth of all sizes appeared in windows and doorways. Without any more trouble, we took the town and captured a few Italian soldiers.

The battalion continued its push westward along the southern coastal road. Italian troops surrendered in bunches, often without a fight. On the few times we came under fire, we'd send out a flanking element, and the Italians would either run or give up.

Instead of sending them all back to PW cages, we kept a few prisoners with us to interpret the local idiom and help with digging and menial grunt work. They seemed happy to be out of combat and caused us no problems.

The few Germans and Italians still fighting in western Sicily began to feel the squeeze. They blew up bridges as they retreated.

Late one morning, we came under fire as we approached a blown bridge on a small river that emptied into the Mediterranean. I sent a patrol across on a flanking maneuver to get behind whoever had fired at us, but the enemy had already pulled back.

I didn't want to put more troops across the river to chase them until I could build a decent ford. It would do no good to get infantrymen on the other side until I had a way to get support across for supplies and to evacuate the wounded—all the logistical considerations that go with combat.

I put a bunch of Italian prisoners to work clearing rubble and filling in the riverbed enough to drive trucks across. After an hour, one of my men pointed out a jeep and some tanks coming up the road behind us.

Tanks? We didn't have any tanks attached to us. I looked through my field glasses and saw a jeep leading four tanks. When they got within a hundred yards of us, I could tell it was General Patton in the jeep. I had a man run back and stop them from getting any closer. I didn't want them drawing fire down on us.

The general got out and walked up. He didn't have on that showy uniform he'd worn in Bizerte, but he still had the ivory-handled revolver strapped on.

"Who's in charge here?" he demanded.

"I guess I am, sir. I'm the operations officer."

Patton looked at me as if he were expecting a major or colonel. "What are you doing here, son?"

After I explained our situation, Patton watched the PW Italians filling in the ford for a few moments, then turned back to me. "We're going to cross here," he said. "Let the armor through."

Anybody who wanted to fight in front of me was welcome to it. But I knew damn well that Patton was not going to ride across the river in one of those tanks. And I knew sure as hell they were likely to get fired on.

"Sir," I said, "can I talk to your tank commander before they start across?"

"He's in the first tank."

As I walked back, a lieutenant climbed out of the turret.

"Would you mind crossing upstream a couple hundred yards? If you cross here, a lot of return fire might come in on my outfit."

"Yeah, I can do that," he said.

We shook hands and I trotted back to where Patton was standing with his hands on his hips. I got the prisoners out of the riverbed.

I couldn't help thinking of what Patton had said about not taking prisoners. I felt myself getting mad all over again and thought about asking him what he wanted me to do with my prisoners, but I had sense enough not to.

Instead, I turned to my driver, a private, who had already dug our two-man foxhole. "Dig a hole for the general," I said.

We were on soft ground a few yards from the sea. The private began throwing dirt and sand and soon had another hole dug.

By this time, the tanks had pulled off the road and were clanking and screeching along, headed upstream. I edged closer to my hole as I watched the lead tank maneuver down the shallow east bank and enter the river, crossing easily in water that came only halfway up its tracks. At the steeper opposite bank, the tank slipped and hesitated, gunning its engine, slithering in the mud, struggling for traction. Then the tracks grabbed and the tank lurched up the bank.

In its most vulnerable position, its front end pointed up, the tank was fired on. A small artillery round clanged sharply off the armor and cartwheeled up and over the tank, landing some yards behind it, red-hot and glowing.

Patton didn't bail into his foxhole, but he took a step toward it.

The tank slid back into the river and reversed across to our side, engine roaring and smoking. Then all four tanks retreated.

"Lieutenant," said Patton, "go ahead with what you're doing."

He didn't run back to his jeep, but he moved at a smart pace. He and the tanks turned around and headed east.

Serves him right, I thought as I watched them leave. Wearing three stars, this guy's got no business being up here talking to a junior officer in combat.

We finished the ford and crossed the river. No one fired on us or held us up in any way. The infantry carried the day.

I never saw Patton again. He went back and wheeled north somewhere behind us and entered Palermo in triumph. But our standing joke, every time we saw a tank, became "Let the armor through."

The battalion pushed on across the south coast, capturing the airfield and some large German transport planes at Castelvetrano without drawing fire. I never liked being around buildings in a combat zone so I stayed at the edge of the airfield while a couple of company commanders took some men and searched the hangers. They were empty. Someone had left in a hurry. That was all right with me. Following the road out of Castelvetrano, we moved back toward the sea.

A bedraggled civilian population started to show itself along the dusty roads and in the villages. Starved-looking children in rags gave us the V for victory sign and begged candy and cigarettes whenever we slowed.

I was happy enough with the inaction, but the men were getting restless and rowdy. Late one afternoon, as we moved further into wine country, 1st Battalion set up its command post in a house at the western edge of a small town. The rifle companies settled in the vineyards and olive groves a kilometer or so beyond the town.

That evening, lounging around the command post, we heard explosions and gunfire out where the companies were. We radioed to see if they were under attack.

They told us that, after drinking a lot of wine, soldiers from two companies had started throwing smoke and concussion grenades and shooting over each other's heads. Since I was handy, the battalion CO sent me to get the situation under control.

Fortunately, I had served with both companies and many of the men knew me. I located some officers and noncoms and stopped the fireworks before anybody got killed.

We moved out at dawn the next morning, hangovers and all. The sun came up behind us, promising another hot day. Again, I was in the lead element, ahead of the battalion with a squad of soldiers following my jeep in a truck. We rolled right along; there seemed to be no enemy anywhere around.

It was still early in the morning when we pulled into a small port city. At the town's central plaza, we rousted an elderly home guard commander out of his quarters in a large three-story stone building that opened directly onto the square. It probably doubled as the town hall. The commander was in charge of the port, a largely ceremonial position, more like a mayor than a military commander.

Sporting a trim white beard, the old man stood before us still wearing his long gray nightshirt and an old-fashioned nightcap. I had one of my men who spoke Italian explain to the commander that he needed to surrender the town officially, so there would be no resistance. We didn't want to hurt anyone unnecessarily.

The old fellow, who must have been in his seventies, looked confused for a moment, then gathered himself and straightened to attention. Through the interpreter, he asked if he might return to his quarters and put on a uniform so he could surrender in proper military order.

Sure, we could do that.

He nodded stiffly, made a precise about-face, and walked back into the building. We took a break and waited. I sat down on the curb and talked with some of the men.

We lolled about for twenty minutes, and the old man was still inside. I hadn't sent anyone with him because I felt he wouldn't give us trouble. Finally, it occurred to me that he'd had plenty of time to change clothes, so I went to take a look.

I pushed open the door, stepped into a short hallway, and walked up two marble stairs into a large foyer. There, above and to the right, I saw the old man. Wearing his dress uniform, black boots, and a ceremonial sword, the honorable commander had hanged himself with red drapery cords tied to the second-story balustrade.

17
Troina

The 39th Regiment rolled eastward across the northern edge of Sicily, a few miles inland from the coast. We passed through the outskirts of Palermo, which Patton had captured a few days before without much of a fight.

We followed narrow dirt roads into the mountains of central Sicily and stopped outside Enna late one evening, so dusty we looked covered in chalk. All through that cold night, artillery rumbled in the hills. Dim flashes sporadically lit the ridge line where the Germans were making a defensive stand to protect their escape port at Messina.

The next afternoon the battalion commander said, "I don't know where the regiment is or even if we're still part of it. Go find them."

My driver and I hopped in our jeep and headed west a few miles to look for the regimental HQ. The sun edged toward a high ridge on our left. Coming back, we drove the pine-forested area of a small valley and saw a formation of a dozen planes flying toward us a few thousand feet up.

We pulled off the road, stopping in the lengthening shadows, ready to jump out and take cover if the planes dove on us. As they flew closer, I could see they were U.S. fighter-bombers. I was about to relax when I saw them release huge bombs from their undercarriages.

We hit the ground. I couldn't believe it. There was nothing else around— no artillery batteries, no supply dumps, nothing but a jeep and two soldiers. First off, if they saw us, why didn't they recognize us as friendlies? Second, why unleash this many bombs on one little jeep? It didn't make sense.

Then I saw these things start to wobble and flutter on their way down and realized they weren't bombs. The planes had jettisoned their empty auxiliary fuel tanks. The nearest one hit the top of a big pine tree a hundred yards away, broke apart with a loud crash, and sheared off the tree's branches.

The planes droned away, unaware, I'm sure, of our presence. We drove back to the forward CP, arriving at twilight. With wispy clouds hovering over its rim, Mount Etna, an active volcano twenty-five miles further east, glowed faintly against the evening sky.

As nightfall enveloped the mountains, we heard a pulsating engine noise coming from the direction of the volcano. It had to be a German twin-engine plane. Our multi-engine planes had synchronized props that didn't pulsate.

The throbbing engine noise moved closer, a little off to our left. Suddenly, a floodlight came on underneath the plane, lighting a large area beneath it. A few rifle shots rang out, but the plane didn't change course, continuing westward past us, looking for who knows what—probably artillery or a supply dump. We didn't have any. No anti-aircraft guns, either. The plane banked at the end of the valley and flew back low and slow, searchlight still on. Nobody bothered to fire at him, and he disappeared toward Mount Etna. But we stayed alert all night for an air attack that never came.

The next day I went to meet the new commander of the 39th Regiment, Colonel Paddy Flint, a 1912 graduate of West Point. In his mid-fifties and normally too old for a combat command, Flint got the job, it was widely rumored, by lobbying General Patton, his old friend and mentor.

I took a jeep back down the twisting road to the regimental CP and sat around with other members of the battalion staff waiting to meet this guy. I hadn't even met his predecessor, who I heard jumped out of his jeep, broke a leg, and was whisked back to Bizerte.

As we sat talking on the slope of a hill, a ragged little Sicilian kid came up and tried to sell us cactus fruit. I gave him a couple coins for a few and he left happy. They were a strange-looking, pale green fruit, a little larger than walnuts, with small stickers on them.

"What the hell do I do with these things?" I said.

"You soak them and pull the stickers out," someone said. "Tasty."

"Here," I said, and tossed them to the guy. "*Bon appétit.*"

As we sat there joking around, up walked an old man, bowlegged, sinewy, wearing cowboy boots, a black bandana around his neck, and a big white colonel's insignia on his helmet.

He slapped his leg with a swagger stick. "Gentlemen," he said. "I'm Paddy Flint, regimental commander."

We introduced ourselves and he shook hands with each of us. When he got to me, he said, "Hell, son, S-3s are supposed to be majors. What happened to you?"

"First battalion's a little short of majors right now, sir."

"Where you from, son?"

"Enid, Oklahoma."

"I was stationed in Oklahoma after the First World War. Used to go up to Enid from Fort Sill." The old man winked. "Stayed up at the Youngblood quite a few times."

I smiled. "Yes, sir."

The Youngblood Hotel was mainly frequented by oilmen and prostitutes. Maybe this old boy wasn't as old as he looked.

With only a few words, the old man connected with all of us. Then he smoothed a small place on the ground with his boot and kneeled. Using his swagger stick, he drew AAA-0 upside down in the dust so we could read it.

He stood up. "Anybody know what that is?"

Most of the men of the 9th Division were from New York or somewhere well east of the Mississippi River. I was probably the only guy in the group who'd been around farms and livestock.

"Looks like a cattle brand," I said.

"That's right, son. How do you know about cattle brands?"

"Well, I know about the 101 ranch up in Ponca City, and my uncle and I worked for the Johnson farm, the Lazy J. We branded its cattle with a J leaning on its side."

"What do you think this one means?"

"Colonel, I have no idea."

"Triple-A-bar-zero." He looked around at everyone. "Do any of you know what that means?"

Nobody said anything.

"Gentlemen, this is going to be our new motto. It means anything, any-time, anywhere, bar nothing." The colonel turned to the supply officer, a major.

"By tomorrow morning," he said, "I want every helmet in the regiment to have triple-A-bar-zero on both sides, 2-inch letters, white paint." He turned and walked off in a funny little bowlegged gait. This old man was going to get us in a hell of a lot of trouble.

The motto Colonel Flint drew in the dirt that day survived the war and is still on the helmets of a training unit at Fort Jackson, South Carolina.

The next day we all had triple-A-bar-zero on our helmets. The battalion moved northeast toward Troina. As we approached Cerami, the Germans retreated and shelled us through a long sleepless night, with our artillery answering back. We dug for most of the night to get as far away from the artillery as possible.

When our rifle companies finally attacked Troina, stories of Colonel Flint's leadership style spread throughout the regiment. He liked to go right up front where the troops were under fire.

Early in the battle, he dragged one battalion commander out of his command post and headed for the forward-most positions. While the commander advanced under small-arms fire in textbook short dashes and then hit the dirt, the colonel kept walking forward in his bowlegged gait, never once ducking or taking cover except when his battalion commander pulled him to the ground.

"It don't make no difference, son." The old man jumped to his feet. "Come on, let's go."

During the fight, the colonel stood up from cover and pounded his scrawny chest in front of the enemy positions. "Hey, you fuckers," he screamed, "we're coming to get you!"

Advancing 200 yards behind a rolling artillery barrage, Flint, without getting a scratch, led the charge that drove the enemy off the ridgeline outside Troina. Taking those kinds of chances boosted the morale of the regiment tremendously.

We moved to the high ground southwest of Troina and tried to dig into the flinty soil. Late that afternoon, the regiment called in air support against the town. Two different fighter squadrons swept down the valley but veered off before they reached their targets, each time scared away in the face of relentless antiaircraft fire.

We kept digging, getting ready to hunker down for another long, sleepless night. Shadows lengthened, and from somewhere behind us, artillery started to boom, sending shells screeching overhead on their way into the town.

Just before sunset, I heard aircraft engine noises over the town and spotted a German FW-190 fighter coming slowly down the valley, flying low, not much higher than the ridge we were on. He passed over the battalion CP on the ridge to my left and continued on without firing a shot.

A few troops popped at him with their rifles, but he didn't waver or change course. He must have been searching for artillery flashes.

In a few minutes, back he came up the valley, flying even lower than before. The plane lifted over the CP and dropped down so he was below where I sat watching him. His canopy was pushed back and I could see into the cockpit. He was not shooting, just cruising along barely above stall speed, a couple hundred yards away.

As the plane came opposite us again, the pilot, in his leather helmet and goggles, turned and looked at us. Then he waved. What the hell was he up to? Was he drunk? A free spirit? Looking for a place to land and surrender?

We waved back. No need to waste ammunition. Our trucks and their ring-mounted .50-caliber machine guns were somewhere behind us, unable to get up the ridge. Firing rifles was a waste of ammunition. We watched the plane fly back over Troina and disappear into the evening shadows. He didn't come back.

The next morning a flight of American P-40s with bombs hanging from their bellies came roaring up the valley and were met with the same intense antiaircraft fire that turned away yesterday's raids. But this time the fighters continued straight and true on their run.

They swept into Troina, engines screaming over the gunfire, and dropped their bombs right on target. The town erupted in explosions as the planes pulled up in a steep climb, fell into a quick sideways turn, and roared back across the town on a low strafing run that ripped into the enemy's defenses.

That pretty much ended the battle of Troina. We attacked shortly after the air raid and walked into town with little opposition. The Germans who survived the bombing had taken off, pulling back to make another stand somewhere closer to Mount Etna in their fighting retreat toward Messina.

As we approached the volcano, I got a radio message from a guy I knew back at regimental headquarters.

"Charlie," he said, "You're from the South, aren't you?"

"Yeah."

"What do you think of Negroes as fighters?"

What was he getting at? "Joe Louis is pretty good."

"I thought you'd like to know the air support you got at Troina the other day was by the first black pursuit squadron in the war."

"That don't mean shit to me," I said. "They did a hell of a good job."

After the war, I learned the air attack was led by Lt. Col. Benjamin Davis, Jr. In the mid-1970s, a few years after he retired as a three-star general, I was in Miami to see Oklahoma play in the Orange Bowl. At the pregame parade through downtown, I slipped out of the crowd and walked behind the reviewing stand where the general was sitting with other dignitaries. Bands were marching and music filled the air. My head barely stuck up above the floor of the stand.

"General Davis," I yelled. "Do you remember Troina?"

He looked around but didn't see me.

I waved. "I was at Troina."

The general spotted me, rose from his folding chair, and walked over. He leaned down and shook my hand.

"Thank you, sir," I said, "for what you did for my outfit back in Sicily."

General Davis died of Alzheimer's at Walter Reed Army Medical Center on July 4, 2002. He was 89.

18
Two Medics

Wary of ambushes, the 1st Battalion edged along, following the retreating Germans around the contours of raw, mountainous terrain. One morning the regiment sent down orders limiting our mortars to firing only a basic load each day—primarily what each mortar team alone could carry. That meant the three rifle companies could not assign men to carry extra mortar rounds for the heavy weapons company, firepower that could mean the difference between victory and defeat.

What the hell was happening? The mortar was a valuable weapon to infantrymen. It could pour indirect fire on the enemy and keep him from overrunning us. Was our mortar ammo going to some other outfit? I hurried to the regimental command post to find out.

"There's a coal miner's strike back in the States," said the adjutant. "The Army put us on a firing limitation."

I couldn't believe it. The strike had shut down the blast furnaces that produced metal for the munitions we needed to fight.

"Those guys ought to come over here and do my job," I said. "I'll gladly go dig coal."

Apparently, President Roosevelt thought so, too. He nationalized the mines and threatened miners with being drafted into the military. That ended the strike and our firing restrictions lasted only a few days.

In the flow of war, we had to be, if anything, flexible. The 39th Regiment came to Sicily as part of an ad hoc task force. First, in a loosely knit provisional command on our swing through the west, and then attached to the 1st Division chasing Germans to Messina. We didn't rejoin the 9th until after the Sicilian Campaign.

It was the same at the battalion as we tried to control the chaos of combat. Using standard Army procedure, the commander filled holes at his companies with men he thought he could count on. Ranking sergeants led platoons that had no officers. Decimated squads were combined into one unit under the senior enlisted man.

And so I came to command B Company when its CO got wounded. We had been in Sicily for three weeks, and we still wore the same wool long johns we had landed in. It was now August, hot in the daytime, though still cold at night without blankets. The men had come ashore with only combat packs, easily filled up with a few toilet articles and a change of socks.

Operating on our own as a regimental combat team, the 39th got little of the logistical support normally provided by the 9th Division. And we got no time off to clean up or change clothes.

We were orphans, really. We bathed in the Mediterranean or in streams and rivers we happened to stop near. Every now and then, we had enough time to draw water from a farmhouse well to wash up and shave out of our helmets, but we hadn't changed clothes since Tunisia. They were rotting on us and we were rotting in them, fungus rashes in our crotches and on our feet. I even had sores on my hands that scabbed over from clawing at them.

The first thing I did when I walked into B Company was look up the supply sergeant, who'd been with the company since Operation Torch the previous fall. He spoke Italian and was a real scrounger. I already knew him from when I was a platoon leader in the company back in North Africa. In fact, I had served in all the battalion's companies at one time or another.

"Get us some new underwear, Sarge," I said, "and some socks. We're in bad shape."

Unfortunately, I didn't get new clothes. B Company's commander returned and I went back to the battalion the next afternoon. But a few days later, I heard the sergeant scrounged new underwear and socks for the company from an artillery unit. You can't beat a good supply sergeant.

Despite the inspirational leadership of Colonel Flint and the heroics of the Tuskegee pilots, capturing Troina came at a heavy cost. Two days before the fighter-bombers pounded the town, I watched from my S-3 observation post as one of our companies lost over twenty men crossing open ground. The Germans let the company advance down a barren slope into the middle of an exposed field before shelling it.

Almost immediately, the attack fell to pieces. Men were blown apart, thrown into the air, or scythed down by shell fragments as they fled panic-stricken in all directions. One platoon was particularly hard hit, as men cringed in the exploding field and died where they lay. Others scrambled for any cover they could find. A few ran back toward the departure line and the safety of the ridge. The enemy shelled until nothing moved. It was a slaughter.

By the time the Germans pulled out of Troina and we advanced through the area, many of the dead had already been buried in shallow marked holes where they awaited the division's graves registration unit to process them into a temporary cemetery. As we drove up the road, we passed a corporal who told us several 1st Battalion soldiers were buried nearby.

We stopped the jeep and walked over a small rise to find almost two dozen bodies exhumed, lying bloated in shallow open graves, ripening in the sun. The stench overpowered us and I started cursing. Then I saw the bodies were missing only their shoes. I thought of all the ragged, barefooted Sicilians I'd seen, and that calmed me some. If I were desperate, with war raging all over my homeland, I'd take shoes off dead men, too. We radioed the location of the graves back to the regiment. They needed to hurry.

That evening, I briefed the four company commanders on the next day's objective, an attack on Randazzo. The operation I had planned would begin at dawn. By midnight, I was in my foxhole trying to sleep, when the commander's runner rousted me.

Stiff and miserable, I dragged myself to the CP and got orders to take over A Company for the morning attack. The commander had stepped in a hole on his way back to the company in the dark and couldn't walk.

There seemed to be a pattern developing here. Two rifle company command assignments in a week. Was my boss trying to get rid of me? Careful where I stepped, I followed commo wire a quarter mile up to A Company's CP, arriving at 0100 hours. Dog-tired, I lay down in a trench and told the first sergeant to wake me at 0300 so we could get ready.

It was still dark when I gathered the four platoon leaders together. Two of them were sergeants, temporarily in charge. A lieutenant I didn't know commanded another platoon. I'd known the other lieutenant as a rifle platoon leader in Tunisia.

"We're taking Randazzo this morning," I said to the only man there I knew. "You lead the attack with first platoon."

"I'm weapons platoon," he said.

"We'll sort that out later. Right now, I need you in the lead. I'll be right behind you, then the other—"

"Why the fuck are you trying to get me killed?"

"Look, I'm in command here," I snapped, "and you're the only guy I know."

"I'm heavy weapons; I ought to be following the other platoons."

We stared at each other. No one else said a word. Suddenly, it occurred to me that this must have been how I sounded when I questioned my battalion commander's orders back in Tunisia. I took a deep breath and touched his arm.

"Listen," I said, "I need you at the point. I'll be right there."

The man dropped his gaze; the issue was settled. He was a good officer, just stretched thin. In the end, the lieutenant went where I ordered him to go. That's the only way the Army can work.

At dawn, we started for Randazzo, seven miles away, not knowing what to expect. We advanced onto the lower slopes of Mt. Etna. Vegetation thinned out and the lava grit and ash began to bog us down. I put the lead platoon a hundred yards up the slope to walk along a narrow-gauge railroad track, while the rest of the company followed down on the road in a column of platoons. I wasn't worried about Germans being above us. Nobody could maneuver or bring up support in the lava sands. Even mules would have a hard time carrying supplies up that volcano.

After a mile, we heard sporadic small-arms fire ahead of us. A few artillery rounds screamed over and exploded behind us. Time to leapfrog the mortar team. I let them set up to cover us in case of a firefight, and we advanced until we were out of their support umbrella. Then I brought the mortars to the front and we did it again, a long, plodding maneuver.

After the third leapfrog, I heard a German burp gun open up not far ahead. I moved the platoon down the slope off the road and we waited.

In a few moments, two medics came running down the road, away from the shooting. This was definitely not right. They were supposed to move to the wounded, protected by their medical badges, even though the large red crosses did not always shield them in the heat of battle. My two medics didn't slow down when they got close, and it was obvious they were bugging out.

"Stop!" I yelled.

The medics glanced at me but kept running. I scrambled up onto the road, chambered a round in my rifle, and swung the barrel toward them.

"Goddamn it, I said stop!"

They did.

"Where's your kits?"

They had abandoned their medical supplies. I picked up one of the crates of mortar shells we were lugging and threw it at the nearest medic. It weighed over twenty pounds, but he caught it. I motioned for the other kid to pick up a crate. Then I tore off their red cross medic bands.

"You fuckers are now mortar men," I said. "You stay with me. Everywhere I go, you go."

I did everything I could for the next 24 hours to get those guys killed. They humped mortar ammunition all afternoon. When I later checked on the platoons, I deliberately took routes that might expose us to enemy fire. I figured I could make it but I hoped maybe they'd get hit.

Stupid. I let anger take away my perspective. Luckily, the Germans were busy retreating toward Messina and a boat ride across the strait. We walked into Randazzo without being attacked.

The town seemed deserted and eerily quiet. Other than a couple of bomb craters near the railroad tracks, we saw little damage. Some bullet pockmarks on the stone buildings and a few collapsed walls, but the town was not totally destroyed. Had the Germans just disappeared? Where were the civilians?

Randazzo was a fairly large town, with lots of places for ambushes and snipers. I sent patrols in every direction. We had to clear the town before we could relax. One patrol reported hearing people in the church, a large stone structure in the middle of town.

With my two ex-medics in tow, I followed the patrol to the church and broke open a side door after the heavy front door wouldn't budge. We found over 200 women, children, old men, and cripples in the basement. They must have been there for several days. The place stunk of urine and excrement. It was pathetic. We helped them upstairs and gave them emergency chocolate bars and what C rations we could spare.

The next morning I sent the ex-medics out to separate platoons. They were now riflemen. I never did trust those guys to be medics again, a job that called for a lot more bravery under fire than they had shown.

After the campaign, I got them both transferred out of the 9th Division and into a unit gearing up for the invasion of Italy.

19

R and R

A British unit relieved the 39th at Randazzo, and we rejoined the 9th Division, bivouacked near Cefalu on the coast. Almost half the Germans escaped to Italy, and the Sicilian Campaign later became known as our bitter victory and their glorious retreat. While Allied generals bickered and grandstanded, the German high command took care of business and got thousands of their troops across the Strait of Messina to fight again.

At Cefalu, we settled into an easy routine, but our diet remained poor. The troops in the rear siphoned off the best food, leaving us with whatever they didn't want and what little we could scrounge. We made do with C and K rations. By this time, I had lost over 30 pounds and weighed only 150, even with beach sand in my pockets.

Colonel Flint was in his element. His bravado had won over the men, who accepted his enthusiastic training without bitching too much. They believed he would help them succeed when we faced the enemy again.

One morning, the colonel marched the regiment into the mountains and demonstrated a coordinated attack behind walking artillery fire. While the rest of us watched from a hillside, he led one battalion 200 yards behind the advancing shellfire. The object was for the explosions to keep the enemy's head down while the attackers got close enough to finish off any survivors before they could rise up again and defend themselves.

It was a striking demonstration. Fortunately, no short rounds fell near the battalion. In an actual battle, the attack would have continued, short rounds and all.

Between training sessions we swam in the Mediterranean, watched movies, wrote letters, gambled, and tried to keep the troops from getting too drunk and clapped up.

The Italian invasion started without us, but quickly bogged down. Italy officially surrendered that week, but the Germans fought to push the invasion force back into the sea. Soon the 39th was practicing landing attacks. We marched to the water's edge and simulated attacks back to high ground a mile off the beach. We wondered what assignment these maneuvers were preparing us for.

One evening a headquarters team, led by a colonel I'd never seen, briefed us on a mission to rescue the Salerno beachhead. At daybreak the next morning, loaded down with gear, we marched four miles to an airstrip next to the beach and waited while C-47s landed. By 0800, forty were parked nose to tail. The Luftwaffe would have gotten a bagful had they attacked this gaggle, but they must have been busy elsewhere.

In full combat gear, we waited to board, each rifleman with two bandoliers of ammo draped across his chest. I was sitting out of the sun under the wing of one of the transports when a single-engine seaplane landed on the mirror-smooth sea. A small motor launch raced out to the plane and picked up a bearded man in plumed headgear and a white, gold-braided uniform. The launch took him straight to shore and a staff car whisked him away.

I don't know who the man was or why he was in such a hurry, but our boarding time came and went. Maybe he had something to do with the delay. That afternoon the rescue mission was scrubbed and we marched back to camp. Whatever saved us, I was grateful.

We continued to worry about being thrown into the battle for Italy, but in early November 1943, word came down that the 9th Division was going to England for R and R. Giddy with relief, we moved into a tent city outside Palermo. The second night, a storm flattened our tents, but that was okay. We weren't going to war, so waterlogged and muddy was just fine.

We sailed for Greenock, Scotland, and encountered nothing worse than a storm at sea. After docking, we remained on board for three days, awaiting ground transportation. Finally, we left by train for Barton Stacey. As we clacked along, icy raindrops lashed the windows, and the drab countryside looked the same as when I'd last seen it. Had Operation Torch only been a year ago? We had come a long way since then, and were now combat veterans.

At Barton Stacey, an old World War I camp near Winchester, I moved into a drafty Quonset hut with three other lieutenants. We paired off on either side of a thin wall that split the hut across its middle. Our side had one naked light bulb and a pot-bellied stove that provided almost no heat from the poor-quality coal we fed it. We spent most of our off-duty time drinking beer at the officers' club where it was somewhat warmer. We returned to the hut only to climb into the sack, often with our clothes on.

We rested for a week before getting back to work. Early on, we had a parade for Churchill and Eisenhower, who reviewed the regiment with Colonel Flint. The colonel had them stop in front of a soldier he had planted in the front row.

The kid had on the helmet he'd worn in Sicily when a bullet went through it, piercing it just above its front rim. The bullet deflected upward and around the outside of the plastic liner, swerved off the rear lip of the liner and blew an exit hole through the back of the steel helmet, all without touching him. While the soldier beamed, both Churchill and Ike examined the helmet, then shook his hand.

The kid later died in Normandy.

The military continued stockpiling equipment for the coming invasion of France. Tanks, trucks, assault boats, and munitions of all sorts lined up in every open space. There seemed to be no room to grow crops. No wonder our rations were so paltry. The joke was that if one more piece of heavy equipment came ashore, the whole island would sink into the sea. Yet the massive buildup continued, and we knew the big show was coming.

During daylight hours, we watched C-47s tow gliders across the southwestern skies around Stonehenge. At night searchlights probed along the paths of German bombers attacking the ports on the southern coast. Anti-aircraft tracers arced into the night sky, converging on enemy planes caught in the lights. We often heard the far-off whine of straining engines and the rattle of machine-gun and cannon fire as British night fighters darted at the edges of bomber formations and raked them with tracers.

For some reason, Colonel Flint had taken a liking to me and gave me a plum job as regimental police and prison officer and post fire marshal. This gave me lots of screw-off time to roam around in my own jeep as I coordinated with local police and fire stations in the area. I reported to the old man weekly.

The stockade was a three-acre compound located in a remote corner of the post. An ancient stone building sat in the middle, surrounded by a chain link fence and rolls of razor-edged concertina wire. The old building looked almost medieval, with walls more than a foot thick and a massive oak door at the entrance.

I knew most of the assigned guards. I had fought with them in North Africa and Sicily. I knew a lot of the prisoners, too. Most of them were there for typical stuff that happens around Army camps: AWOL, pub brawls, drunk and disorderly.

This was supposed to be R and R and none of us wanted to put up with chickenshit garrison rules, so I ran a pretty loose operation. I didn't bother locking anybody up unless MPs brought them in still drunk. Then they went into a cell to sleep it off. Mostly the prisoners played ball, wandered around the compound, or lounged in the office area, smoking and joking, playing cards with the guards.

To cut down on gambling, I didn't allow prisoners to keep money. Most of them didn't have much anyway by the time they got to the stockade, so it was not a big deal. But one day a sergeant showed up with over 100 dollars in American bills, won in a dice game off some replacements before they had time to make the mandatory changeover to military scrip. This was a lot of money, over three months' pay for lower-ranking enlisted men. On the black market, greenbacks went for a large premium in exchange for scrip or British pounds.

I took the money off the sergeant, gave him a receipt, and tossed it casually in my unlocked desk drawer. Of course, next day the money was gone. As a finance major, I should have known better. This theft could become a major problem for me. If I didn't find the money before it came time for the sergeant to leave, I would have to pay him back myself.

Fuming, I set about finding the thief. I had the guards search everywhere and everybody. I opened all the straw-filled mattresses and dumped them on the floor. Nothing. Then I interviewed the prisoners and guards individually. One name kept coming up, a private from 2nd Battalion who was in the stockade for being absent without leave. I called his commander.

"Yeah," he said, "the guy's a fuckup. Gives me nothing but problems. Why? What's he done now?"

"I think he stole some money, I'm not sure yet."

"I wouldn't put it past him."

It was late in the day. I called the kid in and questioned him again, but he wouldn't own up. "Private, if you don't tell me where that money is, I'm going to put your ass in solitary confinement. Are we clear?"

"Sir, I didn't take any money."

I yelled out the door. "Sergeant, come get this man and lock him up in solitary."

The solitary confinement cell was in the rear of the building, down a long hallway. About ten feet square, the cell had a heavy oak door with a small opening at eye level through which the guards could observe the prisoner. No bunk or blanket, no toilet, no heat. Just a bare floor and solid stone walls except for a foot-square opening ten feet up on the outside wall. A cold, damp, miserable place to spend time dressed only in fatigues and without a coat.

The sergeant came back into my office. "What do you want me to give him?"

"Nothing. Leave him just like he is."

It was cold the next morning when I looked into the cell. "Where's my money?"

"I don't have it," the kid said, pacing the floor, rubbing his arms against the chill.

"A lot of people say you do." I could see my breath in the air.

"I want out. You can't keep me in here."

"Like hell, I can't. You're staying in solitary until I get that money back."

I went to my office and, after thinking about it for a while, had half a loaf of bread and a tin can full of water sent to his cell. Bread and water. Not even a canteen.

By midafternoon, I wasn't all that sure of my authority, so I drove to regimental headquarters to brief Colonel Flint on the situation.

"You can keep him confined for three days but hell, son, I can hold him as long as I want. You sure he took it?"

"No proof, sir, but everything points to this guy."

"Well, keep him a couple more days and see what happens. Maybe he'll own up to it."

I didn't go see the kid that evening. Let him think about it a while. I sent him bread and water and went to the club.

The temperature was in the mid-40s again. I sent the sergeant with the kid's morning bread and water. He came back and said the prisoner was yelling he needed to take a crap.

I didn't budge and neither did the private. He crapped on the floor and tried to throw it out his little window. He missed and some of it stuck high on the wall. I began to doubt that any of this was going to work. Was I abusing this prisoner?

That evening, increasingly frustrated, I decided I'd let him go the next morning. I didn't know what else to do. His three days were up and I didn't want to continue on the colonel's authority. I felt bad enough about it already.

Early the next morning the private asked to see me. Maybe he was going to confess after all, so I made him wait another hour, then told my sergeant to go get him. Even though he looked tired and filthy, the kid snapped to attention, and rendered a crisp salute.

I returned it. "Well?" I said, waiting.

He looked me in the eye. "Sir, I didn't take that money."

And I knew then that he hadn't. Hell, it could have been anybody. It could have been one of my own guards.

I stared at him for a long moment. "Do you think you can go back and soldier? Stay out of trouble?"

"Yes, sir."

"I don't want to see you in here again."

And I didn't. I checked with his commander a couple weeks later and he said his soldier was doing better. I never found the missing money and made it up out of my own pocket.

This kid died somewhere in Normandy, too.

It was a good thing that German air raids during this period never got up to our area. The pumps attached to our small water tanks were not big enough to fight large fires. Even more pitiful was the local home guard, made up of British men too old to be in the military. Without firearms, they drilled with pitchforks. We'd see them patrolling villages in their farm clothes, marching around with their pitchforks on their shoulders.

I stopped a group of them on the street one day. "What are you supposed to be doing?"

An old man jabbed his forked prongs toward me. "Paratroopers," he said. "We'll poke them before they can get out of their bloody chutes."

I wasn't so sure. Still, I'd have hated to be an enemy airman forced to bail out and have those old guys come at me with pitchforks.

On one of my first leaves, I visited an old friend stationed at an airbase on the Salisbury Plain, southwest of Barton Stacey. I'd played semi-pro baseball with him back in Oklahoma. He enlisted a year before me and became an Air Corps pilot flying transports. We spent the day catching up and talking about old times. His wife lived in Enid, a few blocks from where Ruth was staying with her parents.

That was the last time I saw my friend. He died ten months later dropping paratroopers to capture bridges in Holland during Operation Market Garden.

After a few weeks in my police and fire marshal job, I'd seen everything there was to see in the villages around Barton Stacey. Even though London was still a favorite German target, I started going into the city, two hours away by train.

With all able-bodied Englishmen off somewhere in military service, London was overrun with unattached females. And of course there were thousands and thousands of young American males on the island with nothing but sex on their minds.

On my first overnight pass, I rode into an underground station in the central theater district and climbed the long stairs into a blacked-out Piccadilly Circus. In the darkness, I felt my way along the wall of a building and bumped into a woman standing alone.

Before I could apologize, she opened her coat and moved against me in her flimsy dress. "Come with me," she said.

The shock of her warm softness left me speechless. She reached down to my crotch and gave me a squeeze. I put my hands on her hips and slid them up her body until I was pushing against her breasts. It had been so long, I wanted to sink down in her.

Then I pushed her away. "I can't."

I don't know why I didn't take some comfort there. I was a virile young man with an uncertain future, about to go off to battle again and maybe die. I have not always been a perfect husband, but at that moment, I thought of Ruth and determined to stay true to her, at a time when I most needed to find solace, when I most needed to be held by a woman.

Instead, I got my ass off the street and went to see an Agatha Christie play.

That spring, civilians and all sorts of Allied soldiers packed the trains to London. I rode in four or five more times and saw all the latest plays and musicals. The bottom of the playbills at all theaters bore a notice saying that, in the event of an air raid, the audience might wish to seek shelter, but the performance would continue.

The first time I heard air raid sirens go off, I looked around and saw hardly anyone leaving. If these people could stay, so could I, though I never heard any bombs falling or explosions near the theaters. I'm not sure what would have happened then.

In early April, I went on temporary duty to Birmingham, a large city well north of us. I was the junior member of a team of five 9th Division officers sent to brief over a thousand officers of the newly arrived 90th Division about what to expect in the coming invasion.

Colonel Barth, the division's chief of staff, led our small group, including the division's artillery commander, a medical officer, a major from one of our battalions, and Lieutenant Scheffel. Of course, I was last on the program, scheduled to speak on infantry tactics at the company and platoon level.

The seminar, held in a large school auditorium, began with our introductions. When my name was called, several men at the back of the room stood up and waved. "Hi, Charlie," they yelled.

"At ease," barked a staff officer down front.

When we broke for lunch, three guys who had yelled at me rushed up, all brand new second lieutenants in this untried outfit. After a moment, I recognized them from my ROTC classes at Oklahoma A&M. They had been a year or two behind me.

"What are you going to talk about, Charlie?"

"What do you guys want to know?"

"We want to know how the hell you stay alive."

The eternal question of the soldier in combat. I decided right then to talk about crack and thump, two-man foxholes, and the importance of having a batman. I was supposed to talk for an hour, but by my turn, I had only fifteen minutes left. It had been a long exhausting day. What was the most important thing I could tell them? As Americans, what did they know least about?

I climbed on stage and said, "I suggest each of you get yourself a batman."

From his seat in the front row, a two-star general from the 90th jumped up. "Lieutenant, I'll have no mention of batman."

I didn't know what to do. They needed to know this to survive in combat.

After a few seconds of silence, Colonel Barth stood up. "General," he said, "that officer is under my command." Then he looked at me. "Lieutenant, go ahead with what you want to say."

"Gentlemen," I said. "I hope all of you make it home. I know some of you. We were schoolmates and personal friends. And you've asked me to tell you how to stay alive in combat. It's not easy, let me tell you. The infantry had a terrific loss of platoon leaders and company commanders in North Africa and Sicily. I want to tell you a few things you can do to improve your chances for survival. You have to stay alive to carry out your responsibilities as officers."

I had their attention. When I finished telling how a batman could help them survive, my time was up, but they wanted to hear more, so I spent another twenty minutes talking about crack and thump and two-man foxholes. It must have helped them, because a recent unit history of the 90th Division mentioned our briefing on that day long ago, before the D-Day invasion of Normandy.

Southern England continued to fill up with men and equipment. Embarkation camps blossomed along the coast. I left my job with the police and fire departments as we began to train with serious purpose, although we no longer practiced assault landings on the beach. This gave me hope that we would not be in the initial wave of the invasion.

On the first of June, Colonel Flint, wearing fatigue coveralls and his usual black bandana, assembled his officers on a grassy hillside near the camp and began recalling our past actions in North Africa and Sicily.

"Gentlemen, that was just schooling for what's ahead of us. Now it's time for us to graduate. We're about to embark on the greatest invasion in history. We're going to liberate Europe."

The colonel paced back and forth, calling on us to do our best in the coming fight. He reminded me of Coach Iba giving the basketball team a pep talk before a big game. Then the colonel stopped and spun to face us, standing tall, hands on his hips, eyes narrowed.

"Some of us will not make it," he said, "and some of us will get wounded. Some of us will come through okay, but it don't make no difference. It's something we got to do."

No one said anything for a moment. Then, from somewhere in the back, came a lone voice. "Colonel, it might not make any difference to you, but it makes a hell of a lot of difference to me."

The old man went to pieces laughing and the rest of us did, too. That was exactly how every one of us felt in those uncertain days before the invasion.

20
D-Day + 3

By June 1944, we were restricted to camp, but we didn't study maps of landing beaches or initial invasion objectives. This was different from our preparation for the invasions of North Africa and Sicily and gave us further hope that we would not be in the first waves going ashore. Although secrecy remained tight and no one told us anything, most of our bullshit sessions centered on our being a floating reserve, committed where needed.

Replacements had flowed into the battalion all spring, bringing the companies to authorized strength of two hundred enlisted men and six officers.

Three new captains cut off any chance for me to command a rifle company. But as a senior lieutenant, I had my choice of second-in-command slots. I knew and respected the commander of D Company, the heavy weapons unit, so I became his executive officer.

The commander and I and one of our four platoon leaders were the only officers with any combat experience. Fortunately, many enlisted men were old hands, which helped. In the days before embarkation, we checked and rechecked our machine guns and mortars and our twenty or so assigned jeeps and trailers.

When we joined the mass movement to the ports, the roads were clogged with every sort of vehicle imaginable, from bicycles and motor-bikes, to huge trucks pulling trailers of supplies and equipment. The thirty-five-mile trip to our embarkation camp near Southampton took four hours. Movement officers fought to keep traffic flowing on England's ancient and narrow roads. Trucks squeezed through the villages and eased around corners, often clipping off parts of houses that sat too close to the street.

None of it seemed to bother the British civilians. They cheered and waved flags and handed up little cakes and drinks when we sat stalled or crept through their villages. GIs in the back of the trucks whistled at pretty girls and threw chocolate bars and gum to kids running alongside. Red Cross girls stationed on the route passed out coffee and donuts, while loudspeakers on their vans blared Big Band swing music. It was chaotic and heady, lifting everyone's spirits.

Near the port, we pulled into a field and set up tents. For two days, while other units moved past us toward the loading docks, we listened to the BBC report heavy bomber raids deep into Germany.

On the night of June 4, a heavy thunderstorm knocked down tents and drenched us. Sunrise burned off a low mist and revealed a sea of mud. We sorted ourselves out, expecting movement orders at any moment, but none came. Units camped nearby continued to load and move out.

Waiting to go into battle is sometimes as tough as the fight itself. We cleaned our gear and puttered around, trying to keep the men busy. On June 6, announcements came over the radio that the invasion of Europe had begun, and finally, on the evening of June 7, we got orders to move. We spent the next few hours winding our way through the packed streets of Southampton. We cleared checkpoints, and military police waved us toward the pier where we boarded the British assault ship, *Empire Lance*.

We waited in darkness while the holds of the 8,000-ton ship filled with food, ammunition, and a multitude of other war equipment. At daybreak we pulled away from the pier and, low in the water, moved slowly into a protected area between the Isle of Wight and the mainland and anchored among a solid mass of ships.

As we organized ourselves and got the troops fed and settled, we watched ships streaming back from Normandy, empty and riding high in the water. We took roll call and issued everyone kapok life vests. They hung from the neck onto the chest with a cloth tie-down strap that wrapped around the back to hold everything in place. They looked pretty flimsy to me.

That afternoon the ship's captain, a large, bearded Englishman in his sixties, came off the bridge and briefed us on general quarters and emergency procedures. I looked up at the lifeboats hanging in their rigging out over the water and hoped we wouldn't have to find out if those eight boats—four on each side—would hold all of us. I cinched my life vest tighter.

Just after dark, the 300-foot-long ship raised anchor and we fell in with others and convoyed out into the channel. Normandy lay a hundred miles almost due south.

The company commander and I ordered the few troops lounging on deck to go below. Then we retired to our cabin just under the bridge and tried to get some sleep. After tossing and turning for several hours, we went down to check on the company and then walked around the main deck. The ship was running smoothly without lights in a gentle swell.

Though hundreds of other ships were in the darkness around us, we saw no lights. When we walked near the bridge on the port side of the deck, we heard the captain talking with the watch crew about what they might expect when the sun rose.

Looking forward, I suddenly saw a massive dark blob, taller than our ship, a hundred yards off our bow at the 11-o'clock position.

I grabbed my commander. "Look out!"

The other ship, coming fast, loomed abruptly over us and we ran away from the rail. A whistle screamed and our ship slipped to the right. Just as we reached the opposite rail, the *Empire Lance* rocked sideways and shuddered, and a terrible screeching noise shattered the night.

Both ship whistles continued to shriek and a metallic grinding sound moved along the other side of the *Empire Lance* toward its stern. The lifeboats near us swung violently in their harnesses. I grabbed the rail to keep from falling.

Then it was over and we heard nothing but the whistles still screaming. We crossed back to the other side of the ship, stopping ten feet from emptiness at the edge of the deck. The lifeboats, their rigging, and most of the railing were gone, wiped away.

General quarters sounded and I looked up and saw the captain. "Are you blokes okay?" he yelled.

"Yeah. What hit us?"

"Something big. We're lucky."

Everyone but the crew had to return to their sleeping areas, which for us was only a few steps away. We left our cabin door open until we heard the crew determine we would remain afloat, though crippled. If we had abandoned ship with only half our lifeboats, most of us would not have made it through the night.

At daybreak, we looked directly south at a coastline that curved around us to the eastern horizon. Ships were everywhere. Through my field glasses, I watched a battleship firing toward shore. Its huge guns belched flames and reddish smoke that rushed downwind.

Closer to us, some destroyers and cruisers poured smaller shells inland. I could see no flashes of explosions on the beaches, but a deep rumbling came from wherever the shells were landing. The captain announced that the collision the night before had damaged his ability to unload, and the ship was to stand by five miles off Utah Beach and await further instructions.

We anchored near a rock island the size of several football fields and watched the action. Soldiers on ships near us scrambled over the sides and down nets into landing craft bobbing in the waves. Moving toward shore, some of the larger boats shot flurries of rockets ahead from launchers bolted on deck; the shells traced long red arcs through the sky.

The battle went on all afternoon. Enemy artillery batteries still firing raised huge plumes of water around the ships. One small landing craft blew apart in a bright flash and another spun crazily from a glancing blow. No shells hit near us, but we watched anxiously, wondering when we would get involved.

I was on deck most of the day, going below only for meals. Allied forces were on double daylight savings time and, near the summer solstice, the sun wouldn't set until midnight, rising again about five in the morning. We set up a standby watch so we'd be ready to unload if the beach control officers gave us orders to move.

All day, Allied aircraft, wearing black and white invasion stripes around their wings and fuselage for easy identification, roamed unchallenged through the skies, flying protective cover for the armada or else streaking inland to bomb and strafe enemy positions. That evening, I stood on the stern near a 40mm gun mount with one of our better noncoms, pulled from a platoon to act as a runner back to the rest of the company confined below.

Would we get ashore tomorrow or would we limp back across the channel and transfer our equipment to another ship? Daylight had started to fade when a flight of twelve German fighters dove out of the sky, strafing the beach and making runs on ships near shore. My NCO and I stood at the rail as antiaircraft tracers arced up from ships a few miles away.

We found ourselves yelling, "Get the bastards, get the bastards!" We cheered when the wing of one diving plane sheared off, throwing it into a crazy spin before it slammed into the water.

Anchored away from the other ships and sheltered near the little rock island, we never thought to get off the deck or take cover beneath the canopy of the gun mount a few feet away. We watched the show and rooted for the good guys. I put my glasses on one of the Messerschmitts diving at a large LCT a mile or so due east, tracers moving ferociously up and down between the plane and the landing craft.

Under heavy fire, the plane suddenly banked and turned toward our ship. He swung level a few feet off the water and came straight at us. Lights started blinking from the center of the plane.

I leapt sideways away from the rail. "That sonofabitch is shooting at us!"

The 40mm gun behind us began rapid firing at the plane. The concussion and noise of the outgoing shells rang and pounded in my ears as I scurried for the cover of the gun mount. Cannon shells burst along the deck in a line of explosions running toward me. A light flashed almost at my feet and I felt hot stabbing needles all over the right side of my body. A searing pain in my groin folded me over and knocked me down.

I must have passed out. When I looked up, two medics were kneeling over me. My face felt raw and my right leg and arm burned. But intense pain and wetness in my groin worried me the most. Had my genitals been blown off?

I heard the sound of tearing cloth and the pain began to dull after they shot me with morphine. Someone said, "You'll be fine," just before I sank into the warm safety of the drug. I didn't get to ask them how bad I was hit.

When I faded back in, I was hanging in the air in a litter basket, being lowered over the side by a small crane. Sailors waiting below on a bobbing Landing Ship Tank unhooked the litter and carried it to the stern, securing me on the LST's deck in a sheltered passageway near the bridge. Were they taking me ashore for treatment? Would I get shelled again?

I grabbed at a sailor. "Where are we headed?"

"Back to England, sir. We've got a couple hundred PWs down on the cargo deck."

That was a relief. We sure weren't going to land on the beach with prisoners aboard. By this time, it was semidark. I lay listening to the sound of the engines, wondering if my wounds were bad enough to get me shipped back to the States.

As the morphine wore off, I began exploring my body. I felt tears in my clothes and small wounds on my face where fragments had hit me, but my pain seemed to be focused directly in my privates.

21
Vital Parts

Someone had stripped off my pistol belt. The .45 automatic, canteen, and other equipment were gone. I had blood on my jacket and a lot of it on the front of my pants. I looked at the luminous dial of the fine Swiss watch I'd bought at Camp Robinson two years before. A jagged shell fragment was embedded in its face.

Sometime later, a young medical officer came by and wanted to see my wound tag. Normally it would have been attached to my uniform to give basic information on time of injury and when I'd last been given morphine.

"I don't have one," I said.

"What do you mean? How am I supposed to know what I can give you?"

"You can give me another shot of morphine right now." The pain in my genitals was getting worse and I didn't feel like messing with a doc who'd obviously never been in combat.

Instead of giving me a shot, he took out a wound tag and began filling it in. I answered questions for what seemed like hours, even though it could only have been a few minutes. Then he reached inside my shirt and checked the dog tags hanging around my neck.

"How about that shot now?" I said, gritting my teeth.

"When we're through. What time were you hit?"

I snapped my hand up and looked at my watch. "Eleven twenty and nineteen seconds."

"Don't be so goddamn smart. I've got other wounded to tend to."

I turned my arm around so he could see the ruined watch. The annoyance seemed to drain out of him and I got my morphine.

I fell asleep under a Navy blanket and awakened later to the sound of gunfire. Tracers flew back and forth across the sky. The LST's 40mm gun opened up from somewhere above me. I heard the crack of small-arms fire going over the ship. The roar of a large shell passed over, and then another, too close.

Aw, shit. Here I was an infantry officer, wounded on one ship and about to die on another. If I'd been in better shape, I'd have gotten the hell out of there. Where to, I didn't know, but I felt exposed and vulnerable just lying there.

Battles usually start and stop suddenly. This one didn't, and our ship continued to fire after incoming fire ceased. When our 40mm finally quit, one of the ship's officers came down a ladder from the bridge.

"You doing okay down here?"

"Yeah, I made it. What the hell was all the shooting about?"

"German E-boats, but we chased them off," he said. "They never got close enough to hit anybody."

The officer then told me how they had formed a convoy of different kinds of ships to protect each other on the trip back across the Channel. It was a good thing. E-boats were lightly armed speedboats, and a ship alone stood no chance against them. They darted in close and fired their torpedoes at point-blank range. Our little convoy had enough firepower to keep them at bay. Finally, after swarming around us without finding an opening, the E-boat commanders gave up.

So did I, and after a few minutes of hearing only the sounds of the engines and the sea, I fell asleep again.

I awoke with sunlight in my eyes, thinking of the woman I had turned down in Piccadilly Circus. Had she been my last chance? I still had no idea how badly I was hurt, and worry skittered through my mind. What would Ruth think if I came home with no ability to have sex, no way to have a family? What would happen then?

As I fought self-pity, the ship's engines slowed noticeably and a crew member told me we would dock in a few minutes. We passed through a breakwater into the harbor of the small port of Weymouth. At the pier, medics and Red Cross workers came aboard and carried us litter patients down the starboard gangway and onto a waiting train. I was loaded into a windowless car with other wounded, most of them German prisoners.

The attendants fed us tea and biscuits, and the train pulled out, headed north for an unknown destination. We clacked through the countryside for an hour before a British doctor came by to check my wounds. I was hurting by this time, but I wanted information more than drugs.

"How bad is it, Doc? Am I going to lose anything?"

He loosened the bandage, took a look, then patted my arm. "You're going to be okay," he said. "You've got a fragment in the head of your penis. I don't think you'll lose any vital parts."

The head of my penis? "Everything's vital down there," I said.

"You'll be okay." He gave my arm a squeeze and moved on to the next litter.

I felt a little better. At least nothing had been sheared off or mangled, and I knew now what was causing all the pain. Still, I worried about what they might try to do to me when I reached a hospital. I certainly wasn't going to give up any part of my dick without a fight.

It was a long, tiring trip, with frequent stops for traffic and to unload patients. Sometime in the afternoon they took the Germans off the train, and around dusk we moved into hills that made the wheels screech around curves. They unloaded several of us at Malvern, near the Welsh border, and field ambulances waiting at the station drove us to a U.S. Army hospital a few miles away.

After I endured a series of painful erections throughout the night and examinations during the day, a major stood at my bedside reading my chart.

"Why don't we try to remove that fragment?" he said.

I was almost ready to agree to anything he could offer. "What all's involved? We're talking about the family jewels here."

"I'm not sure," he said. "The fragment's only about half the size of a pencil eraser, but I've never done this before." He smiled. "I'll be gentle."

They had found no other serious wounds and I knew I would be going back into combat. So much for the million-dollar wound and a ticket home. A Red Cross worker came by later and helped me send a canned message to Ruth that I was okay and I loved her.

The next morning I was wheeled into a large Quonset hut and met the surgical team. First, they removed fragments from my right arm and leg and cleaned up the right side of my face, which was peppered with dirt and debris blown into it from the ship's deck. There must have been nerve damage, because whiskers didn't grow on my right cheek for years afterwards.

After the minor surgery, the docs proceeded with the delicate operation to remove the lead from my penis. "It should be routine," I heard the surgeon say just before they sedated me.

I awoke slowly, late in the afternoon, becoming aware of more and more pain as I regained consciousness. My hands were tied down and I had a tent over the lower half of my body.

"Nurse!" The pain in my groin was intense enough to bring tears to my eyes. "Nurse!" I yelled again.

The ward nurse, a buxom woman about my age, came running to my bed.

I yanked against the restraints. "What have they done to me?"

"Calm down," she said, and explained that they tied my hands to keep me from tearing at the stitches while unconscious.

"What did they do to me? I'm hurting like hell."

She peeked under the canopy. "You're hurting because you've got an erection pulling at your stitches. You had one on the operating table, too. It was all they could do to stop the bleeding and get you sewed back up. They couldn't even take out that fragment." She chuckled. "You've still got lead in your pencil."

"It ain't that funny."

"I'll get you a shot," she said, "but I've got the only thing that will relieve your suffering, and you can't have any of it right now."

"What's that?"

She cocked her hip at me, slapped herself on the butt and, laughing, walked off to get my shot.

That night, I woke from another drugged sleep in time to talk to the doctor making his rounds. I listened to him explain again what had happened during the operation.

"Let's see if it will heal with the fragment still in it," he said.

I couldn't have agreed more. I didn't want anyone cutting on my pecker again, not then, not ever.

And today, after fathering three children, I still have lead in my pencil.

22
Ashore in France

While I recuperated over the next few weeks, the 9th Division helped capture the Cherbourg Peninsula. By early July, the division was fighting in the hedgerows south of Carentan, and its battalions won several Distinguished Unit Citations.

I took long walks on the landscaped paths surrounding the hospital and later hiked into nearby hills to build my strength. The area was lovely, with large old trees dotting the rolling countryside, much like genteel rural Virginia.

This peaceful land seemed a long way from the war, but with serious casualties streaming back from France in increasing numbers, the hospital kept it real. Beds were scarce, and by mid-July, litter patients lined the halls. Pressure was on those of us on the mend to make way.

While waiting for my travel orders, I increased my walks and physical activity to toughen up, even though my groin was still tender. By this time I had met several other wounded 9th Division soldiers, although none from the 1st Battalion, 39th Regiment. Still, with the division in common, we tended to spend time together.

The hospital commander pinned Purple Heart ribbons on all of us, and two days later, I got orders assigning me to the replacement depot at Southampton, travel orders to follow. Assignment to a repo-depot was standard Army procedure for soldiers returning to the war zone. From there I'd go to any unit needing a combat officer. I knew there were plenty of empty slots to fill, and I didn't look forward to joining a new, inexperienced division. I had come too far with the battle-tested 9th.

One morning, walking the grounds with other 9th Division soldiers whose wounds had almost healed, I gathered the men around me.

"How would you guys like to go back to your old outfits when you get out of here?" I asked.

"I don't want to go back to the war at all," someone said.

A man snorted.

"Fucking A," said another.

Well, of course. None of us wanted to go back to the war. We'd seen too much of what war could do to a human body. It was all around us daily, the hospital filled with the sightless and the maimed—limbs missing, terrible burns—inconceivable agony. Nobody wanted any more of it. We'd been lucky. Our wounds might not be so minor next time.

"Look," I said, "we're all going back. Most of us have already got orders. There's no way out of it. Do you want to take your chances at a repo-depot, or would you like to go back to your old 9th Division units?"

Put that way, they were all for staying with the units they knew. That afternoon, I walked into the hospital commander's office.

"Sir," I said, "I know you're hurting for space. I've got a dozen 9th Division soldiers, all of us about as healed as we're going to get. We want to go back to our old units."

"You've already got orders to a replacement depot."

"I know that. But if you'll change the orders to get us back to our old units, we'll get out of your hair tomorrow."

With more wounded arriving every day from the ferocious fighting in the hedgerows, it was an easy choice for the commander, and he got his adjutant right on it.

The Army being what it was, our departure didn't happen quite that fast. I had time to get over to supply and draw combat gear. I scrounged up another old Springfield rifle, even though the M1 Garand had replaced it in the Army's arsenal. I wasn't about to change weapons now.

Two days later, in the early morning hours, we loaded our gear onto several trucks and headed for the port at Southampton. England was still without lights at night, and had been that way for five years. We crawled along dark roadways with a sliver of taillight and tiny blackout lamps on our front fenders.

Daylight came slowly without our running into each other or anything else on or off the roadway. Military traffic still clogged the roads and the 90-mile trip took most of the day. We stopped often in small villages where Red Cross workers or tireless English women served whatever refreshments they had. We appreciated their efforts, but none of it cheered us much. We knew what we would be facing in a few days, and the mood was funereal. We had been there before.

At Southampton, we settled into a tent city and went immediately on standby alert. Late the next night, we loaded onto lorries and made our way through the blacked-out city to a British freighter with enough spare room to take our small group.

Since we were surprise passengers, the Navy didn't have enough life jackets for us. I hoped we wouldn't need them. They stacked the enlisted men in the rear hold among some British vehicles, and squeezed me into a tiny cabin with the ship's medical officer. We joined a convoy between the Isle of Wight and the mainland and eased into the gentle swells of the Channel's open waters.

Halfway across, I learned we would go ashore at Omaha Beach. The Allies had built an artificial harbor, called a mulberry, a mile off shore. It lay parallel to the beach to calm the waters and make offloading men and equipment safer. The mulberry had worked for a while, but a strong storm had torn it apart and the sea was now as rough as ever in the loading area.

We sailed through an armada anchored off the coast, their barrage balloons floating overhead to keep enemy planes at bay. As we eased around the left end of the wrecked mulberry, I could see hulls of scuttled ships lying haphazardly where the storm had strewn them. Over half the structure had been breached and most of the floating piers were gone.

With my field glasses, I scanned the cliff just back of the beach, thankful I had not been one of those who stormed it on D-Day. In the sky behind the cliff, planes dove on enemy positions that seemed only a few miles away. The muted crumps of exploding bombs rumbled off the coast toward us.

A few artillery rounds screamed in from large German field guns still firing, splashing up huge geysers in the harbor. The guns, firing on map coordinates and without artillery observers to adjust their aim, produced only a random shot pattern. I felt caught up in some giant Russian roulette game played by the gods and hoped no rounds had our names on them as we moved toward shore.

At high tide, we dropped anchor a half mile off the coast. The wind picked up and large swells peaked and rolled over into white-capped waves. Using bullhorns and blinker lights, the Navy signaled landing craft to come alongside. One chugged in, bobbing in the swells, trying to stay close to the landward side of the ship while it waited for us to scramble down the nets hanging above it.

Loaded with combat gear, we knew boarding the little craft wouldn't be easy. Besides helmets, rifles, and packs loaded with rations, socks, and toiletries, the men had bandoliers draped around their necks. Hanging from each man's pistol belt was an entrenching shovel, a first aid kit, and a canteen filled with water. Like deadly ornaments, hand grenades festooned each soldier's uniform. Instead of bandoliers, I had field glasses and a map case hanging around my neck and a .45 automatic on my hip next to a magnetic compass case. We had everything but the life jackets I hoped we wouldn't need.

Facing the side of the ship, we climbed cautiously down the nets, looking over our shoulders and trying to measure the fluctuating distance to the slippery deck heaving below us. The roll of the sea swung us back and forth in the net and slammed us into the side of the ship.

When to let go? Time it right and a soldier could almost step right onto the boat, no problem. Mistime it, and he could drop ten feet or more onto the deck and break a leg or his back. Worse, a man could fall into the dark waters between the boats and sink like an anvil.

Somehow, all twelve of us got aboard without anyone getting hurt. I positioned the men evenly on each side and moved to the rear, a step below the sailor manning the helm. He eased the landing craft along the side of the ship, entered open water past the stern, and headed for shore, engine roaring and spewing fumes.

The swells got larger and the tide hid all sorts of defensive barriers installed by the Germans. Halfway to the beach, still in deep water, a huge wave lifted the boat and dropped it into a trough. With a loud, screeching, metallic crunch, we lurched sideways and came to a halt at an odd angle. Immediately, water gushed into the boat low on the left side.

I grabbed the side of the boat to steady myself and hurried forward to find a railroad rail sticking through the hull. Yelling men bailed with their helmets in a growing frenzy, but couldn't keep up with the water pouring in. The helmsman reversed the engine, then gunned it, rocking the boat forward, trying to get us free.

Nothing worked. We sank lower, impaled on the rail, oily water rushing into the boat. One man pulled socks and underwear from another man's pack and stuffed them into the hole, trying to stem the flow. The boat shifted again and he yanked his hand out of the water, screaming, his fingers gashed open and bleeding.

Without life jackets we'd drown, even if we shucked all our gear. I looked for something, anything that would save us, and saw movement to my left. Fifty feet away, an empty landing craft headed out to sea.

I swung my arm, motioning wildly for the other boat to come closer. The sailor standing at the helm slowed down, but he stayed where he was, not sure he wanted to get his boat near whatever mess we were in.

I motioned again. "Get over here, goddamn it!"

He still didn't turn toward us. I unslung my Springfield, and moved the bolt to chamber a round. I yelled again. Still, he hesitated. I whipped the weapon to my shoulder, aimed six feet over his head, and pulled the trigger.

That got him moving. We scrambled off our sinking boat onto one riding much higher in the water. As we neared shore, our new landing craft dropped its ramp in the surf and we waded onto a beach littered with burned-out tanks and wrecked equipment from the invasion six weeks before.

We were back in the war.

23
Operation Cobra

We made our way between rusting, bulldozed heaps of equipment, stacked coils of wire, and piles of supplies waiting to be moved inland. We trudged up a small gully on perforated steel plate the engineers had laid. At the top of the cliff, I looked out to sea, past wrecked barges and smashed equipment still clogging the landing area, trying to imagine the carnage that took place here.

I thought of the men who died on these beaches and their grieving loved ones back home. How crazy it now seemed that Ruth and I had married before I shipped out. Though I was still determined to get home safely, being wounded shook my confidence.

It took a day of walking and hitching rides to get to Carentan, only twenty miles from the beaches. One of the major road junctions of the area, Carentan was a hub of activity. When it was captured, the units moving up from Utah Beach had quickly linked with those landing at Omaha. Supplies, men, and equipment now poured through in a tangle of noise and exhaust fumes.

An MP directed us to a transportation office where they looked over our orders and gave us general directions to our units. I said my goodbyes to the men; they looked somewhat scared and uncertain—just as I felt. They would have to make it back to their units without me, and I walked off alone, heading south to find the 1st Battalion, 39th Regiment, last known location somewhere west of St. Lô. I never saw any of those men again.

About 1900 hours one evening in late July, I found the regimental headquarters in a large pyramidal tent at the edge of a clearing. The atmosphere was grim. Word had just come down that Colonel Paddy Flint had been shot in the head by a sniper, knocked off the lead tank in an attack to root Germans out of the hedgerows. I wasn't surprised. It seemed a fitting way for the old man to go out. He would linger for a day before succumbing to his wound.

Besides losing our commander, the air attack meant to soften the enemy for Operation Cobra had been a disaster. Several planes in the massive raid dropped their bombs short, decimating units that hadn't pulled back far enough, and scattering others along a 20-mile front.

My new regimental commander had no idea where his units were. He stood up from behind a small field desk in a back corner of the tent and motioned me over.

"Stick around, Scheffel," he said. "We'll get you a job. Meantime, get with ops and find out where the hell my companies are. We've got to be ready again tomorrow."

The infantry's responsibility in Operation Cobra would be to break out of the hedgerows against whatever was left of the *Panzer Lehr* and other German divisions facing us. Desperate to hold their lines, the enemy knew that if we ever broke through, our tanks would roam free, and the rout would be on. The Air Force had pulled its bombers off missions deep into Germany to soften up the enemy dug in against us. Too bad the heavy bombers botched their first attempt at close air support.

With the 39th in reserve, the 9th Division's two other regiments would lead the push in our sector. It would be a huge operation. Two other infantry divisions were on the line with the 9th, all of us supported by extra artillery, while two armored divisions waited in reserve to exploit any breakthrough we could make.

Tomorrow, if the weather stayed clear enough, over 2,000 bombers would fly in again to pulverize the ground, hopefully dropping all their bombs in front of our lines this time. Then the infantry would jump off across the St. Lô-Périers Road and surge out of the peninsula. At least that was the plan.

It took me most of the evening to pinpoint several of the regiment's companies, marking their locations on a map I got from the operations officer. Along the way, I passed one of the division's artillery battalions firing shells filled with surrender leaflets. One side had instructions in German on how to surrender safely. English directions on the back told Allied soldiers to treat the bearer in accordance with Geneva Convention rules for prisoners.

Under cover of darkness that night, our troops, wary of the next day's air raid, pulled back well over 1,000 yards from the departure line along the road, moving as quietly as possible, hoping Jerry wouldn't infiltrate into the ground they were vacating. Surely, the flyboys would get it right this time and bomb the bastards good.

By 0930 the next morning, I had gone to ground in the sparse woods a mile behind the line of departure. Sitting in a foxhole, I watched through binoculars as the first waves of several hundred U.S. Thunderbolts and British Typhoon fighter-bombers flew in from the northwest with a muted roar. They peeled off and screamed down to attack German anti-aircraft positions firing up at them.

A Thunderbolt, caught by the German gunners, exploded in a fireball, scattering fragments across the field. The pilot never had a chance. To my left front, a tiny U.S. spotter plane hung in the air, radioing target information to an artillery fire-control center nearby. Large field guns opened up somewhere behind me, and big shells came over on their way to hit the German guns, ripping through the air with ferocious screaming sounds.

Several fighters dropped bombs with yellow smoke to mark the target area for the big bombers that would follow. Typhoons fired rockets with great bursts of smoke and fire, each missile trailing white sparks and flame on its way to the target. Thunderbolts raked the German lines with .50-caliber machine guns. Rocket and artillery explosions and the rattle of gunfire went on for half an hour before the fighters disappeared to the west.

It wasn't long before formations of two-engine medium bombers appeared at about 10,000 feet, just below the gloomy overcast hanging in the sky. Soon they were overhead, bomb bay doors open, releasing strings of bombs. Massive clouds of smoke and dust rose as explosions rumbled along the front. Waves of concussion flapped my uniform sleeves and compressed my chest. The ground trembled and the booming noise became a continuous roar.

Somehow, despite all the shelling and strafing and bombing, the Germans managed to throw up scattered bursts of flak. With our planes filling the sky, it was hard to miss them, and the Germans didn't. Fire flashed in the left wing of one bomber, folding it up over the fuselage as the plane began a sickening tumble toward the ground. Parachutes blossomed in the sky. More planes were hit on their lumbering runs over the target and fell in twisting balls of flame and smoke.

A little before noon, I saw a thin pencil line moving across a clearing sky behind me, coming in from the northwest. Through my field glasses, I recognized the distinctive twin tail fins of hundreds of B-24 heavy bombers, flying in formations of a dozen or more, white vapor trails streaming behind.

Large bombs began falling, filling the air with high-pitched whistles on their way to pound the Germans some more. Waves of heat rose from the explosions, creating a wind that scattered the marker smoke and blew it back over our lines. More parachutes opened above the target area. One bomber, its load hung up for some reason, disappeared in a brilliant flash when flak set off the rack of bombs in its belly, vaporizing the plane. Another B-24 exploded in a shower of sparks. Large chunks of debris, blown upward and outward, turned slowly in the sky before falling.

The boundaries of the target area blurred, then vanished in the smoke, and planes in later waves began releasing their bomb loads earlier. The screaming whistles grew louder and clearer as they came closer. I looked up and saw a string of bombs I knew would fall on me. I curled up in the bottom of my hole and explosions started walking toward where I lay helpless. Then I heard more blasts behind me.

On my left, a crashing boom slammed me against the side of my foxhole and bounced me off the quaking ground. Pain knifed into my ears and squeezed the air out of my lungs. I sucked in dirt and choked trying to breathe. Spitting, I opened my mouth against the deafening roar. Mother of God, they were going to kill us all.

Dirt and debris fell on top of me. Something heavy slammed hard into my back under my right shoulder, numbing my arm. I turned sideways and pushed a massive piece of dirt and sod off me. It hurt to inhale.

On and on came the planes. I didn't dare move, staying pinned in my hole until midafternoon, never knowing where the next bomb would fall, no way to call it off or do anything about it. I prayed somebody somewhere was on the horn telling these guys what they were doing to us down here.

After lying stunned and shaken for a long while, I realized I could no longer hear airplane engines. I pulled myself out of my hole, ears ringing and back hurting enough to make me wonder if I had a cracked rib. Feeling lucky to be alive, I made my way through the choking smoke, past bomb craters and shattered tree stumps to the regimental command post. It had not been hit.

I stumbled into the tent as bomb damage reports and rumors began to trickle in from along the line. Packed close together in preparation for the follow-on attack, some units had escaped unhurt, but others were not so lucky. One regiment in another division lost over 130 men, the equivalent of more than half a company. The highest-ranking officer killed was a three-star general, blown out of his slit trench some two miles behind where I had been holed up.

All I could do was fidget and rage. My back hurt and my teeth ached as I listened to incoming reports. The whole operation was just another shitty disaster, even worse than the screw-up the day before, planned no doubt by staff weenies sitting somewhere safe. Disgusted, I hoped that at least enough bombs had fallen on the other side of the St. Lô-Périers Road to kill every German there.

24
Taking Over C Company

The morning after the bombing, I went over to the medics to have the docs take a look at my back where the debris had fallen on me. Nothing but a bruise. Then I stopped by the dental tent to see if I'd cracked a tooth during the raid.

A lieutenant colonel was in the portable chair, a dentist peering around a stainless instrument into his wide-open mouth.

"That tooth needs to come out, sir, but we don't have any anesthetic."

The colonel pushed the dentist's hand away. "When are you going to get some?" he said. "This damn thing hurts."

"Maybe tomorrow. They've been promising us for a week."

"I can't wait that long." The colonel got up, walked to the tent opening, stopped, then spun around. I could see his jaw was swollen.

"You got any whiskey?" he said.

"Yes, sir. Scotch."

The colonel sat back down. "Give me a drink and pull the goddamn thing."

The dentist poured him a stiff one and went to work. Bracing himself, he pulled and twisted on a lower molar with what looked like pliers. The colonel grunted softly as his tooth came out, and after the dentist packed some wadding into the hole in his jaw, he got out of the chair, a little unsteady on his feet. He reached up and touched the side of his face.

"I believe that'll do it," he said through clenched teeth; then he walked out, headed back to duty.

I followed the colonel out of the tent. My teeth didn't hurt near bad enough to go through something like that. When I got back to the regiment, I had a new assignment.

"Charlie," said the commander, "Go take over C Company."

"Where are they?"

He waved his hand vaguely toward the front. "Somewhere over there. Go find them."

I looked forward to commanding troops again, the only real way the Army measured infantry officers. I gathered my combat gear, left word with regimental supply to send my officer's roll up to 1st Battalion's command post, and headed south. Crossing the St Lô-Périers Road, I walked into the moonscape left by the air raid. Overlapping bomb craters covered the area. Tanks and artillery pieces that had not fled were burned and blackened wrecks. It was utter destruction.

As I moved further into the killing zone, the stench of death grew. Nothing lived that I could see, and animal carcasses not blown apart had swelled so that their legs stuck straight up or out to the side. I passed a horse that had dragged its intestines along the ground, ripping them open before it collapsed and died. German positions were totally demolished, with dead bodies and parts of bodies strewn and splattered across the torn ground. Large clouds of bluebottle flies were buzzing everywhere. Where did they all come from?

I tied my handkerchief across my face against the smell and wished I had brought a gas mask. Climbing through the bomb craters and avoiding caved-in bunkers, I saw no foliage, no color anywhere except black and brown and dull shades of gray. No trees, just shattered, leafless stumps. The cloudless sky had the only real color, almost shouting its blue down on the destroyed earth.

I made my way through this wasteland until I ran into soldiers wearing the 9th Division patch. With their help, I located the forward command post of 1st Battalion.

I reported to my commander, a major I knew from Sicily. I was his S-3 when he had previously commanded the battalion, before a replacement lieutenant colonel bumped him back to executive officer. Now here he was again, in charge but still a major. Same old story.

"Congratulations," I said. "Where's your silver leaves?"

"Same place as your captain's bars, up the Army's ass."

The major dragged out a map, and his new S-3 gave me some idea where C Company's advance had taken them. Soon I was on my way again, following commo wire to the company's forward CP a mile further south. I walked up to find the first sergeant and two other enlisted men.

"Any officers here?" I said. "Who's in charge?"

The sergeant hesitated. "The exec's in charge, sir, has been ever since the captain got wounded in the air raid."

"Well, I've got verbal orders from the regimental commander to take over the company, so get the exec and platoon leaders up here."

"Yes, sir," the sergeant said and sent a private to round up my key personnel.

Verbal orders of the commanding officer, or VOCO, were as good as written orders on the battlefield. I was now the "old man," as subordinates referred to their commanders.

While we waited, the sergeant told me the company's kitchen had taken a direct hit during the air raid. All the cooks were killed; the truck, stoves, everything wiped out.

"Have you reported it?"

"Yes, sir. They know about it at regiment."

"When do we get replacements?"

"They said it would take a couple days."

"I'd be surprised if it's that soon. It's total chaos back there."

When the officers showed up, I recognized my exec and two of the platoon leaders from North Africa. But a new lieutenant just in from Officer Candidate School headed up one rifle platoon, and a staff sergeant I didn't know had replaced his wounded officer in another.

This unknown quality of leadership in two of my rifle platoons caused me some concern, and I spent two hours checking defensive positions. The enemy seemed to have retreated out of the area ahead of Patton's tanks, and the night was fairly quiet, but you never knew.

The company was spread astride a narrow dirt road that cut through small fields bounded by hedgerows. I made a complete tour of the area, chatting a moment with the men and letting all the newcomers get a look at their commander.

I made sure the new men were paired with old-timers in two-man foxholes, located so they could defend against any German counterattack with interlocking fire. I ordered the platoon leaders to do a good foot inspection of their troops and see that they had enough field rations for tomorrow's advance. I knew it would be a long day. Finally, I was satisfied with our preparations.

My orientation tour not only let me familiarize myself with the company, but also gave me a chance to lay out the duties of the company's runner and my radiomen. The runner, an 18-year-old draftee, had been in the job for several weeks, which made him a veteran.

"Besides your duties as runner," I said, "you're also my batman."

"What's that?"

"Basically, when we come under fire, you're going to dig a hole big enough for the both of us while I'm busy trying to figure out what to do."

He grinned. "What if it's really hot and heavy, sir?"

I grinned back. "Then I'll be down there digging with you."

His attitude seemed right. I knew I had the good man I needed. When the going got tough, he would dig holes for me to bail into and be my last resort for getting messages out if all else failed.

My walkie-talkie carrier, a private first class, was also a veteran. He knew his job was to keep his radio near his commander. The walkie-talkie was a cumbersome and somewhat heavy rectangular box, fitted with a micro-phone and earpiece and a push-to-talk switch on its side. Its range was short, at best only a mile. Generally, that was good enough to keep the platoons and company headquarters talking to each other.

The communications sergeant carried a longer-range SCR-300 radio strapped on his back. He stayed in the command post to provide a link with the battalion. When we were on the move, his job was also to stay near me.

After I made sure these three men knew what I expected of them, I lay down not far from the CP on my one blanket and tried to sleep. Artillery batteries rumbled in the distance behind us and an occasional answer-ing round swooshed high overhead from somewhere miles to our front. I shifted around, trying to get comfortable. This was the first of several long nights I would spend on the hard ground before my officer's roll and air mattress caught up with me.

In the early hours next morning, one of the CP guards shook me awake. "Battalion's on the horn, sir."

I made my way through the darkness to the CP and picked up the tele-phone handset attached to the SCR-300 radio. The battalion commander came on and gave me map coordinates for the day's objective, a village three miles farther south.

"Charlie Company will lead the battalion advance in a line of companies at daybreak."

Roger and out. I sent my runner around to wake up the platoon leaders. The night was over and my first full day as C Company commander had begun.

25
Looking for the Enemy

We moved out at dawn, advancing cautiously south in a line of platoons. I sent scouts out on each side of the main column and leapfrogged the platoons every few hundred yards to keep the company from stringing out along the road. I kept my command group moving behind the lead platoon.

I stopped the company for a midmorning break during one of these changeovers. There had been no sign of Germans, no small-arms fire or artillery anywhere in the area, but as a precaution, I moved the troops off the road, out of sight along a hedgerow.

While I studied a map, word filtered back that someone was walking down the road toward us. Keeping out of sight, I moved to the front of the column and looked through my field glasses at a man 100 yards away. There was a rustle around me as men shifted into firing positions.

"Easy," I said, still watching the man through my binoculars. He had no weapon that I could see. "Nobody fires until I give the word."

We waited while the man walked closer, limping slightly. He wore a leather flying helmet, heavy boots, and a flight suit. He looked like he might be one of those airmen who bailed out during the big raid. At 100 feet out, he still hadn't seen us.

"Halt!" I yelled.

Startled, he stopped immediately and threw up his hands. "Don't shoot!"

"Keep your hands up and get over here. Slowly."

When he was fifteen feet away, I halted him again and stood up so he could see me. He was anxious, hands still above his head. "Don't shoot. I'm an American."

By this time, I was positive he was. "Where you from?"

"New York City."

"Name the two baseball teams there." I couldn't resist.

"Yankees and Dodgers."

I laughed. "Ever heard of the Giants?"

He relaxed, dropped his hands, and ran toward me. "Boy, I'm glad—"

I pointed my rifle at his chest, stopping him again. "That's a good way to get yourself killed," I said.

The airman was a sergeant, a B-17 waist gunner. He had unbuckled his harness and tumbled out of his burning plane before it exploded. Landing behind enemy lines, he had buried his parachute and hid in a hedgerow for two days and nights, watching the Germans retreat south.

"I figured they were all gone by this morning, so I started looking for Americans."

"How'd you know we weren't Germans?" I asked. "What made you leave your hiding place?"

"I knew you were Americans. I heard one of your guys tell his men to get their asses on the ground for a break."

I asked the sergeant about enemy troops and equipment. Based on his answers, I figured he must have seen elements of a retreating tank division, possibly the *Panzer Lehr* supposedly in the area.

After we got all the information the sergeant had, we did what infantry soldiers normally do and relieved him of everything we could use: his Air Corps watch, his gloves, and an escape kit containing a few hundred French francs and a silk map. I stuck the map in my case. It was better than most of the ones I had. In the end, the airman kept not much more than his dog tags before we sent him to the rear for his official debriefing and a free trip back to England.

The Germans had abandoned Marigny by the time we got there, and we took over without a firefight. Our responsibility was the eastern edge of the village and I set up a defensive perimeter with an outpost on a slight rise 100 yards away.

Later that evening a dozen replacements showed up, including new cooks. That didn't bring us to full strength, but every little bit helped. The 9th Division had lost over 3,500 men since landing in Normandy less than two months before. That's over one casualty for every five men assigned, the equivalent of more than a regiment and a pace that was starting to outstrip the manpower pool being trained back in the States.

My first problem was to get the kitchen squared away. We needed a mess sergeant to ramrod our new cooks and get decent hot meals prepared. While I ate canned C rations for supper one night, I remembered a good sergeant in one of the rifle platoons, a tall kid from Philadelphia, where I'd played in a college basketball tournament. Coach Iba never skimped on food, and we ate at some of the best restaurants in the country on road trips.

I sent for the sergeant. "You ever eat at Bookbinder's back in Philly?"

"Yes, sir."

"How'd you like it? Great food, huh?"

"Yes, sir, it's real good."

"Okay, you're my new mess sergeant."

The man was struck dumb. Finally, he said, "I don't know anything about cooking."

"Don't have to," I said. "You've eaten at Bookbinder's."

"Sir?"

"You know what good food tastes like. That's all you need to know. The cooks know how to cook. Your job will be to make sure it tastes good. Think you can do that?"

The sergeant decided he would give it a try. It got him out of his job as a squad leader in a rifle platoon and into something normally a lot safer. He became one of the best mess sergeants I had during my time in the Army.

The next morning the battalion commander and his staff briefed his four company commanders on our individual responsibilities for the day: The operational boundaries and adjacent friendly units, which company would lead, time of departure, radio frequencies, supply points, and evacuation routes for the wounded.

Finally, they gave us what little intelligence they had. Generally, knowledge of enemy forces in front of us—their size and combat capability— never seemed to get down to the foot soldiers. The decisions left to a company commander had to be loose and open-ended, because he never knew in advance what the situation would demand. He only knew the enemy was out there somewhere, wanting to kill him.

Back at the company, I briefed the platoons, and about noon, we set off across country, looking for the enemy. Over the next few days, we met little resistance, but German land mines slowed our progress. Trip wires waited in the foliage. A sudden blast one morning, followed by men screaming and writhing on the ground, put us all on edge.

After the mine casualties, my new troops shuffled along in numbed silence, bunching up, violating their recent training. This was too real for them. Nothing in basic infantry training can prepare a man for the first time he sees what explosives can do to the human body.

The squad leaders and platoon sergeants hounded the men to maintain their intervals. At the noon break, while the medics gave us typhus boosters, I made the rounds to pair my new men with more experienced soldiers.

We had no armor support, not that we needed any yet. After crossing the Operation Cobra departure line, most of the tanks had swung west along the main roads so they could enlarge the breach. Artillery followed along back there somewhere, but we hadn't needed them either. That left us with only small arms, light machine guns, and mortars.

Our real job, though I would never say it so bluntly to my men, was to get shot at so we could engage the enemy, who kept retreating before us. The Brits called it FFF: Find him, fix him, and finish him. But we hadn't even been able to find the enemy, much less pin him down so we could kill him.

So we kept walking. Small-arms fire crackled sporadically in the distance. That was the scary part, knowing they were out there somewhere. What's in that gully? Check out those buildings. What's over that rise? Flank that crossing. Is there a machine gun in that hedgerow? Where the hell are they?

That night we bivouacked in an apple orchard, frustrated, waiting. My new mess sergeant and his cooks had followed us all day with their new kitchen truck. They soon came forward with a hot meal and fed the enlisted men spam, beans, coffee, and jam.

Then the officers ate the same meal, but the sergeant set up chairs and served us on a folding table covered with a white sheet. A small touch, but it made me feel better.

The sergeant poured another cup of coffee. "Not quite the same as Bookbinder's, is it, sir?'

"Tastes great, sergeant. You're doing a good job."

Although it seemed like Charlie Company moved in its own little world, someone back at regiment or division or corps level must have been keeping track. Often, for no reason that I could see, our movement would be held up all afternoon. Some days we'd advance only a couple of miles even though we hadn't come under fire. Other times we would rush along and make six, eight, even ten miles in a day.

Each morning I briefed the platoon leaders and sergeants on our location and how we fit into the advance. On nights the BBC broadcasts skipped in on our radio, I'd mark a large-scale map with whatever progress I could figure out and go over it with the men. They seemed to take comfort from my updates. Plotting the capture of cities on the map and seeing the Germans being squeezed into a shrinking area on both fronts gave us hope that someday the war would be over.

Meanwhile, the enemy retreated before us. Sometimes they left a small delaying force to slow us down. One of their favorite tactics was to set up a machine gun at a crossroads to cover both directions. When we appeared, they'd fire a burst and we'd hit the ground. By the time we flanked them, they had usually packed up their MG-42 and disappeared. We'd find spent cartridges, a few empty sardine tins, and maybe a pile or two of shit they liked to leave for us.

We moved on, mostly by ourselves, my operational area bounded by visual landmarks, today a small lane on our left and a wheat field on our right. I moved the company in a line of platoons, with one squad leading each platoon and a point man out front.

It takes a special person to walk the point. It's a lonely, scary position, one that frays the nerves and freezes the minds of most soldiers. But several seemed to thrive on it, like the18-year-old kid leading this morning's advance.

I stopped him just before we headed out. "I'm curious," I said. "Why the hell do you want to be point man?"

He grinned. "Sir, it's the safest place to be. I figured out that when we're advancing, the Germans never shoot at the point man. They always fire at the bunch of guys following him. So I want to be the point man."

I liked the kid. "Stay alert up there today," I said.

About midmorning, out of sight around a slight bend, a single shot rang out, followed by a crescendo of small-arms fire. By the time I got to the front of the column, the lead platoon was spread out along a hedgerow, pouring fire over the top into a line of trees 200 yards away.

Crouching, I moved along the line, but couldn't tell if we were taking any fire. Not surprising. Usually, if we put enough firepower on the Germans, they'd quit shooting and bug out. We might not have seen them, but they didn't know that. Firing so many bullets in their general direction was often enough to make them duck and run, especially a rear guard who knew their buddies were already gone.

It's the natural reaction of a soldier under fire to feel he's being targeted individually, even if he has no idea where the firing is coming from. It takes a lot of combat experience before a man can overcome the fear of death and hold a position while bullets are cracking the air and tearing up the ground and foliage near him.

"Cease fire," I yelled up and down the line. The firing slowly died. Sure enough, no shots were coming our way. But one of my riflemen was moaning, shot in the upper body.

He was a new guy, wide-eyed and terrified. A bullet had torn open his left shoulder, shredding muscle and shattering bones before exiting through his armpit. A medic came up, shot morphine into him, and worked to stabilize him for evacuation.

I knelt beside my wounded replacement troop as the drug took hold and he began to calm down. I had no doubt his war was over.

"You'll be okay, son," I said. "They'll get you back to the doc in a couple minutes. They'll fix you up. You'll be fine."

While this was going on, two soldiers dragged my point man back to our side of the hedgerow. It was too late for him. Shot in the hip, he had slid face first down the opposite embankment where he'd been shot again through the top of his helmet, blowing his brains out across the back of his uniform.

When we moved on, I couldn't help thinking about my earlier talk with the young scout. His theory of walking the point just hadn't proved out. This time the Germans shot the first American they saw. And sometimes all it takes is to be wrong once.

At the next intersection, about a mile farther on, a Catholic shrine stood by the side of the road. Miraculously, an undamaged, life-sized Christ looked down from a ten-foot cross.

As we passed in silence, a few men genuflected and made a small sign of the cross. All of us took whatever comfort we could from it.

The next day was muggy and warm. Without opposition, we advanced through what used to be peaceful farmland. Now, dead and bloated animals lay rotting in churned fields. The houses and farm buildings were burned or blown apart. We passed an old farmer in filthy clothes leaning against a tree near an ancient stone farmhouse with a barn attached. The roof of the house had caved in, and something big had blown down most of the front wall. A dead horse lay on its side amid scattered household debris and splintered timbers. Open to the elements, the inside of the house was a shambles.

The old man took a swig from a wine bottle he held by its neck and raised it in a kind of salute.

"I'm sorry for your loss." I said, pointing to the house and shaking my head.

He shrugged his shoulders and waved his bottle toward the house. "C'est la guerre," he said, and took another drink.

Outside another village, the battalion commander called with orders to check a large building off to the left of our advance.

I was reluctant to send out a patrol to this unknown building. I was still a new commander, untested in the eyes of the replacements and some of the old-timers.

Okay, Scheffel, time to prove yourself if you want these men to follow you. I decided it was worth the risk of getting a commander killed for me to gain the company's trust. When I gave a tough order in the future, I didn't want the men hesitating and thinking I wouldn't do a hard job myself. Failure to follow orders could get soldiers killed.

So rather than send out a foot patrol, I called my jeep forward. The jeep's windshield had been lowered onto the hood and covered with a canvas shield to cut down reflections. Mounted on the front bumper was an angle-iron pole, five feet high, with notches on the front side to knock down wires that might be strung across the road. The jeep had a .50-caliber machine gun mounted on a pedestal, but I ordered a BAR rifleman into the backseat for extra firepower. Then we headed off through an open pasture to check out this building.

As we got closer, I noticed a faded red cross on its dark tile roof. A low stone wall, looking centuries old, surrounded the main building and another structure behind and to the left. The main house had three stories of windows spaced regularly across its massive stone front. I wouldn't want to clear the place room by room.

We drove up to an ornate iron gate more than the length of a city block from the building, but close enough for snipers to pick us off easily.

"Stop here," I said. "You guys cover me. I'll see if I can find out what's going on."

The driver climbed behind the machine gun and the BAR man braced his weapon over the covered windshield on the hood.

Carrying my rifle loosely in my left hand, I walked slowly through the gate and up the path toward the front door, trying not to look threatening or concerned. The well-kept grounds showed no signs of war that I could see, although I primarily looked for movement at the windows. When I got halfway to the building, the front door opened and a man in a heavy dark robe walked out.

By the time he got to me, my heart had slowed its pounding. In halting English mixed with French, German, and Spanish, the monk explained he was a Trappist, and the building was a monastery that had been turned into a hospital. Only a few Germans remained, too wounded to be evacuated.

Glancing again at the windows, I held up my rifle. "No combat soldiers?"

He shook his head. "Come. You see."

I looked into his serene face. "No, I believe you."

The monk handed me a card the size of a bookmark. On the front was information in French about the Trappists and their work. On the back was a picture of Saint Christopher, the patron saint of travelers.

I stuck the card in my jacket pocket, where it stayed throughout my tour in the war. I was not necessarily superstitious, but I was a long way from home in a perilous situation and needed all the help I could get.

When I got back to the company, my first sergeant asked why I didn't check out the monastery.

"It's the perfect place for an observation post," he said. "They could bring all kinds of shit down on us from up there."

He was right, of course, and I didn't have a good answer, certainly none that would satisfy standard military doctrine. But something made me trust the monk.

"Just get the company formed up, Sergeant, and let's advance on down the road."

That night we dug in along a hedgerow at the edge of a field. I hacked at the side of the mound with my entrenching shovel and smelled something earthy, but sharp and familiar. I glanced up but didn't recognize any plant in the tangled foliage on the hedgerow. I kept digging and cut deeply into a damp root. I sniffed at the wet shovel. I had smelled that fresh odor before.

I grabbed the root and yanked and followed it to the surface. At the top of the row, I found a four-foot geranium bush, much larger, but otherwise the same as the ones that grew in Enid.

Tears sprang to my eyes. All of a sudden I was transported through time and space, past Ruth and past A&M, all the way back to my childhood and the safety of my parents' house before my father died.

Across an ocean, in war-torn France, I sank to my knees before the geranium bush growing in that ancient hedgerow. For a long moment, I felt as a bereft child, alone and far from the protection of my mother and father, far from the shelter of home.

26
Walking Fire

Around the first of August, the 39th Regiment went into division reserve, bivouacking near a stream that flowed by a small town. While our nearby field artillery units boomed harassing fire eastward toward the Germans, the quartermasters brought in portable equipment for hot showers. Chattering pumps sucked up cold stream water and piped it through roaring heaters.

Inside four tent walls, showerheads hanging from a contraption of planks and ropes drizzled hot water over us. I stood under the open sky on a wooden cargo pallet that kept me out of the mud, lathered up with QM soap, and got clean for the first time since leaving England. Then, feeling somewhat human again, I put on a freshly laundered uniform and new socks, also courtesy of the quartermaster.

That afternoon regimental HQ requested me to transfer a lieutenant to F Company, 2nd Battalion. The choice was easy. I picked a platoon leader I'd known less than a week and whose platoon had an experienced sergeant. I'd take my chances with the sergeant, who had been in combat since North Africa. That left me with three other officers in the company—my executive officer, one rifle platoon leader, and the weapons platoon leader. I'd keep the two rifle platoons led by sergeants near me.

Thirty new replacement privates arrived, and we stayed busy getting them squared away and paired with veteran soldiers. I emphasized two-man foxholes and made sure they knew how to zero their M1 Garand rifles at various distances. The M1 was now the Army's standard issue weapon and supposedly a fine one, holding eight rounds in a fast-loading clip; that proved handy when the going got tough. Still, I kept my old bolt-action Springfield. It held only five rounds, but it had never failed me. After carrying the Springfield for so long, I didn't trust anything else.

The next day we walked six miles east with no intelligence except "the Germans are out there somewhere." About 1400 hours, the battalion commander radioed for us to halt and take a defensive position. Half a mile east of a small village and facing a forested area, we buttoned up in a circle of foxholes and outposts that defended in all directions.

Elements of the 1st Division were supposedly on our left flank, but I had no idea where anybody was, not Jerry, not other Americans. I sent a patrol in search of friendly units, but it returned without seeing anybody.

Then orders came down for the regiment to flank the Germans farther south. By the time we walked to the road and loaded onto two-and-a-half-ton trucks, it was after 2100 hours, almost dusk. We headed south down a narrow paved road, big equipment and other transports clogging and slowing the way.

A soft rain began to fall. Our convoy jockeyed for position, motors gunning, gears grinding, trying our best to stay on the hardtop. Vehicles slipped into ditches and held up traffic while men and winches struggled to pull them back on the road.

We finally pulled into a field east of Juvigny at 0400 hours in the damp early dawn. It had taken us over six hours to travel less than fifteen miles. Just before noon, the battalion commander and his staff briefed us on the day's objective. The mission was to push the Germans off le Mont Furgon, a sparsely wooded hilltop at the end of a low ridge northeast of Cherence le Roussel, five miles north.

Able Company would attack the opposite side of the hill while Charlie Company attacked from the south. In reserve, B and D Companies would trail behind, followed by Headquarters Company and the battalion command group.

To my surprise, the operations officer told me I would pick up a platoon of four tanks and a tank destroyer from a nearby armored battalion to support our advance.

"Be ready to move out on short notice," the commander said and dismissed us.

By late afternoon I was standing at a gravel crossroads two miles north of Juvigny. We'd just emerged from a wooded area, and I met with my platoon leaders while we waited for our stragglers. I had already lost my tank destroyer, bogged down in the mud just after we moved off the paved roadway. I had to leave a squad of men to protect the crew until someone came to pull them out.

I looked down the wide slope of the shallow draw before me. My objective lay three miles due north, straight across the field. I didn't like the openness of the ground.

As I scanned the field with my binoculars, two artillery rounds, one right after the other, shrieked across the sky from the east. They landed farther west, but it unsettled me. I didn't want to get caught in the open by artillery fire.

I looked east at a distant ridge where the big guns had to be firing from, then told my radio sergeant to get battalion on the horn.

While the sergeant fiddled with the radio, a lieutenant in the lead tank climbed out of his turret. "What's up?"

Another shell screamed over and I pointed to the exposed terrain in front of us. "We need to skirt this field. I don't want artillery shooting at us in the open. We'll stay on the high ground by these woods."

"Sir, I can't reach battalion," the radioman said. Then small-arms fire started popping, also from the east. Shit.

"Forget it," I said. "Battalion will just have to figure it out for themselves."

I put my glasses on a cluster of farm buildings half a mile away. Helmeted men scurried around the structures, frantically digging in. Muzzle flashes winked at me; I ducked behind the tank to brief my leaders.

"Okay, we're going to attack those houses in a skirmish line behind the tanks."

"Wait a minute," said the tanker. "What about antitank weapons?"

"They ain't got any, or they'd already be firing at us," I said. "I'll be behind your tank with one platoon. Hook up a sound-powered phone line so I can talk to you."

The tank commander climbed back into his tank.

"Second platoon will be on my far left, third next to me, all of us behind the tanks. We stay as close to the woods as we can. I want the men firing on the move. Tell them not to fire into the ground. I want bullets hitting tree branches and cracking over those fuckers' heads. Let them know we're coming and keep their asses pinned down." I poked a finger at my heavy weapons lieutenant. "Set up the mortars here and fire at will, as soon as you're ready."

I looked around the circle at their tight faces. No one said anything. "Are you with me?"

They nodded.

"Okay, let's do it."

The weapons platoon set up quickly, and by the time the tanks swung into a line abreast facing the enemy, 60mm mortars were coughing out shells that exploded on and behind the buildings ahead of us. The front portion of a roof blew apart, dust and smoke rising above the trees.

Holding a telephone handset, I stood behind the lead tank on the right end of the line. A wire connecting the phone to the tank snaked up and across the rear deck and disappeared into the open turret. I looked to the left. The men were spread out and ready. I brought my arm up and slashed it forward. "Let's go, let's go!" I shouted into the phone.

The tank lurched and clanked forward, its engine roaring, and exhaust fumes engulfed me. The tank to my left recoiled as it fired its big gun. Then my tank fired. Smoke and dust from the concussion wave billowed around me. I stumbled and almost lost my footing. What if we were advancing into a minefield? I moved over into the tank's tracks.

"Fire your machine gun!"

A muffled staccato erupted from the front of the tank. To my left, I heard a few rifles fire, then more. My soldiers were moving forward, firing from the hip.

By the time we had gone fifty yards, the men started walking faster. They began screaming. It was spontaneous and contagious, a primal yell rising up from somewhere deep in our warrior past. The rifle fire became a roar mixed with ancient battle cries. My skin tingled. I felt the hair on the back of my neck lift, and a wild, primitive joy grabbed me.

The noise was deafening. I could no longer hear any incoming fire. The Jerries were whipped. Thrilled, my heart racing, I yelled into the phone, "Fire, fire!"

At 200 yards, the enemy broke and ran. I saw men moving near a tree at the edge of the compound. "Shoot the bastards by that big tree on the right!" The tank's cannon fired, exploding a shell near the tree. "Yeah!"

It was exhilarating to do all the shooting with nothing coming back at us. The men kept moving forward, screaming, firing and reloading, firing again, their voices insane.

"Pour it on! Keep firing, keep firing!" Then I realized I was yelling into a dead phone. Somewhere the line tying me to the tank had broken.

We were near the buildings now, still firing. There was no resistance. The tanks had shot the place to pieces. They stopped, their motors idling, turret guns still aimed toward the compound. Rifle fire trailed off to a sporadic crackle.

We counted over sixty bodies scattered around the compound. Some of the enemy died in their holes and firing trenches, but we also found small groups who died without their weapons, panicked and running for the high ground and ridges to the rear. Three more died in one of the shelled houses, remnants of their uniforms still burning on their blackened bodies. The smell of roasting meat mixed with cordite in the air.

I spent the next couple of hours regrouping. Amazingly, we had only one casualty, a new man with a minor wound. We had the high ground, now what? We were at least a mile too far east, stuck out by ourselves with no other outfit coming behind us. We were vulnerable.

Adrenalin still flowed through our veins. We were high from our victory, but I knew we needed to get out of there before the Germans counterattacked us. I made one final attempt to contact the battalion CP but couldn't raise them, so we moved north on our own, leading our tanks and leaving the dead where they lay.

We continued slowly north along a narrow gravel road, scouting ahead, probing for the enemy, always seeking higher ground. The weapons platoon and our jeep caught up with us, and I stopped the company on a slight rise.

We'd stay here if we had to, but I needed to know what was ahead of us. We hadn't run into any more enemy, and we had several more hours of daylight. I spread my map on the hood of the jeep and saw that the little community where we'd routed the Germans was la Hardiere.

Ahead of us, five miles northeast, lay Sourdeval, on the map a fair-sized town sitting astride a major road junction. Whoever controlled Sourdeval could control traffic movement in the whole area.

Still feeling the rush of our victory at la Hardiere, I made a snap decision. I would take the jeep and a squad of men and head toward Sourdeval. Maybe we could get there before the Germans. The rest of the company would wait here and keep trying to reach battalion on the SCR-300 radio.

I climbed into the passenger seat, put a soldier in back to man the .50-caliber machine gun mounted between the seats, and we took off, a squad of ten riflemen following on foot. Now and then we passed a few cattle or sheep grazing in the fields, but farmhouses were deserted, no people anywhere. A mile farther, we approached a small hill, and I sent scouts to check the other side. Nothing.

At the crest, we pulled to the side of the road. I got out of the jeep and scanned ahead with my field glasses. I thought I saw spires and buildings in the distance that might be Sourdeval. I scanned slowly back down the road and across the fields. No traffic or movement anywhere.

Feeling a little uneasy, I thought about turning back, but decided I'd come this far, I might as well go on, though I'd leave my foot soldiers here.

"If we're not back in an hour, you guys take off without us." The riflemen spread out and took defensive positions on both sides of the road. I nodded to the squad leader and we drove slowly down the hill.

The whole area before us seemed empty. No dust trails in the distance or heavy equipment tracks anywhere, no enemy commo wire strung along the ground. A few head of livestock grazed in the fields, but we saw no people. We came to an intersection where another road angled into ours from a slight rise on the left.

As we passed this junction, the gunner in the back seat swung the machine gun to the left. "Someone's coming," he said.

It was a jeep, barreling down the side road toward us, dust rising behind its rear wheels. I put my hand on the gunner's arm. "Wait. They're American."

My driver slammed on the brakes and we moved to the side of the road. The other jeep kept coming fast. Soon I saw it carried two men. Where the hell were these guys going in such a big hurry? They downshifted, careened around the corner, and pulled up a few yards behind us. Identification markings on the front bumper showed the jeep belonged to XII Corps, the major command that controlled all the combat divisions in our sector. They were a long way from home.

A tall lieutenant colonel, wearing a clean uniform and an overseas cap instead of a helmet, got out of the jeep. These guys were definitely not infantrymen. They didn't have any combat gear. Carrying my Springfield, I walked back to meet the colonel.

"Where you headed, sir?" I said, without saluting—standard procedure in a combat zone where snipers might be lurking.

"I'm on my way to Sourdeval, lieutenant."

"You are?"

The colonel nodded. "I'm taking over their city administration." This guy was a civil affairs officer, corps echelon or above.

"Well, that's where we're headed, too. We need to check it out."

"What do you mean? Hasn't the town been cleared?"

"Not that I know of. That's why I'm on this patrol."

He looked puzzled. "They told me it's already been cleared."

"Well, we're on our way for a look-see, if you want to come along." I pointed over the colonel's shoulder. "My company's up this road a ways where we just had a big firefight."

The colonel glanced back, then looked up the road toward Sourdeval, pondering for a long moment. "No, lieutenant," he said abruptly, "we don't want to interfere with your duties. You carry on with what you were doing."

The colonel climbed into his jeep and told his driver to turn around. I stood and watched while they drove back up the road and disappeared in the distance.

As we pushed on, thinking about meeting the civil affairs officer gave me more confidence. Maybe an outfit out of our zone of action had already captured Sourdeval and sent back to corps headquarters for someone to come forward to keep the civilian government functioning.

But where were the civilians? We passed several farms and saw no more livestock in the fields, no chickens in the yards, no farmers. We drove through a tiny cluster of houses straddling the road that, according to my map, must have been la Forge. Not a person in sight.

By the time we neared the outskirts of Sourdeval, I was having doubts again about our situation. It reminded me too much of my motorcycle ride into Bizerte the year before.

"Slow down."

My driver downshifted and the jeep crawled past three shuttered houses. If an American unit had captured and cleared this town already, we'd have run into checkpoints or guard posts or other activity by now. This was way too much of a good thing. Something was wrong.

"Turn around," I said. "Right now."

The driver made a U-turn in the middle of the street and we drove slowly out of the town. Nobody fired on us but I held my breath until we were on the open road again.

That civil affairs officer was lucky he ran into us.

27
Finding B Company

When I got back to the company, the tanks were gone and I had a message to radio the battalion. Before I could make the call, the S-3 drove up.

"Charlie," he said, "you're stuck out here a mile in front of the rest of the battalion. We're already the most forward unit in our sector."

"Where'd my tanks go?"

"I've pulled them back. And you need to get your ass out of here before you get cut off. What are you doing way over here anyway? Why the hell did you go so far east?"

"I'm not taking my company across open ground. Besides, you didn't give me a border, so I figured it was up to me to do what I thought best. Anyway, now we're on this high ground and I don't like giving it up."

"Look, Jerry's already past you on the north, and a whole panzer division's been spotted on the other side of Sourdeval."

"So that's why we didn't see anyone there."

"You went into Sourdeval?"

"Just got back. Drove in to check it out."

The S-3 shook his head and took out a map. He pointed at a spot a mile west of where we stood. "You need to withdraw to somewhere around this little farm here at la Gallerie. That's where your tanks are. Be sure you link up with B Company. They'll be somewhere behind you."

As much as I hated to give up my position, he was probably right. It would be stupid to stay out here by ourselves.

Over the next hour we moved into la Gallerie, an abandoned farm on the edge of an apple orchard. The single story farmhouse sat thirty yards off a dirt road from Sourdeval that ran west to Cherence le Roussel, a mile or so behind us. The battalion CP was somewhere back there. I sent three men with a walkie-talkie to set up an outpost in the cellar of the farmhouse to keep an eye out for anything moving on the road.

Across the road, the land was open, sloping down to a small river a couple hundred yards away. A half mile past the river another road ran west, larger and looking paved. I scanned it with my glasses but didn't see anything.

I sent my only lieutenant and his rifle platoon to spread out along the river and protect our right flank. I kept the other two rifle platoons with me. Their veteran sergeants knew what they were doing and soon had the men digging foxholes in a more or less square pattern, 200 yards on a side.

Our defensive perimeter enclosed the outbuildings and a large haystack on its eastern edge.

In the middle of our compound sat a small, squat building made of heavy stone blocks, the perfect place for my command post. My radioman and my runner would be in there with me.

I put two tanks across the road to help protect the right flank and two inside my perimeter, one to the left front. I kept the lead tank and tank platoon commander behind and to the right of my command post. I wanted him nearby in case I needed to shift his tanks in a hurry. From his spot, he could cover part of the road as well as the approach through the orchard. The tanks churned up the ground as they lumbered off to where we would dig them into position.

Small-arms fire began to crackle across a shallow ravine a half mile to our left. On the other side of the ravine, a heavily forested slope rose onto a craggy ridge. Company A was supposed to be somewhere over there. I hoped they could protect our flank.

I still hadn't linked up with B Company, and it was getting late. I hopped in the jeep and we took off to find them. At the rear of our perimeter we came to a sunken lane that wasn't on my map. My driver eased the jeep down a three-foot embankment, and we started west between hedgerows on what appeared to be an old wagon trail. After a few hundred yards we stopped at a fork. The left trail appeared to bend back in the direction we had come from, so we turned right onto a lane that meandered vaguely northwest.

The trail narrowed as it curved north. We drove on until we came to a field that opened on our right. I didn't like the looks of it, but the trail clung to the edge of the field, so we started slowly across. We didn't get ten feet before small-arms fire opened up from somewhere on the right. Bullets cracked overhead.

"Get out!" I yelled and bailed out of the jeep. The driver hit the ground on the other side. We huddled against the tires as more bullets popped over us. A ricochet whined off the front end. There was no way we could get to the .50-caliber machine gun in the jeep to return fire.

A mortar shell exploded somewhere to my right front, and dirt clods clattered down on us. Smoke and the acrid smell of burnt cordite drifted over. Another shell exploded, this time to my left, on the other side of the lane, followed quickly by two more, closer. Angry buzzes filled the air as sizzling fragments snipped leaves and branches and thudded into trees along the hedgerow.

A tremendous concussion wave lifted me off the ground. A shell had hit right above us on the hood of the jeep. I felt, more than heard, the explosion. Shredded metal hung over the fender in front of me and oily smoke poured out of the mangled engine compartment.

I looked under the jeep. "You hit?"

"I don't think so." The driver didn't seem sure, but the debris and fragments had missed me, though my head ached from the explosion.

The shelling stopped and the small-arms fire slowly died away. We waited. After several minutes I crawled around to the driver's side. Keeping what was left of the jeep between me and where I thought the firing came from, I raised up enough to reach between the seats for my musette bag that held a compass, flashlight, a pair of socks, and a few toilet articles. I was operating on instinct. The bag wasn't really worth getting shot at again.

Red-hot fragments had shattered the dashboard, leaving burn holes in the seat backs. The .50-caliber had spun around and rested at a crazy angle, a jagged piece of steel sticking out the side of its barrel.

I grabbed the bag and pushed the driver. "Let's get the hell out of here."

Crouching low, we retreated along the sunken trail to the company perimeter without getting fired on again. When we got there, a few engineer troops were laying antitank mines in front of our position and on top of the road next to us so we could pick them up the next day before U.S. vehicles moved through. My men were busy improving their foxholes with timber and any debris they could find.

Before it got completely dark, I went around and warned my sergeants and squad leaders to watch for infiltrators. I tested the walkie-talkies at my outposts in the farmhouse and at the creek.

Sometime after midnight, the S-3 rang up on the big radio with the next day's orders and coordinates. With B in reserve, C and A Companies would lead an attack east to retake the same ground I'd been ordered off of that afternoon.

When I signed off, sporadic firing broke out to our front. I squatted in the doorway and peeked around the corner. Muzzle flashes on the left seemed to come out of the orchard, although it was too dark to tell for sure. I heard the unmistakable sound of a German burp gun as it raked our perimeter with rapid automatic fire. Men along the line returned fire and the burp gun quit. A grenade exploded with a flash and the firing tailed off. The firefight lasted less than five minutes.

After a few moments I crawled forward, armed with only my .45. When I got close to the perimeter foxholes, I identified myself so my jittery soldiers wouldn't shoot me by mistake. After I was certain they knew who I was, I crawled up and found we had one wounded. A German patrol must have blundered into our position. They'd be back now that they knew where we were.

In the next couple of hours, we were probed three more times, all resulting in brief, intense firefights, one on the other side of the road. Somewhere across the creek, German tank engines roared, their tracks squealing and clanking in the dark. It sounded like they were moving past, trying to get behind us. Then firing broke out on the opposite side of our position. I hoped A Company held. Otherwise we could be completely cut off.

Sometime after 0300, I was back in my CP, leaning against the wall trying to get some rest when a loud noise jerked me awake. What was that? I dragged myself up and went to the doorway. Artillery crumped in the distance.

"Did you hear anything unusual?" I asked the guard standing outside the entrance.

"Something came down the road. Fast."

I made my way to the foxholes along the road. Nobody knew what it was and nobody had fired as it roared by. How had something come right through us without setting off a mine? I passed the word around that I was going to inspect the road.

The mines were still in place. After a quarter mile, a voice yelled for me to halt.

"I'm Scheffel from C Company."

"Come ahead."

I walked toward a sergeant standing in the middle of the road holding a Tommy gun. As I got closer, I recognized him as a man I'd served with in Tunisia and Sicily.

"Did you see something come down this road a little while ago?"

"Sure did. Right back here."

The sergeant led me fifty feet farther down the road where a dead German lay sprawled close to two wrecked motorcycles.

"I shot both of them as they rode through. I don't think this one knew what hit him. The other guy lived. We patched him up and sent him back for interrogation."

"Are you still in B Company?"

"Yes, sir. Ever since North Africa."

We chatted a while longer, then I headed back up the road, wondering how those two motorcycles got past us and through a minefield. I knew I'd never figure out how such strange things can happen in combat, but at least I had found B Company.

28

Panic Is Contagious

At dawn, just before the battalion advanced in the day's attack, my last patrol returned from the north. A favorite German tactic was to probe for weaknesses between units and create havoc behind our lines. My patrol set up an ambush in the ravine separating us from A Company, but hadn't encountered any infiltrators.

At 0700, we followed our tanks forward, while A Company advanced on our left. Sporadically, artillery shells shrieked overhead, landing somewhere back near Cherence le Roussel.

We advanced on two farm buildings and found them empty. Across the ravine, Company A came under heavy machine-gun fire and bogged down as they approached a hedgerow. A thousand yards ahead of us, two German tanks suddenly appeared on the road from around a curve. Our tanks fired on them, the recoil of their big guns stirring up dust and debris. The German tanks withdrew without returning fire.

With our flanks exposed, A Company pinned down, and no other friendly units nearby, I felt uneasy about pursuit. Before I could radio my concerns to battalion, the S-3 ordered us to fall back. Resistance had stiffened, and we needed to get ready for whatever was coming.

"Hold what you got," he said. "Something's up."

Charlie Company fell back to la Gallerie. The World War II infantryman at the sharp end of combat rarely knew more about the war than what he could see in front of him. So we had only hints of the German counterattack underway to break through to the coast and cut off Patton's armor from its supplies, threatening the whole breakout.

That afternoon, an artillery observer showed up and began plotting firing coordinates for our defense. I was glad to see him.

"Where do you think you'll need it?" he asked.

"Everywhere." I pointed out landmarks and likely approaches. The observer called in a round or two until one hit the spot. Then he'd mark and label it on a sheet overlaying his fire control map. It made little sense to me, but I hoped the necessary adjustments were being made at the gun batteries located miles behind us.

My half-strength weapons platoon had only two mortars, a machine gun, and a couple of bazookas. While the observer continued plotting coordinates, I set up my mortars at the rear of the compound and located a bazooka on each side of the road.

Then I made sure the men improved their foxholes and slit trenches, digging them deeper and covering them with whatever logs or timber they could find. I tested the walkie-talkies again and strung commo wire to the perimeter to hook up sound-powered telephones. I would have to communicate quickly with my platoons when they needed artillery fire.

My observer spent two more hours calling in range-finding shells that burst at various distances in front of our perimeter and across the creek on our right flank. Then the firing ended and the observer walked over.

"Okay, it's done," he said.

"Great. So you're confident you'll be able to stop whatever comes at us tonight?"

He shook his head and handed me the map. "This is for you. I've got to go."

I looked at the strange markings on the map overlay. "What the hell am I going to do with this? You're supposed to be my artillery observer."

"No, you'll do fine," he said and walked toward his jeep.

Dumbfounded, I followed him, cursing.

"You'll be okay," he said. "Just call in the nearest fire point and adjust if you need to when the round hits. Then fire for effect. You'll do fine. They'll hit what you call in."

That's what worried me. I watched the bastard drive away, leaving me to cope with a fire map full of artillery concentrations I didn't understand. Just that quickly I had become my own artillery observer. I walked back to my CP, carrying the map, hoping I didn't in some ignorant way kill us all.

I made one last round of our defenses before dark to ensure our firing lanes were clear and our walkie-talkies and telephones worked. I didn't want anything else coming through our positions like those motorcycles the night before, so my instructions to the men were "Stay in your holes and keep alert. Let me know if you see or hear anything unusual."

I had my radio sergeant contact the artillery fire-control center and confirm our call signs. Just after dark, I heard heavy vehicles moving in the distance to the east. Not a good sign. Then a Luftwaffe night fighter paid us a visit, the first one I'd seen since the Allies had, for the most part, driven the Germans from the sky. The fighter roared along the moonlit road less than 100 feet off the ground and fired a burst of cannon shells that sparked in the darkness, exploding in a long line on the road.

At the end of its run, the plane peeled back into the sky and its engine noise faded in the distance. Soon I heard the faint squeal of tracks, the muffled grinding of gears, and the ominous diesel growl of tanks straining and moving in the darkness.

It was going to be a long night.

A steady, ground-shaking rumble unsettled the darkness. Enemy tanks and heavy vehicles streamed west along the road across from the See River where one of my platoons had dug in. Although I couldn't shell all the way to the road, I checked concentration numbers on my map and called for artillery on the closest one.

After a few moments, the round shrieked overhead and exploded with a flash, followed by a satisfying boom. That gave me a little confidence in performing the duties of a forward artillery observer. I continued to call in harassing fire whenever my men reported anything moving in front of them.

Our compound covered three or four acres on top of a small knoll. From my command post, I couldn't see everything around me, so after dark I crept out again to make sure I still knew where my soldiers were. I didn't want to call artillery down on my own men.

I crawled up to a soldier lying behind a Browning automatic rifle pointed down along the side of a hedgerow, its barrel propped up on a bipod stand. I lay beside him, talking in a low voice, when suddenly he nudged me. We heard a rustling noise, maybe ten yards in front of us, toward the Jerries we knew were only a short distance down the slope.

"What is it?" I whispered.

We heard it again, and my BAR man answered by firing a short burst of five or six rounds. Then we lay quietly, listening. It might have been a German scout crawling up to find out exactly where we were. We waited but didn't hear anything else.

After a few minutes, the BAR man said, "You cover me, I'm going to see what that was."

"Okay, if you want to." I wasn't about to order him to go out there. "Stay down. If there's trouble, I'll fire over your head so you can crawl back. Whatever you do, don't get up and run."

He slid from behind the weapon and I rolled over, grabbed it, and raised the barrel slightly. My soldier crawled forward in the grass along the edge of the overgrown hedgerow, stopping every few feet to listen.

Then he was out of sight and I couldn't hear anything but distant gunfire. My heart pounded. My hands started to sweat. I adjusted my hold on the BAR and shrugged my shoulders to ease the tension. I took a deep breath and waited.

Finally, from several yards away, he said, "It's a goddamn pig."

When he crawled back, I asked, "Are you sure it's a pig?"

"I know a pig when I feel one," he said. "It's a fucking pig, and I got him."

A waste of good meat, I thought. Crazy, what will pop into your head under stress. Our kitchen truck was somewhere miles away and, under attack, we couldn't have cooked anything anyway. Besides, I'd seen what a BAR could do, and there was probably not much left of that pig.

Back in my command post, I called for artillery every time we heard or thought we saw anything near us. As the night wore on, our support became spotty. Sometimes we got a round, sometimes we didn't. I didn't know one of the division's artillery battalions was under attack and forced to move. The rest juggled priorities all along the front trying to keep the Germans from breaking through.

The sporadic fire support kept me off balance. I had no real idea how this artillery thing worked, how to call it in, how to adjust it, what was normal, and what was not. I felt increasingly powerless while the darkness around me seemed to bristle with unseen danger.

By the time my battalion commander called to check on me, I was in a ragged, short-tempered mood. "Charlie, how are things going up there?"

"We've got to have more artillery support," I said. "We're not getting half what we call for. Been that way for an hour and it's getting worse."

"I'll see what I can do."

Before we could sign off, the regimental commander came on. He called my battalion commander by his first name and said, "How are things going up there?"

"Well, Charlie's having a tough time. He needs more artillery support." They talked openly. What could the Germans learn from it anyway? They already knew where we were.

Then I heard another voice I recognized. It was General Eddy, who had commanded the 9th Division since before the invasion of North Africa. My whole chain of command was now on the channel. We could all hear each other and talk by flipping a switch.

The general asked his regimental commander the standard question. "How are things going up there?"

And the colonel said, "Oh, just fine."

I flipped my microphone on and said, "The hell they are!" and flipped it back off.

General Eddy said, "Who was that?"

My call signal was Charlie for C Company, Reckless for 1st Battalion, and Red for the 39th Regiment. "This is Charlie at Charlie Reckless Red," I said.

"How're you doing, son?" the General asked.

He probably knew his companies were pinned down and under heavy attack, but just to make sure he fully understood the situation, I took a deep breath and said, "Sir, if we don't get some more fucking artillery fire up here, you're going to have the whole fucking German army in your front yard in the morning."

"Son, you'll get all the help you need."

Things immediately got better. For the rest of the time we were pinned down at la Gallerie, I got artillery fire whenever I called for it. Big stuff, even 155mm howitzers that would lift us off the ground when they hit nearby.

Everybody from the general on down knew we had to hold out. If the Germans reached the coast, the Allied breakout would collapse. They knew C Company and the rest of 1st Battalion had to blunt the point of attack at Cherence le Roussel.

The Germans knew it, too. After midnight, the noise level increased and Jerry seemed to be on all sides of us. Then German flares burst over us and a tank appeared abruptly to our immediate front, grinding forward, firing its machine gun into our perimeter. My two Sherman tanks opened fire with their big guns, and from the doorway of the command post, I yelled artillery concentration numbers to my commo sergeant crouched over his radio behind me.

He screamed into the mike for a fire mission, then yelled at me, "They want to know what they're shooting."

"Tanks! Tanks!" I shouted. "Tell them tanks!"

Within seconds, shells roared over and hit near the tank with deafening explosions and it retreated. But the infantrymen following behind the panzer came on, firing as they attacked our lines.

Then a runner ran up from the platoon leader down by the river. Two tanks with infantry were firing at them from the field on the opposite bank. I ducked back into the CP and shined a flashlight on the map, looking for the right concentration number. It could have been any of three or four locations. Screw it. I called them all in and went back outside. Soon a crescendo of explosions hit south of us. Hold them off, guys. Don't let the bastards cross the river.

The firefight still raged on the eastern side of our perimeter. Rifle and machine-gun fire rose from a crackle to an almost constant roar. Between the small-arms noise, I could hear frightful yells of men in deadly combat. Grenades exploded along the line.

A tank's big gun opened up on us from somewhere out in the darkness on my left. The front of a barn in the corner of our compound burst apart in a tearing flash. The building began to burn, its fire throwing long shadows and casting a flickering light that dimly illuminated enemy soldiers running at our foxholes. My men poured bullets at them from their concealed positions.

Another panzer appeared up the road on the right. The Sherman tank next to my CP was buttoned up, its turret pointing left toward the burning barn. I had to get it turned around so it could fire on the enemy tank before it attacked. I had no phone or radio contact with the tanker inside, who couldn't see much of anything except what was directly in front of him. I grabbed my rifle and ran to the front of the tank.

"Move! Move!" I pounded my weapon against the sloping hull, the rifle's steel butt plate clanging against the metal armor next to the driver's closed window.

Nothing happened.

"Goddamn it, open up!" Screaming curses, I slammed my rifle over and over as hard as I could against the tank. Bullets cracked past me and pinged off its armor.

Then, just as I lunged at the tank again, something else crashed into the hull, caromed off, and exploded. The concussion knocked me flat on my back in front of the tank.

There was a pounding roar in my head and the world closed in. My focus narrowed. I rolled over and struggled to sit up. I looked at the rifle I still held in my right hand. A fragment had sliced through the sling and left it dangling. I dropped the weapon.

My hands were shaking and I couldn't get them to stop. Where was I hit? I looked down to see if my genitals were still there. I didn't see any blood. Now frantic, I began to feel for wounds. My entrenching shovel, sheared off my web belt, lay on the ground next to me. I had to be hit somewhere. I lifted my left arm. The sleeve of my combat jacket hung in tatters, but my arm didn't seem to be hit. I choked back sobs and felt for the wound that would kill me. Where am I bleeding? What am I going to die from? I fumbled around and began to tremble violently. I looked up at the tank looming over me. If it moved, it would crush me, and I couldn't get up.

Then a soldier was pulling on me, yelling into my face. "Lieutenant, I've got to get you out of here."

He dragged me to my feet. I had no idea who he was or where he had come from. It didn't seem like I'd ever seen him before. I just couldn't think.

"Where are we going?"

"Back to the aid station."

"Aid station," I repeated, unable to focus.

The soldier held my arm and led me behind the tank and a few yards toward the rear of the perimeter. Two men ran past us, then another. That didn't seem right.

Someone yelled, "The old man's been hit!" A man running past dropped his rifle.

I turned around and saw more men running toward us, moving shadows backlit by the burning barn. Somehow, that jolted me out of my fog, back to reality. I jerked my arm loose from the man helping me.

"Let me go!"

The noise of the battle rushed in on me. I saw more soldiers abandoning their positions. It looked like half a platoon was bugging out. I didn't blame them. I realized my panic was contagious. If the old man is taking off, then it's time to get the hell out of here. I had to stay. My mind started to function again, and I moved toward the closest man running past me.

"Stop, goddamn it! We're not going anywhere. Get back in your holes."

And they did, not one by one, but as a group. When they saw the old man was going to stick around, they went back to their foxholes.

I walked into my CP and noticed I had stopped shaking.

"Man, I thought you'd had it," said my radio sergeant.

"I'm all right," I said.

Those scared soldiers would never know it, but they had saved me, too. If I had gone back to the aid station and been evacuated with combat fatigue, I believe I'd have been a basket case, incapable of handling pressure or functioning under any kind of serious stress for the rest of my life.

We continued to hold off the Germans throughout that long, sleepless night.

29
Holding Our Ground

Shortly before dawn, distant small-arms fire crackled out in the dingy gray fog. From the south came the creak and rumble of tanks and heavy equipment as I made my way around to check our defenses. Two soldiers, twin brothers from B Company, had hidden in the farmhouse cellar during the night. They said they had come looking for water from our well, heard a German patrol on the road, and ducked into the outpost.

One of my platoon sergeants was also there, half drunk on *Calvados*, a potent apple brandy native to the area. Several cases of the stuff stood along the back wall.

"Get back where you belong," I said to the twins.

When my tipsy NCO started up the stairs after them, I grabbed him by the arm. "Sergeant, I don't want to see you down here again. You need to leave the liquor alone and keep your troops in their holes. Are we clear?"

I had the soldiers on duty in the cellar carry the cases of *Calvados* outside and empty every bottle into the dirt.

To the east, several dead Germans lay within a few yards of our perimeter. According to their *Soldbuchs*, their identification papers, the dead men were *Panzergrenadiers*, armored infantrymen attached to the 2nd Panzer Division. We left the bodies where they lay.

My understrength company had suffered one killed and twenty-four wounded, including several from the platoon by the river. At our aid station, located in shallow trenches at the rear of our compound, two overwhelmed medics did their best to care for the wounded. One rushed around adjusting tourniquets while the other worked to tie a bloody compress on a chest wound so it wouldn't suck air.

Back in my CP, I sent out more patrols to contact Company A, now dug in again north of us. I continued to call for artillery anytime we saw or heard tanks or unusual noises. Periodically, I'd call for a round or two at random concentrations just to harass any enemy that might be out there.

Around noon, in bright sunlight and blue skies, a mechanized convoy moved past us across the river on the unguarded road to Le Mesnil Tove. Through my field glasses, I watched a German truck and staff car pull out of the column. Why the hell were they stopping?

The tanks and armored cars rumbled on, and I watched astounded as orderlies set up a table, spread a white cloth over it, and prepared to serve lunch to four officers. They must have thought the whole area was theirs instead of just a narrow corridor.

I thought I would serve them a mortar round for dessert, but before I could set this up, single-engine planes appeared in the western sky. Soon I could see the wide white invasion bands around their fuselages and wings. They were ours.

I yelled for the tankers to lay out identification panels. Six feet long, two feet wide, and made of different-colored reflective cloth, the panels stayed packed away in the tanks until friendly aircraft flew close. Then the tankers spread them so the planes wouldn't attack. It didn't always work in the ebb and flow of a chaotic battle, so I warned the men to stay in their holes.

The planes circled once, then peeled off and roared down in single file toward the convoy. White smoke spurted from under the wings of the lead aircraft as it fired its rockets. The line of traffic broke apart as wheeled and tracked vehicles scattered. One truck swerved sharply off the road and tipped over, spilling men like so many toy soldiers out of a box.

The fighters finished their attack run and maneuvered to come around again. One plane banked its left wing and headed our direction. I could see British markings on the wings and the large air scoop under the propeller that identified it as a Typhoon, the RAF's feared tank buster, a heavy, well-armed fighter-bomber.

We cheered as the Brits made pass after pass, their rockets and cannons inflicting massive damage. The ground shook. Black, smoke rose into the sky. The turret of one tank blew off in a spectacular explosion that tossed it 100 feet into the air. Flames shot out of the hole on top of the tank. Burning men scrambled from ruined tanks and rolled to the ground. A few rose and staggered a step or two, but most lay where they fell, writhing in death throes.

Still, the Jerries put up what resistance they could, firing machine guns and antiaircraft guns from their trucks and tracked vehicles. Tracers rose against the diving planes. Soldiers fired rifles and automatic weapons as the Typhoons roared over. One plane belched oily smoke out of its engine compartment and wobbled back west, trying to gain altitude. Another plane spewed a thin, pale cloud of hydraulic fluid before plowing into the ground, its wing-mounted cannons still firing.

After a few minutes, the Typhoons climbed and formed up, then headed west again, leaving behind heavy columns of smoke rising across the southern sky. Vehicles in the convoy limped eastward, a glorious sight that gave us hope the Typhoons might have stopped the German counterattack, or at least blunted it.

As the noise of the air attack subsided, from somewhere south, a few miles beyond the carnage littering the road, came the rumble of artillery fire. Intense firing broke out to the north in the vicinity of A Company's position. This was not over yet, and I got on the radio to beg for food and ammunition.

That afternoon more aircraft appeared in a clear sky. From back over Cherence le Roussel, flying about ten degrees above the horizon, the planes made their way slowly toward us. They weren't fighters, but I thought they were Americans and yelled for the tankers to get out their identification panels.

While the tankers scrambled to lay out the panels, I put my glasses on the planes again, but couldn't see their profile. Heading straight for us, too low for me to see any white bands, they looked like twin-engine German bombers.

"Pull the panels in!" I yelled.

The tankers ran around gathering the colored panels. They wadded them into small bundles and dragged them back up on their turrets and down into their tanks. The rest of the company scurried for cover. I edged closer to my stone CP building, watching the planes fly toward us.

No, wait, I see the bands. They're American. "Get the panels out!"

"I wish the hell you'd make up your mind, Lieutenant." The tankers scrambled out to reposition the panels as the planes droned closer.

The aircraft were C-47s, famed workhorse transports of the U.S. Air Corps. As they reached almost directly overhead, they began dropping supplies. Fifteen parachutes popped open and we watched helplessly as they drifted over the German lines, landing half a mile to the east. We couldn't get to any of them.

The wounded began to suffer more as we ran out of morphine. We shared rations and cut back how much we ate. There was no food in the farmhouse, and whatever had been stored in my CP was long gone. At least we had water from the farmhouse well.

Nebelwerfer rockets we called "screaming meemies" roared over us with frightful shrieks. Occasionally a round landed near enough to keep the men pinned in their holes, still digging in and improving their fields of fire.

We could almost set our watches by the enemy patrols trying to flank us and split us away from Company A. Every time we heard or saw anything outside our perimeter, I called for fire missions, so many that I began to memorize the coordinate numbers and corresponding landscape features.

Snipers shot at us sporadically, forcing us to run or crawl everywhere we went. The men looked on edge, haggard and tired to the bone, eyes red and sunk into faces gray with fatigue.

The day ground on toward nightfall, and we were thankful we didn't have to deal with German tanks. The morning's air attack had driven them to cover, but after dark, we heard them again prowling the road. I answered every screech and clank and grinding gear with a fire mission to keep them at bay.

When one of my outposts radioed or crawled back to report a tank coming his way, I didn't ask for just one round. It was fire for effect, and we got it quickly. The artillery kept them off us. I thanked the batteries when they stopped an attack or knocked out a tank.

Even if we heard nothing, I'd fire a round or two along the road every so often, trying to keep the fuckers off balance and guessing, same as we were. The evening dragged on. Exhausted, I slumped against the wall just inside the doorway. Sometime after dark, I heard what sounded like hoofbeats coming down the road toward us. What now? I stepped outside and heard sheep bleating, but the mines on the road were not going off. I walked toward the road but couldn't see anything. By the time I got to our foxholes, the whole flock had run by without setting off a single mine. That worried me.

I squatted next to a hole partially covered with branches and dirt. "Did you see anyone driving those sheep?"

A soldier leaned forward, peering at me through a small opening. "No, they just ran by."

"Well, something spooked them," I said. "Stay awake. Sheep ain't the only thing roaming around out here."

I stopped by several more foxholes to let the troops know the old man was out checking on stuff. Maybe it would give them more confidence. On my way back to the CP, I broke open a chocolate D-bar and gobbled half of it, the first thing I'd eaten since morning.

Things kept clanking in the night and I responded with more fire missions. Shells screamed in and burst in a jumble of noise and light; then it would be quiet for a few minutes as we strained to see and hear the danger around us. Too tired to move, I sat upright, so if I dozed off, my head would drop over and snap me awake. That happened more than once.

An outpost on the left flank sent word they'd heard a tank moving toward us down the narrow swale separating us from Company A. I knelt by the radio and shined a flashlight over my map, looking for a concentration to fire at. None were close to the tank. I hadn't expected to need firepower so far off the road. The RAF's daylight air raids and our artillery fire had caused the tanks to scatter. They couldn't move in groups through forests or rough terrain.

I decided to call in a shell forward on my left flank to let the Germans know they were moving into a fire zone. I took the mike from my sergeant and called in the concentration. The round screamed in and exploded north of my CP. Perfect. The tank should be about a hundred yards east of where that shell hit.

I snapped open the mike. "This is Charlie Reckless Red. Up 100 from that last round. Fire for effect."

In less than a minute came the piercing screams of approaching artillery shells, tremendous roars, louder and louder—too loud! Before I could duck, there were horrific explosions, one after another, almost right on top of us. My CP shuddered violently as the concussions jarred and lifted me, then slammed me to the floor. Dirt and debris blew in the door. I couldn't see or breathe. I gasped for air, sucking in harsh, acrid smoke. My eyes burned and a ringing noise filled my head. The concussion had ripped the microphone out of my hand and I struggled to find it again in the dust and gloom. Finally, my fingers closed around it.

"Cease fire! Cease fire!" I screamed.

"Did we get him, Charlie?"

"Hell, you damn near killed us all. You hit my company."

"We put it right where you wanted it."

That stumped me. "Where the hell are you?" I asked.

"I can't tell you."

"Well, you're goddamn sure not where I think you are or you wouldn't have put those rounds right on top of me."

"I moved them up 100, just like you called for."

"Well, I can't direct any more fire unless I know where you are."

We argued back and forth for several minutes while my frustration grew. What a mess. My lack of knowledge and experience in directing artillery had caused who knows how much damage to my own men. I needed to get out there and see.

Finally, I said, "Look, fella, I don't know where the hell you are, but unless you can put your artillery fire where I need it, you'll be explaining it to the fucking Germans when they roll up to your front door in the morning."

That convinced him, and he gave me his coordinates. I checked the map and saw he was north, way over to our left, not behind us as I thought. I had called in artillery almost directly on top of my own command post.

By this time, my radio sergeant had picked himself up out of the corner where he'd been thrown. I handed him the mike and went to check on my troops. As I walked out of the stone hut, it occurred to me that its south-facing door had probably saved us. Since it opened down range, along the axis of the shell flight but away from where the guns fired, most of the fragments had splattered away from the doorway. The thick stone walls had stopped the rest.

Outside, the stench of burned powder hung in the air. I listened for the screams of wounded men, but heard only the sharp crack of small arms and the dull rumble of more artillery landing somewhere in the distance. Bent low, I headed toward the farmhouse and foxholes south of the command post. I moved as quickly as I could through torn-up ground and past a shattered tree trunk. I circled around to the tank I had pounded on the night before. It looked okay.

Ten yards past the tank, I heard a burst of automatic fire, much closer than before. I hit the ground and saw moving muzzle flashes in front of our eastern perimeter, heard the unmistakable sound of Jerry's burp guns. He was attacking again.

The Sherman tank behind me fired its machine gun, the enemy too close to our lines to use its big gun. Tracers from the tank set a haystack on fire, and from the cover of their foxholes, my men fired at the enemy soldiers it illuminated.

A *Panzerfaust* anti-tank rocket, trailing sparks and fire, swooshed across the compound and over the top of the Sherman, exploding somewhere in the hedgerows behind us. Our mortars coughed out two high-trajectory shells into the orchard less than fifty yards in front of our lines. They didn't seem to scatter or slow the enemy.

Their infiltrators began to run through our eastern perimeter. We fired at them from all sides. Bullets cracked in every direction and the gunfire quickly became a continuous roar, drowning out individual shots. I could see grenades exploding at the foxholes on our eastern perimeter but couldn't hear them in the noise.

Silhouetted by the light of the burning haystack, German soldiers ran to silence the men firing at them from foxholes, then turned to run at others that opened up from a different direction. Shot at, hit, spun around, knocked down, they kept firing and throwing potato masher grenades at our holes as bullets poured out at them. It's harder to kill a man than you might think. Hit a half dozen times or more, he might still come at you, screaming, cursing, determined to kill you.

A flare burst overhead. Suddenly, I saw a lone Jerry running through the middle of the compound carrying a *Panzerfaust* antitank weapon. Fired at from every direction, he ran straight for the Sherman near the CP, passing not fifteen feet away from me. I'd left my rifle back in the hut, and I was too dumbfounded by this solitary charge to reach for the .45 on my hip. Still shaken from calling artillery down on my company, I couldn't focus on what to do. It popped into my mind that this guy must be trying to win the Iron Cross, attacking a tank single-handedly.

In the dying light of the flare, the German soldier seemed fearless, running hard, his mouth open. I know he was screaming, but I couldn't hear him over the gunfire. Bullets popped close past me and kicked up dust around him. Then he stopped a few yards from the tank and knelt on one knee, taking deliberate aim with his shoulder-mounted weapon. But just as he fired, a bullet must have nicked him or passed very close. His head jerked and his body twitched enough to spoil his aim.

The rocket roared out of its tube slightly off target and slammed low into the tank's wheel mechanism, mangling the track. If that shell had pierced the armor under the turret and exploded inside the tank, it would have killed the whole crew. Instead, the tank rocked on its suspension, and after a moment, began firing its machine gun again, still in the fight.

The German dropped his empty *Panzerfaust* tube, ran around the rear of the tank, and disappeared. I don't know what finally happened to him, but he was one brave soldier.

The chaos continued. I somehow rolled and crawled to the CP without getting hit. My communications sergeant knelt in the doorway, firing his rifle at Germans still coming at us out of the orchard beyond the eastern perimeter. The noise filled my head and drove out most coherent thought.

The sergeant, his eyes wide with terror, yelled something I couldn't hear. I grabbed his shoulder and screamed back at him.

"We've got to get some artillery support. They're going to overrun us."

I couldn't tell if he heard me or not, but he didn't move. I pulled him inside where the stone walls somewhat muffled the noise. I put a light on the artillery map, jabbed at it with my finger, and shouted into the sergeant's ear.

"Call in these coordinates. Tell them it's infantry and fire for effect. Got that?"

The sergeant nodded.

I grabbed my rifle and peeked out the doorway. The building partially blocked my view to the northeast. I didn't want the enemy running up on our blind side, so I crawled over and dropped into a foxhole near the CP to get a better view and a more open firing lane.

Germans ran through the front part of the compound, firing in every direction in a desperate fight with our guys in foxholes. I decided not to shoot unless the enemy directly threatened the CP. I didn't want to draw their attention. At all costs, I had to protect the radio. It was our lifeline to the big guns, our only hope of survival.

Soon I heard artillery rounds on their way in, loud screeches tearing the night sky apart on top of the hellish noise already filling the air. It sounded like the end of the world. I hunkered down into my puny hole, careful to hold my mouth wide open and my chest away from the ground, hoping the concussion waves and quaking earth wouldn't blow out my eardrums or damage my insides. God, please don't let them fall on top of us this time.

A half dozen rounds exploded in a series of intense flashes of light and noise, followed almost immediately by another salvo. Smoke and dust blew over me; the acrid smell of burnt gunpowder filled the air. Tree splinters, dirt, and tiny shell fragments rained down, as the noise level slowly lowered from the continuous roar to a staccato of shots that sounded like strings of firecrackers going off.

I peeked over the edge of the foxhole. Through the smoky haze, I saw broken tree trunks and burning branches in the orchard. Our artillery had hit them with tree bursts, shells that exploded before they hit the ground. These ferocious blasts send fragments down and outward, slicing through everything, particularly deadly to exposed infantry.

The barrage broke the back of the German attack. The enemy soldiers inside our perimeter pulled back, shooting wildly as they retreated, while my men poured fire at them. One of my riflemen rose out of a foxhole and let loose a long thumping burst with his Browning automatic rifle. We had them on the run.

The fight was over. We climbed out of our holes, moved the seriously wounded to the rear, and quickly reorganized to fill in the defensive gaps as best we could, getting ready for another attack. It could come at any time.

After I had my troops situated, I checked in again with the artillery fire control center to make sure they were still with us. Then I switched off the radio to conserve batteries.

We waited, straining to see and hear anything moving among the shattered trees and smoldering stumps in the ravaged orchard. Darkness cloaked the hills and from somewhere came the faint growl of enemy vehicles thrashing along country lanes. To the south, shellfire flashed behind the hills, its muted explosions rolling across us like thunder.

Crouched in foxholes, bleary-eyed and dead tired, the men of C Company watched and waited. Tense, nerves on edge, they pointed their weapons toward unseen danger.

Back in the CP, I sat on the hard floor just inside the doorway so I could see outside. I ate the rest of my D-bar and washed it down with half a canteen of water to fill my stomach. I tried to think of what else I could do to improve our defenses, but my mind was a jumble of images from the battle. I wasn't sure we could hold off another determined charge if we didn't get some relief.

At dawn I dragged my aching body off the floor and went to check on the perimeter. It was quiet. Nobody had bugged out. Nobody let his buddies down. The men had endured. They took everything the enemy could throw at them and held. We had made it through one more miserable night.

I was proud of Charlie Company. We had held our ground against overwhelming odds, the best the German army could throw at us. Giddy with fatigue and relief, I slapped soldiers on the back and offered them what words of encouragement I could muster. It was the best part of my job.

Grateful for the breather, we stayed at la Gallerie the rest of the day, getting ourselves together and evacuating the wounded, while I scrounged supplies and tried to find a hot meal for my men.

30
The Chase Begins

That night I posted minimum guards, rotating them every two hours to give the men as much rest as I could. Down to only sixty percent of our authorized manpower, my troops moved around like old men, exhausted to the point of shuffling instead of walking. I was so tired I felt on the verge of hallucination, eyes burning, filthy, overwhelmed with bone-numbing fatigue.

But at 0730 hours we advanced again, walking through the gore and body parts that littered the orchard and roadside. I had learned that it never did any good to think about or pay attention to dead enemy soldiers. They were just another part of the battlefield landscape, but this morning it was hard to avoid the carnage caused by the artillery and air strikes that had supported us. Maybe the war was wearing me down. I almost couldn't remember ever doing anything else.

We passed the twisted hulk of a burned-out tank with a charred body draped half out of its turret. In the ditch by the road there was a leg sheared off high above the knee, boot still on the foot. Farther on, a glob of what looked like fat lay piled in the road. These things stuck in my mind.

We walked back over the ground I had given up before the siege at la Gallerie and came across parachutes from the airdrop that went astray. The crates were empty except for toilet paper notes the Germans had left us. "Thanks for the smokes, Yanks," read one.

We walked for the next few days, setting up standard defensive perimeters in the evenings, but German ground forces seemed to have disappeared. With the company undermanned, I was glad when a few replacements caught up with us along the way, including two new lieutenants for platoon leaders.

I promoted several privates to corporal and a few of the better performers to sergeant. I counted on the noncoms to hold things together and get the replacements settled until my new lieutenants got up to speed.

We kept pushing the Germans southeast. Now that their counterattack had failed, their forces extended way too far west, vulnerable to being flanked, cut off, and annihilated. At night, our artillery, following along behind us, fired safe-conduct leaflets at the enemy, trying to get them to surrender. The Germans answered with artillery of their own, the lethal kind. Hundreds of shells streaked back and forth over our heads all night while we huddled unrested in our holes.

One night, Jerry aircraft killed three of my soldiers with bombs meant, I was sure, for our artillery miles away. None of this stopped our advance. At most, it was a delaying action by a rear guard while their main forces raced eastward, trying to escape the Allied pincer movement closing in on them. The American Army pushed up from the southwest while the Brits and Canadians drove down from the north, forming what became a pocket in the area between Falaise and Argentan.

Finally, we climbed on trucks and moved sixty-five miles one evening to a position outside Briouze, south of Falaise. The battalion linked up with another division, and I got orders to dig in on high ground and hold what we had. I was not to send patrols north.

For three days, British and American fighter-bombers decimated the German armor and trucks jamming the roads and lanes headed east. It was a slaughter. The burning hulks lit the sky north of us, smearing it with oily plumes of black smoke.

This was our first chance to rest and recover after the intense battle at la Gallerie. I lay on the hillside watching a ragged line of men and horses wind their way through the wrecked vehicles clogging the roads that led back to Germany. A truck pulled out of the trees where it had hidden and made its way slowly eastward.

My battalion commander called on the SRC-300 radio and my communications sergeant, always nearby, handed me the phone.

"Congratulations," said the colonel. "You just made captain. Paperwork's on its way. Great job you did back at Cherence le Roussel."

Numb with the strain and fatigue of that battle, all I could summon up was "Yes, sir. Thank you." I was past the point where a promotion or the medals that would come later meant anything. Like most men at the front, I cared little or nothing for medals and honors. My world was too stark. I just wanted the job done so we could go home. By this time, most of the old-timers who'd fought in North Africa felt the same way. The war was wearing us down.

More replacements came up that evening, along with some mail, including several letters from Ruth. It was the first mail I'd received since leaving England.

I was anxious to read them, but my first job was to get the new men paired with veterans. Replacements were at their most vulnerable upon arrival. Alone, scared, knowing nothing about how to survive in a combat zone, they couldn't be left to fend for themselves or they'd die in a hurry. If we could get them through their first few days of combat, their chances for survival went up.

Finally, I sat down to enjoy Ruth's letters, always a luxury and a great comfort. I certainly needed an emotional lift right then. I tried not to think about her too much; I missed her so badly. In lulls like this, when I wasn't busy trying to keep myself and my men cared for and alive, an intense longing for her came over me.

But the last letter I opened was different. "My dear husband," it began. "I can no longer pray that you will be brought home safely."

I felt like something had struck me in the chest. Oh, man, what's happened? What's she telling me? I stared blankly at the paper, trying to concentrate.

The gist of her letter was that she couldn't pray for me while I was doing my best to kill Germans, whose wives were also praying for God to save their husbands while they tried to kill me. It created too much of a problem for God.

Stunned, I tried not to fall apart. A problem for God? What about me? There was no way Ruth could know the problems her words had just caused.

Her letter ended with "So I pray that you won't suffer, but I can't pray that you will come home alive."

I was devastated. All I could do was wish I'd never received this letter.

Sixty years later, long after Ruth died, my daughter, Susan, told me the story of how her mother tried to cope with my being in combat, a story Ruth told her in the 1970s, when Susan was a young wife, waiting for her own soldier to come home from Vietnam.

During the early part of the war, while living with her parents in Enid, Ruth would walk out into the backyard at night, lie down, and take hold of the earth to feel closer to me, knowing that somewhere, at that very moment, I was touching the earth, too.

If I'd known that when I read her letter that evening in France, maybe I wouldn't have felt so alone.

It rained hard all day, pouring into our foxholes and bogging up the ground around us. We waited for trucks, but they never came. Mired in and soaked to the skin, the men waded through soggy mud and tore branches off the dripping trees to stuff in their holes, trying to get themselves and their gear up out of the water before nightfall. It was a loblolly.

The next morning, the battalion convoyed fifty-five miles and bivouacked for two days outside Moulins-la-Marche, where we rounded up twenty Germans who quit without a fight. With over a quarter million German troops trapped around Falaise, the Allies finally closed the gap, but not before a hundred thousand of the enemy escaped to the east through a small opening near Chambois. The comrades they left surrendered rather than face annihilation.

Even so, thousands of Jerries lay dead and stinking for miles along what became known as the Road of Death, strewn amid the tangled and charred wreckage of tanks, wheeled cannons, and horse-drawn wagons. Starving French civilians butchered the carcasses of draft horses, leaving only horseheads and attached hides littering the terrible landscape. The Allies had won Normandy in a final orgy of slaughter, and then moved on, out of the hedgerows at last.

Rumors that we would go to Paris excited us. Then word came down that a division of unseasoned replacements in new uniforms would enter Paris to celebrate with General de Gaulle and his Free French troops. The battle-weary 9th would cross the Seine at Melun, several miles south, and continue pursuit of the enemy.

This pissed us off. Glumly, we rode eighty miles in trucks and dug in for the night. About 1700 hours, we loaded up again and rode another sixty miles before digging in and eating a cold supper. The next morning we had no trucks and walked all day to the assembly point at Melun.

There was no sign of the enemy along the way, hadn't been for several days now, except for their abandoned equipment. We looked inside a Panzer tank that had run out of gas and found it stuffed with cigarettes and no ammunition. That was a good omen.

After getting the company settled and receiving our crossing assignment for the next morning, I walked up a hill in the late afternoon to look for the Eiffel Tower in the distance, but it was too hazy and I saw nothing but the river meandering north. That night we saw lights in the sky from the Parisians celebrating their liberation.

We crossed the Seine the next morning, Sunday, 27 August 1944. The Germans had blown the bridge, but our engineers, working day and night, threw up a pontoon bridge and we bobbed across. I bet a lieutenant from B Company fifty dollars we would be in Germany in two weeks.

A tank platoon and a few trucks joined us on the other side to form an ad hoc task force. As part of a wide Allied push forward, I led my task force northeast with vague orders to "go to Belgium."

We didn't have enough trucks for everyone to ride, and progress was slow. As we passed through a series of small villages newly freed from German occupation, people filled the narrow streets, ecstatic with joy and laughter. Grinning old men clapped us on the back and begged for cigarettes. Excited children wanted candy. Wine bottles were passed to the troops. A woman handed me flowers, then kissed me, beaming.

"*Vive l'Amérique!*" she shouted over the noise and kissed me again.

It was infectious. A delirious human mass pressed in on us, joyous, shaking hands, hugging us amid the bedlam. Some of my men piled out of the truck behind me and into the crowd. Young women led them away by the hand. There was nothing to do about it. The men would catch up later. We were conquering heroes and it felt good; something primitive and exuberant filled us. We were young again and glad to be alive.

As we moved unchallenged through the countryside that day, it became apparent there were no Germans around and a few men began to sing cadence. Every outfit has some joker who's good at making up bawdy rhymes, and so did Charlie Company.

One ditty they came up with: "Oh, we're Captain Scheffel's fighters; we're riders in the night. Wham, bam, thank you ma'am, we'd rather fuck than fight."

At dusk on that hot, humid evening, we finally called it a day. In eighteen hours, we had covered thirty-two miles. It had been a long, tough push. We set up a defensive perimeter and ate cold C rations while our stragglers dragged in. Then we tried to get some rest, the men exhausted, all the wine and song marched out of them.

I was in my command post on the back porch of an abandoned farmhouse, dreaming of Oklahoma, when the guard shook me awake. It took a moment to remember I was still in France.

"Sir, you better get up and take a look."

I'd been asleep maybe an hour. It was barely 0100 and the moon threw pale shadows across the ground. I stepped off the porch and asked the guard, "What's going on?"

He pointed west, down a long slope behind the house. "Look over there."

Two hundred yards away, in the large open field that spread out below us, a column of men moved steadily, parallel to our position. We had dug in on both sides of the road running in front of the house. The enemy column was a third of the way across the field, heading for woods a half mile north.

"Where did they come from?"

"Back over there," the guard said, pointing south.

That was the same direction we had come from the day before. I estimated the size of the column to be 100 men, two platoons. We must have passed them on the march yesterday. For sure, they know we're up here; otherwise they'd be using this road.

With my company spread out in a defensive perimeter, I didn't have time to use more than a few rifles and maybe a BAR. Not enough to do more than scare whoever was out there. I had the men wait until the column got directly opposite us, about halfway across the field.

Wait...wait, "Open fire!"

Our sporadic rifle fire started the Germans running and woke up more of Charlie Company, who joined in the fight. Our firing soon rose to a crescendo. The enemy ran toward the woods, left to right across our field of fire. An occasional muzzle flash sparked among them as they fired wildly up the hill toward us. Soon, their column disintegrated into a mad scramble.

I couldn't tell if we hit anybody, but the Germans must have run headlong into a fence they couldn't see, because several bounced backwards and fell. We kept shooting, but I knew we couldn't hit much at night and I called it off after the last German got over the fence. No need wasting any more ammunition when the enemy was trying to get the hell out of there. I hoped they ran fast and ran far.

It seemed I'd just dozed off again when a sudden grating roar jerked me awake. Something sounding like a giant motorcycle with no muffler sputtered overhead, low in the sky. I rolled out just in time to see a pulsating flash of light come up out of the woods northeast of us and struggle for altitude with a blubbery popping noise.

These had to be unmanned V-1 flying bombs, the so-called buzz bombs that had terrorized England since early summer. Carrying almost a ton of explosives, these monstrosities could level a city block with a powerful shock wave half a mile or more in diameter. Using a primitive guidance system and distance calculator, the short-winged bombs would fly in the general direction of large targets and plunge out of the sky after traveling a set distance. They terrorized the civilian populations of big cities.

Another bomb sputtered across over us and out of sight, followed a few minutes later by another launch. What was going on? I looked at my map and took a compass reading. Were these guys shooting at Paris?

The next bomb cut off abruptly before it got out of sight. A red flash lit the horizon to the west, followed moments later by a shockwave that rattled the house. A short round. The whole company was awake now, wondering what the hell was going on, listening to the V-1s clatter over, hoping another misfire didn't fall on us. We didn't sleep the rest of the night.

At dawn, we ate cold C rations and got ready to move out again. Some of the men wanted to go down in the field to see who we'd fired on but I was in no mood for it.

"If they're dead down there, they're just dead," I said. "If they're wounded, tough. If there ain't nobody there, that's even better. I don't know if we hit anybody, and I don't care. Get your shit together. We're moving out."

After three miles we came to the edge of an open area. Across the field was some strange equipment that it didn't look like anything I'd ever seen on a farm. I sent a squad to check it out. Fifteen minutes later the squad leader radioed back, "There's nobody here. Come on up."

We found two ramps, a couple of trailers with portable control panels on them, and some empty crates. I sighted along the length of a ramp. These had to be mobile launch pads for the V-1s that flew over us last night. The Germans had shot them all and hightailed it.

We didn't see anything the rest of the day except contrails from hundreds of our bombers droning east to pound the enemy's cities and factories.

Get them good, I thought, as I watched the bombers fly over. We'll be there soon.

31
Liberation

We began to see intense, sullen young Frenchmen along the roads and in the villages. They stayed at the fringes of victory celebrations, more observers than participants.

These men were members of the French Forces of the Interior, part of the underground Resistance. In hiding and on the run for years, they frustrated the Germans and the puppet Vichy government by blowing up bridges and rail lines, ambushing convoys, and assassinating Vichy officials.

German reprisals had been swift against the FFI and any civilians caught hiding them. The Resistance especially hated the Vichy secret police, known as the Milice, whose brutality rivaled that of their Gestapo counterparts. With the Germans fleeing, the FFI now sought retribution against anybody who collaborated or committed atrocities. Their presence in the background shaded victory celebrations with a hint of resentment and pent-up rage.

The sun was still high in the sky when we stopped for the day in a small village, tired and worn out. Civilians celebrated and waved flags along the street. I parked my jeep at the edge of a small plaza where a crowd of people were shouting at a man sawing wood. He wore a heavy coat and a long beret. In this heat? With everyone else in shirtsleeves?

An old man shuffled forward and hit the man in the coat sharply on the shoulder with his walking stick, staggering him. I got out of the jeep and started across the square. A young man in the group glanced at me, then pushed the older man away. He turned to say something to the onlookers, and I saw a pistol in his hand. Another man stepped out of the crowd and walked toward me.

"Welcome to our village," he said in heavily accented English.

I motioned past him. "What's going on over there?" The crowd was already moving the man in the coat out of the square.

"Milice," he said, "Secret police. The man is a traitor."

"Where are they taking him?"

"He will be dealt with," the man said, smiling.

"Quickly, I suppose."

The man shrugged. "*C'est la guerre*. He is a pig."

I had other things to worry about and set up my command post at the corner of the square in a building formerly used by the Vichy town government. When I checked in with battalion, I asked what to do about any reprisals we saw.

"Nothing. It's a French matter. Stay out of it. Our fight is with the Germans. How the French handle their internal affairs is up to them."

I kept one platoon in reserve and set up two-man outposts on every side of the village to make sure nobody sneaked up on us. Everyone else was free to enjoy the victory celebrations.

It was a carnival of people laughing, singing, and dancing in the square and the side streets. They brought wine to the command post, and I distributed it among the platoon leaders so everyone not on duty got a drink.

An hour later, a soldier stuck his head in the door and yelled, "Captain, you need to see what's happening down the street."

I followed him around the corner and turned into a side street half a block away. A few yards from the corner, a group of people stood jeering at a dozen naked women cowering before them. The women were covered with what looked like syrup and feathers. Two men pulled another young woman forward and a third went at her hair with what looked like sheep shears.

After the clippers gouged her head a couple of times, drawing a trickle of blood, the woman stopped struggling and submitted to an ugly shearing that left her a few ragged patches of hair. Then they ripped off her clothes, laid her down, and cut off her pubic hair while the crowd yelled.

It was like something medieval, almost tribal, and I half expected her to be stoned. Instead, they dragged her up, painted a swastika on her cheek, and poured something thick over her head and shoulders. As it dripped down her body, an old woman in black stepped out of the crowd. She reached into a sack, pulled out a handful of feathers, and flung them at the shorn woman.

Waving French flags and shouting, the crowd marched up the street past us, driving the naked women before them. It was a disgusting spectacle, as if they were channeling their pent-up anger, frustration, and hatred for the German occupation against these defenseless women.

The procession turned toward the center of town. They paraded the women, these horizontal collaborators, through the streets to the square where they were publicly ridiculed and spat on.

I had seen enough. I might not be able to do anything to stop it, but I didn't have to stick around and watch the French people turn on their own. Back at the command post, I looked at my map. We weren't far from Château-Thierry, site of a fierce World War I battle, where two U.S. divisions helped stave off a determined German offensive, possibly saving Paris. A couple of kilometers to the north lay the American war memorial and cemetery. It took only a second to make up my mind.

"Let's go for a ride," I said to my driver. I would try to locate the grave of a friend's father who had died in the war that was supposed to end all wars. Now here we were again, fighting over the same ground.

We turned onto a short roadway lined with poplar trees, tall and undamaged by the war. At the end of the road, on the right, stood a small stone building. An American flag flew from the flagpole. No one seemed to be around.

I slung my rifle and walked through the gate. The cemetery was laid out in the general shape of a T, the crossbar slightly curved across the top of the stem. A few yards past the building, I could see crosses in the distance, fanning out in an arc, perfectly aligned and falling away gracefully on either side of the wide walkway. It was achingly beautiful in the lengthening shadows. In the middle of my own war, here I stood among soldiers at rest from an old one. I couldn't help feeling the futility of it all.

The door of the little building was open. Inside, on a sturdy table near the rear wall, lay a large book; others filled a shelf on the wall. They had to be the graves registration records. I reached for the book on the table, then pulled back. It might be booby-trapped.

I looked at the heavy oak tabletop and decided maybe it would protect me from a small explosion, so I unslung my rifle, knelt down, and ducked my head below the table. Holding the rifle barrel, I shoved the butt against the book hard enough to move it several inches. Nothing happened.

I flipped open the front cover of the book. It was a graves index, all right. Across the first page, a German soldier had scrawled "Heil Hitler" and signed his name with a swastika underneath.

It took only a few minutes to look up the grave I had come to visit. As I stood before the final resting place of my friend's father, I wondered what desperation could have driven the German soldier to desecrate the registration book.

What futility he must have felt for his part in our war.

The next day our little task force refitted. Badly needed food, equipment, and ammunition came up from Cherbourg, still the only Allied port open on the continent. Three more jeeps, two half-tracks, and several more trucks joined us. We now had enough vehicles so that no one had to walk.

After a hot breakfast, we headed north in a ragged column, my jeep following the lead scout car. Those unlucky soldiers who couldn't get into deuce-and-a-half trucks rode in the bright sunshine on the outside of the tanks and TDs. We wasted no space. Ammunition and spare gear filled every vehicle.

My orders were to sweep ahead and reconnoiter a two-mile-wide path all the way to Germany. I was free to roam anywhere in my lane. The idea was to keep the regiment from running into major ambushes. In essence, we were a trip wire, and I felt like a piece of raw meat dangling at the end of a thin tether, bait for whatever beasts lurked out there.

We stayed twenty or thirty miles ahead of the massive Allied force moving northeast in a wide swath toward Belgium and northern Germany. We moved at a deliberate pace, so that our armored vehicles didn't outrun their fuel supply.

One sunny morning we stopped for a break on a ridge top and watched a column of helmeted Germans on bicycles a half mile across a valley. They could have been out for a Sunday ride—no trucks or staff cars, no armor, no heavy guns anywhere around. My troops started taking potshots at them, and they wheeled off the road and disappeared into a stand of trees.

Major road junctions began to slow us. To buy more time, the Germans targeted the crossroads with mortars, machine guns, or maybe a lone tank. As soon as they saw us, they'd open fire, and by the time we flanked their position, they were gone.

One afternoon, a gasoline truck caught up with us and we pulled into a field to refuel. A herd of cattle, the first we'd seen, grazed near a large chateau across the road.

Since leaving Normandy, we'd mostly come across nothing but carcasses, flyblown, stinking and bloated, their legs stuck in the air. The French had probably hidden some of their cattle, but as the war ground on, the Germans had no doubt shipped a lot back to Germany as spoils of war to feed their own hungry people.

Now here was this unlikely herd of live animals. Some of the men wanted to shoot one and cook it for supper. These were city boys who knew nothing about aging beef or letting it cool. I tried to tell them it wouldn't be any good, but they wouldn't hear it.

"Sir, we haven't had any fresh meat for months. The cooks said if we'd kill one, they'd butcher and cook it."

"All right," I said, "we'll stop here for the night."

I walked across the pasture with several soldiers. We approached three men in farm clothing who stood near the herd looking warily at the weapons we carried.

I could buy, but I couldn't steal. Taking civilian property in a combat zone was not only against Army policy, it was a war crime. I had 200 dollars in French francs to buy eggs, chickens, whatever we needed that was available. One soldier spoke a little French, so I negotiated with the boss to buy one of his yearlings, which I thought would be enough to feed the company.

I don't know what language he was speaking, but it wasn't French or German. These men must have been shipped in from somewhere in Eastern Europe, maybe Poland or one of the other Slavic countries, to run this farm during the occupation, a job that beat their alternatives back home.

I used hand gestures and pointed to a yearling. I was sure the man knew what we wanted, but he kept shaking his head.

"I'll pay you," I said. I pushed my interpreter on the shoulder. "Ask him how much he wants for that calf. Tell him we're going to pay him."

It was no use. We were getting nowhere. Frustrated, I reached toward the .45 on my right hip, intending to get a stick of gum out of my pants pocket.

The man flinched and looked at my holstered weapon. When I came out with a pack of Wrigley's Juicy Fruit, he grabbed the gum out of my hand and pointed at the yearling.

"*Nehmen Sie.*"

You take. I understood that.

The man gave us a short rope, and we headed back across the road leading a calf I bought with an unintended threat and a pack of chewing gum.

While one soldier held the rope, another walked up and shot the calf in the head with his rifle. The cooks soon had the carcass strung up and skinned. Impatient troops got the fires going while red-armed cooks sawed and sliced at the beef.

The men carried freshly cut slabs of meat, still warm with body heat and filled with blood, to the fires and pestered the cooks to hurry. Soon it looked done enough to suit them.

The cooks gave in and passed out half-raw meat. I took a bite of the spongy, bloody mess and spit it out, but the men wolfed it down, declaring it good.

That night was a different story, though. After weeks and weeks of eating almost nothing but canned and powdered food, soldiers found their stomachs rebelling. Some retched and some had diarrhea, while the really unlucky ones dealt with both problems.

It was quite a feast, not to be repeated.

We moved out early the next day. About midmorning, our scout reported a downed airplane ahead. We followed him until I saw a tailfin silhouetted against the clear blue sky. The markings and configuration identified the plane as an American B-26, a two-engine bomber. The crash landing had collapsed its nose gear.

With a BAR man and the scout, I moved closer to the wreck until we could see bent propellers and a long furrow where the fuselage had plowed the earth. A wingtip had touched the ground and spun the plane around. It still had faded invasion stripes from D-Day.

As we approached the wreckage, men in baggy flight coveralls rose from behind a small knoll and holstered their pistols. "We're Americans!" they yelled.

"Seen any Germans?" I asked.

"No. You're the only people we've seen."

The airmen had sustained only minor injuries. After I questioned them briefly, we helped ourselves to their foreign currency, watches, and pistols. I had them escorted to a crossroads a few miles back to wait for the battalion command group.

During the first week of September, we advanced at a brisk pace. Without opposition other than minor shelling and piled debris at road junctions, we crossed into Belgium. As we moved through the countryside, Belgian men, many wearing white coveralls, met us on the road. They belonged to the *Armée blanche*, the White Army. Like the French underground, they had blown up bridges and rail lines, sabotaging whatever they could to harass the Germans.

A few joined our task force and provided information on what we might encounter in the towns and villages ahead. They seemed anxious to take the fight directly to the enemy after their long hit-and-run campaign, and we were glad to have them with us.

The countryside was wooded and hilly, interspersed with a few open areas. Approaching one hilltop town, we took sporadic fire from houses in the outskirts, muzzle flashes sparking in the windows.

Our tanks lumbered into a skirmish line and advanced on the town, firing their big guns. They set one house on fire and put large holes in others. The facing wall of a two-story house collapsed, exposing structural supports and scattering its contents like some giant child's dollhouse.

The firing stopped abruptly and the enemy faded farther back into town. What were they thinking, firing rifles against tanks? Were they leading us into some sort of trap? I sent two tanks and a rifle platoon on a flanking maneuver to the right and the rest of us moved forward cautiously. I still hated built up areas. Not knowing what was around the next corner or behind the next door was a good way to get killed.

As we entered the town, a priest wearing a black robe ran to meet us, shouting, "Kill them! Kill them!"

We calmed the priest enough to get a sketchy story of massive reprisals. A few men of the Belgian underground had attacked a retreating German unit and killed a soldier. An SS officer had lined twenty men and boys against a wall and executed them. Their bodies still lay in the street.

I sent one tank down an alleyway to the left. With a thunderous crash, it tipped forward and fell into a cistern, dumping the radioman I had riding on top into two feet of stagnant water. Luckily, the tank didn't land on him, but he lost the radio and climbed out dripping and smelly. He and the tank crew were now infantrymen.

We followed another tank, its engine revving, pouring hot exhaust fumes over us. A rifle shot from somewhere ahead pinged off the turret and whirred past my head. The buttoned-up tank ground forward to the edge of a small plaza. Its turret began to rotate, moving its big gun, looking for something to shoot.

A few men crouched behind the tank. The rest of us hugged the walls on either side of the street, searching for movement in windows. The tank's cannon stopped traversing, tilted slightly upward, and fired into a building across the square. The recoil rocked the tank on its suspension; dust and grit swirled around us. A chunk of the building flew off, caving in a corner of the roof.

A white sheet fluttered at a window, followed by shouts of "*Kamerad. Kamerad.*"

One of my sergeants yelled out, "*Kommen Sie hier*, you kraut fuckers. *Hände* fucking *hoch!*"

A German officer walked out briskly with his hands in the air and surrendered what was left of his command, less than half a company. He handed me his pistol with a formal little bow. A few minutes later, while we collected weapons and searched the prisoners, another German officer came out of a building fifty yards away and ran across the road to a small shed. He crawled under the shed, shouted something, and fired his pistol at us.

Suddenly the priest was at my side again, grabbing at my sleeve. "That is the man who killed our people," he said. "He is evil. You must kill him."

I looked into the priest's wild eyes. I didn't know what to say to a man of God who would ask me to kill.

Our lightly armored scout car drove slowly up the street. The German fired his pistol at the car and it stopped close to the shed. The sergeant behind its .50-caliber machine gun called for the German to surrender. The officer hesitated, then lifted his pistol and fired.

The machine gun erupted in a burst of flame and noise. Its huge bullets tore into the man's body and set it bouncing and twitching as blood and pieces of flesh splattered into the air.

When we started to move the prisoners to the rear, the German captain insisted I should provide a jeep for his trip. Typical Prussian arrogance. He did not want to walk back with his men.

I was about to explain bluntly just what his rights were, when a man in civilian clothes came out of a house and ran up to an enlisted man standing near. The man reached down his collar, pulled up a set of dog tags, and waved them at my soldier.

"I'm an American officer," he said. "Give me your weapon."

"Sir?" The soldier looked at me.

"Give me that goddamn rifle!"

My soldier stepped back as the man grabbed for his weapon.

"Hold it!" I yelled and moved toward them.

The man turned toward other soldiers, screaming again for a weapon. "I'm going to kill that sonofabitch!" He pointed at the German captain.

"You're not killing anybody," I said. "This man has surrendered. He's under our protection."

The German officer stood still, looking at the American as if he were something less than human.

"Don't smirk at me, you bastard!"

Before I could stop him, the man stepped up to the German and slapped him hard, knocking his head to the side.

I grabbed the American before he could hit the prisoner again. The man screamed and ranted at the German, his fists clenched. He sank to his knees, cursing and choking back sobs.

I nodded to a sergeant and jerked my thumb toward the German captain. "Get his ass over with the other prisoners and get them the hell out of here."

It took a long time for us to get the American's story. Shaking and pacing, he told us he was an airman, a lieutenant, shot down on a bombing raid several months before. The Belgian underground had been hiding him ever since, moving him from place to place a step ahead of the enemy.

Trapped when the retreating Germans came through, the airman had witnessed the massacre. He told us the captain had as much to do with it as the SS officer who had refused to surrender.

His voice began to quiver again as he told of the slaughter. He seemed on the verge of a complete breakdown, so I put him in a jeep and sent him to the rear. His war was over.

After our defenses were squared away, my men helped the town bury its dead.

32
Dinant

Outside the village, the road opened onto a scene of ghastly carnage. The retreating Germans had seized Belgian draft horses to pull their guns and equipment wagons, and American fighter-bombers had bombed and strafed the defenseless column.

Bloated dead men and horses lay amid buzzing flies. The overpowering stench made us throw up as we pushed through the torn bodies and broken equipment. I held my breath, trying not to retch again as a dead Jerry burst noisily under the treads of a tank. We hurried on, our tires sticky with gore; we were glad to move out of the killing zone.

Screening ahead of the division, we moved into the hills of central Belgium. That afternoon, we topped a rise on a two-lane gravel road and saw a long flat straightaway. Four paved lanes stretched in front of us.

Where the road cut through a small hill, someone spotted buildings back in the trees: the camouflaged hangars, barracks, and workshops of an airfield.

We searched cautiously, looking for booby-trap wires across openings, careful about closed doors. Combat soldiers in a hurry don't have time to set up traps much more elaborate than trip or pull wires. We set off no explosions and found mostly trash and empty gas cans. No planes or vehicles of any kind and nothing we could use. The Germans had packed up everything and fled toward their Siegfried Line fortifications.

Back on the two-lane road, we had gone less than a mile when I heard a loud engine roar behind us. I turned to see a plane bearing down on our convoy. Shells thudded and exploded in flashes on either side and beyond me. I bailed. How had this guy missed me?

Flames shot out of cylinders under the plane's wings while it stood on its tail, rocketing straight up. Then the plane nosed over, pirouetted gracefully, and headed back toward us for another pass, wearing black and green camouflage paint, a white cross on its side, and a swastika on its tail. There were no propellers on its huge, noisy engines.

The men fired rifles, and a truck-mounted .50-caliber machine gun chattered, but the plane stayed 1,000 feet up and zoomed back along our column at an incredibly high speed, not shooting at us again.

I had just seen my first jet airplane and learned after the war that it had to be one of the early combat flights of the Messerschmitt Me-262. We might have been the first ground targets that pilot ever shot at, because he did very little damage. Maybe he didn't make that second pass because he didn't want to risk their precious new jet fighter. I never saw a German airplane in the air or on the ground after that day.

The next morning the battalion command group radioed me to probe north and find a way across the Meuse River, a formidable obstacle to our drive eastward. Our task force was almost due west of Dinant. The Meuse ran north from Dinant for 12 miles and turned east at Namur, where it formed a T with the Sambre River. The Division would have to cross the Meuse on the stem of the T, somewhere south of Namur.

The bridges south of Namur were probably already blown, either by bombs from our planes trying to keep the enemy from crossing, or by the Germans to keep us from following. Our only hope of finding an intact bridge seemed to be in Namur.

Rather than take the whole task force with me, I decided to go to Namur in a jeep with a mounted machine gun, accompanied by one tank. At the last second, I tossed a bazooka into the back of the jeep. For what, I really didn't know, since bazookas were not that effective against German tanks, but I felt safer having one.

Leaving my executive officer in charge, we took off, heading generally northeast through the hilly countryside. The day was gray, the roads empty. I kept looking at the map, wishing I had a Belgian White Army guy with me to show the way. After ten miles, I figured the Meuse River had to be half a mile or so across a forested ridge to our right, and the Sambre straight ahead to the north. We climbed around a curve to the left, following the contour of a little valley. As the road snaked back to the right, a tunnel came into view.

I walked to the entrance. Twelve or fifteen feet high, the ceiling consisted of large, rough-hewn rocks that looked damp. I couldn't see the other end or any light coming through it. I backed out and moved to the side. I didn't want some guy lurking in the darkness to shoot me while I stood there gawking.

But I had to see what was on the other side. We turned the vehicles around. My driver got behind the mounted .50-caliber and swung it so that it pointed toward the tunnel. The tanker swiveled his turret and aimed the big gun into the tunnel.

I stood next to the jeep. "If you see me running back here, fire a burst over my head to slow down whoever's chasing me."

I looked up at the head poking out of the tank's open turret. "How about you?" I asked. "You think you can fire that cannon over my head without killing me?"

"Maybe," said the lieutenant, "if you don't count ricochets and the concussion." He smiled down at me.

I walked into the tunnel, wearing a .45 on my hip and carrying my Springfield rifle. Around a bend I saw a circle of daylight another fifty yards ahead. Hearing no sound but my breathing, I walked to the end of the tunnel and peeked into an empty walled courtyard the size of a baseball infield. I seemed to be inside some kind of fortress. An old building on the right was empty, but I could hear faint traffic sounds beyond the courtyard wall.

Made of huge stones, the wall was about twelve feet high, rising from a broad base to taper slightly at the top. Steps on the left side led up to a platform and what looked like firing ports. As I climbed the steps, a church spire, then more of Namur came into view. Traffic noise grew louder. Crouched on the platform, I eased up to have a look.

First, I saw two bombed-out bridges on a wide river 100 feet below. We wouldn't be crossing here. Beyond the river, foot soldiers shuffled along in a ragged column of twos. Motorcycles snaked in and out of a jumble of trucks, staff cars, tanks, and huge self-propelled guns. Horses pulled wagons, carts, and artillery pieces. In an endless rush of grinding gears and gunned engines, what looked like the whole German army crossed in front of me and disappeared behind buildings on the right. I'd never seen so many Germans before.

I had no way to call in an air strike or artillery or even tell anybody what I'd seen. Too bad. I was in a perfect spot for an observer. It would have been a turkey shoot and could have saved lots of American lives.

I made my way back through the tunnel, slowing to a snail's pace until assured my driver and tank commander recognized I was not running from anything. I really didn't want them trying to shoot over my head.

Although worn to a frazzle by the time we got back to the task force, we moved eastward toward Dinant. Dark clouds rolled over and a steady downpour soaked us. For over two weeks, we'd lived in foxholes. Up early, stopping late, exhausted, eyes scratchy, staggering with fatigue and lack of sleep, we hadn't been out of our clothes the whole time.

With rain pouring down, I pulled off the road to confer with the tankers and my platoon leaders, whose haggard faces and bloodshot eyes told me we needed to call it a day soon. None of us wanted to spend another night in the open, but we didn't want to go into Dinant after dark and stumble into a firefight, either.

An hour later, we came to a large farm compound with a big house, some small outbuildings, and a two-story barn. It had stopped raining and the sun dropped below the clouds behind us, casting long shadows across the wet ground. We'd stay here, still a couple of miles from Dinant. The tanks would guard the perimeter while the men pulled guard duty and took turns sleeping in the barn.

I walked toward the main farmhouse and a man came out to meet me. I asked, "Do you speak English?"

"Yes, a little."

"Have you seen any Germans today?"

"No, not for some days. I think they are now across the river."

I explained to the farmer what we wanted to do.

He looked at the tanks, already churning the muddy ground as they maneuvered into defensive positions. Some of the troops had climbed down from the trucks and stood around smoking.

"All right," he said. "But please to have your men not smoke inside the barn. There could be fire."

"I'll give the order. Thank you for your hospitality. I'll make sure we don't bother anything."

The farmer looked at me for a long moment, measuring this unwashed American officer standing before him in a filthy uniform.

"Would you please to have dinner with my family this evening and stay as a guest in my house?"

"I would be honored."

I put my command post in the barn. Loose hay filled the top floor and lay piled against the back wall. Set this stuff ablaze, I thought, and we'll draw artillery fire from every direction.

"No smoking," I told my lieutenants. "Let everybody know that anyone caught smoking in the barn will dig foxholes all night."

I poured water from the well into my helmet and washed up as best I could with a little bar of soap from my box of K rations. At least my hands and face felt reasonably clean.

The farmhouse had an oven on one wall that opened to the outside. As I walked near, I could smell bread baking, a rich, wonderful aroma. Inside, I met the lady of the house and two children, a boy about six, and a girl three or four years older. None of them spoke English.

While the woman finished preparing the meal, her husband led me upstairs to show me the guestroom. Then we sat down to a plain but generous meal of meat, potatoes, boiled cabbage, and hot buttered bread. After a couple glasses of wine, I was ready to call it a night.

Inside my room, a washstand stood against the wall, a mirror hanging over it and a straight-backed chair beside it. A chamber pot sat at the foot of the comfortable-looking bed set against the opposite wall. I would never need that pot. I hadn't slept in a bed since England and I knew I'd be asleep as soon as my head hit the pillow.

I took it all in for a moment, then hung my pistol belt across the chair and took off my boots, something I never did in a combat zone, afraid I might not have time to put them back on. I slipped off my pants, too. I sat on the side of the bed, and promptly sank a foot into a feather-filled mattress.

I crawled under the covers and tossed and turned. The bed was too soft. Sometime after midnight, I rolled out and finally fell asleep on the hard floor.

I went back to the barn at daybreak to get ready to leave for Dinant. We tidied up as best we could, tossing our trash in the holes we'd dug the night before, then filling them again. While we loaded up, I took a lot of ribbing from my executive officer and first sergeant about going soft and being spoiled by sleeping in a cushy bed.

I never did tell them how I'd really slept that night.

Our side trip to Namur gave other outfits time to catch up. We still led 1st Battalion into Dinant, but other 9th Division units crowded toward the river north and south of the town. With the bridges likely blown, these units would have to cross in assault boats the engineers were bringing forward.

The Meuse River winds through rugged country around Dinant. Heavily wooded hills and deep gorges leave only a few possible crossing points for an army. We knew the Germans would defend them well, setting up mortars and machine-gun crossfires. I was glad my company wouldn't be the first to try out those boats.

With the early morning sun in our eyes, we stopped on a ridge overlooking Dinant. The road fell off steeply on its way to intersect a riverfront road near a narrow bridge. The middle of the bridge was down in the water, its support girders poking up at odd angles. On the other bank, a huge citadel towered over the surrounding buildings. Looming beyond its spires, an even larger rock cliff rose from a wooded area. I could see nothing moving anywhere; it was a good place for an ambush.

I left the main body of troops and all the vehicles and walked into town with one undermanned rifle platoon. Only four blocks long, Dinant's main business district hugged both sides of the river. Its buildings faced each other across a river that looked less than 100 yards wide at that point.

We fanned out and searched the buildings on our side, entering through back doors, kicking them in if we had to, so nobody could see us from across the river. When we didn't find anyone, I called the rest of the company into town and sent a patrol to cross the river at the water line, using the rubble from the destroyed bridge to pick their way across.

Almost immediately, the patrol came under small-arms fire from the area around the citadel. The men hurried back under our covering fire. Jerry's bullets hit the water and pocked into the bridge timbers around them. From somewhere behind the buildings across the river, a mortar round arced lazily over the rooftops and exploded upriver from the bridge, spewing a large geyser into the air just as the patrol climbed the bank. Bent low, the men crossed the riverfront street and ducked quickly around the corner where I crouched. Bullets cracked past us, but nobody was hit.

Crack and thump. Thousand and one. My patrol was back safely and now we knew where the Germans were.

We pulled back and I set up my command post in a house on a steep hill three blocks off the river, one of those houses where the front door opened on the first floor and the back door on the second. We found an old couple hiding in the basement. They wouldn't leave.

We were still moving in when three artillery shells screamed over from somewhere behind us, landing across the river. A few minutes later, a lieutenant from a field artillery battery showed up at our back door. He walked over and peeked quickly out the front windows.

"This is great," he said. "You can see the citadel, the bridge, the approach roads, all the way north past that low water dam. Everything I've mapped."

"Was that you firing those rounds?"

"Yep. One–five–five Long Toms, four of them. All zeroed in to keep Jerry's head down while we're getting set to cross the river."

"You gonna be here for that?" I asked, knowing better.

The lieutenant left his firing map marked with concentration targets, and I sat out of view against the back wall, looking through the windows across the room with my field glasses. I called in a few rounds to see if I could hit the citadel. A couple of shells sailed over the top, crashing into the rocky cliff behind. Another hit in the trees to the right, splintering wood with a huge flash. Then one hit above a large arch halfway up the facade, doing little damage that I could see. At least I hit the damn thing.

One of my tanks tried to sneak down to the river on a side street, but came under artillery and mortar fire as soon as it emerged from behind a building. A runner reported that a column of U.S. Army trucks towing antiaircraft guns was coming down the hill toward the river.

I took a back street out of sight of the river and walked up to a lieutenant colonel sitting in a jeep at the head of the column of towed guns.

"Captain," said the colonel, "I've got to head south on that road down by the river and set up my guns a couple of miles out of town."

"Sir, if you get much closer to the river, you'll be exposed to German artillery fire."

I told him about my tank getting shot at, but I couldn't convince him, and he proceeded on while I headed back to my CP. By the time I got there, firing had already started.

It was a disaster. Just as the column turned south onto the river road, artillery rounds hit two of the trucks, disabling one. In the chaos of being shelled, other trucks tried to back up or turn around and jackknifed their trailers, snarling everything. Another 1st Battalion company, still up on the high ground behind Dinant, began firing across the river to support the trapped vehicles and men, some of whom had climbed on their guns and were returning fire. One gunner on a twin 20mm ack-ack mount, confused by the firing behind him, swung the guns around in a panic and began pumping rounds up the hill at the Americans trying to help him.

The firefight lasted only a few minutes, but when it was over, vehicles were burning, men hung dead in their gun mounts, and the unit had suffered over 100 casualties, including many with battle fatigue. The colonel I had tried to stop sat on the floor in the battalion aid station, his head in his hands, moaning, muttering over and over, "What have I done, what have I done?"

One of their captains assumed command and the whole unit withdrew to the rear.

The rest of my company continued to disperse. My weapons platoon leader set up his mortars in the backyard of a house two blocks behind me and reported in. "I've got my spotter back in the woods. He can see the whole town."

"Good," I said. "Drop a few rounds across the river every once in a while and let's see what Jerry does. I'll try to call in the Long Toms on whatever you stir up."

I sat in a straight chair against the rear wall of my second-story observation post, the firing map on a table in front of me. The large window on the opposite wall gave a full view of the citadel, and I tried to catch some movement over there while we traded random mortar rounds with the Germans.

The glass had been blown out of the window, and I had no idea why the couple who owned the place stayed around, but they were still in the basement. Meanwhile, men had found an old waffle iron and were cooking up waffles and pancakes in the kitchen just off the room I was in. They smelled pretty good and a runner and three other enlisted men were hanging around hoping to get some.

German artillery shells started roaring over us from across the river, trying to dislodge or harass our troops up on the ridge behind us. I scanned the citadel with my field glasses and decided there must be a spotter in the narrow spire topping the structure. I called in the Long Toms, and their rounds screamed over but missed repeatedly.

Then I saw the barrel of a small artillery piece sticking out of an archway a third of the way up on the right side of the citadel's face. With a flat thud, the gun fired a round and rolled back out of sight. A few minutes later, the barrel poked out of the archway again and fired another round.

I gave up on the spire and started lobbing shells at the archway hiding the gun. I called in a dozen rounds that missed badly. Leaning forward, I propped my elbows on the table and steadied the binoculars, concentrating on getting the correct adjustment. I never scored a direct hit, but I got close enough to give them something to think about, making pockmarks and chipping splinters off the thick facade. Those walls were built to last.

This game of long-range marksmanship went on for several frustrating minutes until one of my men stuck his head in the door from the kitchen.

"Take a break, sir," he said. "Come eat some waffles. They're pretty good."

"Talked me into it." I motioned to the four enlisted men lounging on the floor. "Got enough for all of us?"

"Yes, sir."

"Well, I'm ready. Let's go." I laid my field glasses on the table and walked out of the room.

Just as I cleared the doorway, a tremendous explosion threw me face down on the kitchen floor. Dust and debris and the pungent smell of cordite filled the air. I rolled over and opened my mouth wide, trying to stop the loud ringing in my head. It was the only sound I could hear for several moments.

Someone pulled me to a sitting position and I checked myself over. I didn't seem to be injured, only shaken by the concussion, but four men in the other room were down, one of them thrashing and kicking against the floor.

By the time I was on my feet again, a medic had come with litter bearers and taken all four wounded men to the aid station. One died two days later.

The artillery round had come in the window I was spotting through, passed directly over my table, and blew a four-foot hole in the wall I was sitting against. I looked through the gaping hole and saw a huge elongated crater in the street behind the house where the shell's payload exploded. An armor-piercing round, the kind that concentrates explosive force forward to penetrate armor, had spared us. A high-explosive shell, one designed to explode with maximum effect upon impact, would have destroyed the house.

In combat, every day can bring its own special chance to die. This time, waffles saved me.

33
The Siegfried Line

Early the next morning, the battalion ordered me to hold my position. A rifle platoon from another company was going to cross the Meuse on a low water dam 400 yards downstream. They would need our support to establish a beachhead on the other side.

I scanned the area through my binoculars. A few inches of water flowed over the dam, enough to slow anybody trying to cross. On the other side of the river, a road came down the bluff out of a stand of trees and ended in a large open area that provided almost no cover.

I double-checked my artillery map for concentrations near the dam, wanting to keep Jerry's head down if he started firing on the men as they crossed. I sent runners to alert the company and we waited.

A few minutes later, twenty or so men, at five-yard intervals, crossed the dam without drawing enemy fire. This was too good to be true, but as soon as the last man got across, they dropped their weapons and raised their hands. Somebody I couldn't see captured them without firing a shot.

Almost immediately, two open-bed trucks came over the hill behind the area and started down the road to the river. The captured Americans stood in the open, held by someone out of sight to us. The trucks reached the dam and turned around. Enemy soldiers moved out of concealment and herded their prisoners into the trucks.

The best time to escape is right after capture, when everything is still in flux, so I had to do something quick to create a diversion. The Germans climbed into the trucks and got ready to drive off. I picked out concentrations halfway up the hill and called in two fire missions.

The rounds tore through the air and hit right on target, exploding on each side of the road a couple hundred yards up the hill. The Germans bailed out and dove for cover; Americans jumped out the back of the trucks and ran for the dam.

I called in more artillery concentrations. "Fire for effect! Fire for effect!"

Then I called in the 60mm light mortars from my weapons platoon, everything I had, trying to keep Jerry's head down while his ex-PWs dashed for safety on our side. A dozen shells exploded around the vehicles. A building collapsed. One direct hit blew a truck apart, sending a tire soaring 100 feet into the air. Metal parts splashed into the river. It was amazing, but every one of the Americans got back safely.

We traded artillery and mortar rounds with the Germans all afternoon. Around midnight, the engineers had their pontoon boats at the river's edge north and south of Dinant. While C Company stayed in place, the rest of 1st Battalion began crossing at a hairpin turn downriver, sustaining almost 100 casualties when the enemy caught the boats in midstream with machine-gun crossfires that wiped out most of A Company. In the chaos and counterattacks that followed, the battalion was unable to secure more than a small beachhead until noon.

We found out later that the 9th Division commander used our battalion as a sacrificial diversion to draw the enemy away from the main crossing several miles to the south. Though a bitter loss for 1st Battalion, the rest of the division crossed with minor resistance, and engineers immediately built bridges to get our heavy equipment across. The 39th Regiment swung in behind Dinant, trying to outflank and trap Jerry's troops dug in there, but they were too late. The enemy slipped away again.

We moved sixty-five miles in trucks the next two days, racing to catch a front line that kept melting away before us. We searched the mines and slag heaps around Sendrogne for enemy fortifications, but we found nothing. Next, we investigated a resort formerly used by German officers, complete with prostitutes. My men liberated some liquor and shared it with several girls still in the area.

A few miles further, our tanks caught up and we regrouped into a reconnaissance task force, operating out front of the division again. We advanced into dense, forested country, the ground boggy and sodden, oozing a spongy dampness. Green moss grew up the trunks of dark fir trees. As we moved closer to the border, everything looked gloomy and more German. We began to see half-timbered houses with livestock barns built onto them. The people no longer welcomed us, but stared sullenly as we passed.

Our advance squad came under a machine-gun attack, easily identified as German by its high rate of fire. The long bursts made me think an inexperienced soldier was behind the weapon. I ordered the lead platoon to flank both sides of the shooter.

They overran the gun and captured a young German in a makeshift uniform that made him look like a boy scout. Only about fourteen years old, he was a belligerent Hitler Youth, totally indoctrinated by his Fuehrer. Except for the fact that he could have killed a lot of us, he would have been laughable. I felt like spanking the kid and sending him home to his mother.

One of my German-speaking soldiers questioned the boy. He stood ramrod straight and told us he was proud to defend his country, exactly as his superiors had ordered him to do. Disgusted, we patted the little Nazi down, gave him some K rations, and sent him on his way west, away from his fanatical homeland. Then we scattered the ammunition and destroyed the gun.

Toward evening, another rear guard slowed our advance. As we moved along a narrow forest road in a column of squads, the armor following behind, I heard a single shot. By this time, I could identify almost any German weapon by its sound, but this one I'd never heard before.

Our advance scout quickly captured another German, an old man dressed in hunting clothes who appeared to be in his late seventies. He stood in the middle of the road where he'd fired his single-shot muzzle-loader at the point man, and then surrendered meekly. We smashed the old man's weapon against a tree, and told him to go home.

We moved cautiously ahead through the dark woods while a misty rain soaked us. We walked along the narrow road until we came to an empty guard post at the outskirts of Roetgen. Our scout raised the pipe barrier and we crossed the border, among the first U.S. ground forces to enter Germany.

The small town looked empty. The vague orders we'd received that morning came with no intelligence report and no specific instructions. I pulled out a Michelin road map I had taken from a dead German officer in Normandy and studied what lay ahead. We had to run into the enemy again soon, but where?

I sent a patrol into the village, but they found no one, and we walked toward a small train depot ahead on the left. On the far side of the station, a rail line crossed the road. We heard the sound of a train coming around a bend to the north and took cover on both sides of the tracks, waiting for what might be a troop or artillery train.

Pouring smoke out its stack, a small steam engine chugged slowly into view around the curve and pulled into the station. The doors on its three ancient railcars opened, and a tired group of women, children, and old men climbed off. We saw no soldiers, no men of military age.

Carrying small suitcases, boxes tied with rope or string, and various odd-shaped bundles, the weary refugees walked out of Roetgen and across the border. They didn't seem to care about us and I didn't try to stop them. They disappeared into the Belgian forest and the empty train pulled away from the little station.

But German troops could come in on a train as easily as civilian evacuees. It was almost dark and I didn't want a firefight in a built-up area where we couldn't see what we were doing. More than a little uneasy, we headed back into Belgium.

I called it a day near a small farmhouse we had passed earlier. I established a roadblock with the four Sherman tanks and ordered the platoons to dig in astride the road. As darkness descended, we lost radio contact with units behind us. We were alone, and it began to rain again, a cold, steady drizzle.

The first sergeant moved the farmer and his wife into the basement and set up the company CP in a corner of the covered back porch. I put a guard on the door and ordered my men to stay out of the house.

It had been another long day, but we settled in and things seemed to be under control. I spotted a small open shed a 100 feet from the house and told my runner I was going to bed down there. He was to wake me an hour before daybreak.

The shed, closed on two sides, was relatively dry under its sloping roof. I was a little surprised when I waded across the barnyard muck and found no other soldiers there, but I was too tired to think much about it.

I saw an inviting pile of hay in the back corner and leaned my rifle against a wall. Exhausted, I dropped my musette bag and pulled the map case and binoculars over my head. Then I took off my pistol belt and everything hanging from it: the holstered .45 automatic, the half-filled canteen, a trench shovel, and my first aid pack. I collapsed onto the pile of hay and covered up with the raincoat I carried looped over the belt. I slept snug and warm until my runner shook me awake just before daybreak.

"P-yew, Captain, you sure do stink."

I had slept in a pile of manure-filled straw. No wonder I had the place all to myself. The command group, after they got through laughing, helped me scrape most of the stuff off my uniform. I knew I'd smell pretty rank for quite a while.

The rain had slowed to a fine mist sometime during the night, and the dark fir trees dripped water in the pale dawn light. They didn't look like they'd ever been dry, same as I felt. As I sat on the porch eating a cold cheese and bacon K ration, a runner came up and said the new battalion commander wanted to see me. He'd taken over a few days earlier after shellfire wounded the previous commander.

I walked up the road to meet the new guy. When I got close, I recognized him. A lieutenant colonel now, and a college jock like me, he'd been my company commander for a while back in North Africa. Was that only last year? It seemed so long ago.

The colonel pulled out a small-scale tactical map. The day's objective was Dueren, a German town twenty miles northeast. To get there, we would have to follow a narrow road into the Huertgen Forest and clear four small villages, starting with Lammersdorf.

I stabbed a finger at the map. "Are these two cross-hatched areas what I think they are?

"Yeah," he said. "The Siegfried Line."

"That's what I thought. It's going to be a long day."

The Siegfried Line, sometimes known as the West Wall, consisted of lines of heavy fortifications snaking north and south along the border—sometimes singly, sometimes in double rows, depending upon the terrain. The Germans had worked on these emplacements for years. Concrete tank barriers stood in front of massive pillboxes with interlocking fields of fire. About four feet high, the "dragon's teeth" barriers were shaped like pyramids with their tops cut off. An intricate system of trenches connected the pillboxes and supporting artillery and mortar pits. Jerry meant to keep us out of his homeland.

Charlie Company, with four tanks attached, would be in the lead, A Company on our left, B in reserve. Company D would trail with their mortars and heavy machine guns to support the advance wherever needed.

The colonel handed me the map and shook my hand. "Good luck," he said.

We took off in a column of platoons, the four tanks leading with a squad of riflemen beside each. I kept my runner, my walkie-talkie guy, and my radio sergeant near me. I could need them at any time. The runner, a private, kept me in touch with my platoon leaders, and the walkie-talkie was my link to the mortars and machine guns in Company D. The SCR-300 the sergeant carried on his back was supposed to get me support from artillery batteries set up miles to the rear.

We crossed the border into Germany again and turned onto a road that took us around Roetgen to the south. Lammersdorf, a few miles further, looked to have a population of maybe 300 people. Stone buildings and stores clustered along the narrow main street. No white flags or people anywhere. It would take only one man with a *Panzerfaust* to knock out a tank and clog the street, stopping us in our tracks.

I held the tanks back and sent the lead platoon into town to clear the way. They didn't find anybody. We walked through the village and stopped again at the far edge of town. High ground a mile ahead, labeled Hill 554 on my map, looked like a good place for an artillery observation post. Anyone up there could control the whole area. The map showed the hill surrounded by fortifications of the Siegfried Line. I didn't like it.

A good infantryman always looks for potential cover, and I took note of three-foot-deep bar ditches on each side of the gravel road. On the left, railroad tracks ran parallel to the road. Company A was supposed to be somewhere over there, but I couldn't see them.

In single file, engines throttled back, the tanks and their assigned squads led us up the road. They would take out the pillboxes. I followed the last tank with my three-man command group, while the rest of the company trailed at ten-yard intervals, strung out, some men still back in the outskirts of Lammersdorf.

Suddenly I heard a short piercing shriek, and the nearest tank careened toward me in reverse, churning gravel, its engine roaring. Close to a tank is the worst place to be when it comes under fire. I dove into a ditch with my runner and my walkie-talkie guy. The radio sergeant jumped into the ditch across the road.

A German machine gun opened up from somewhere in front, and mortar and artillery shells began exploding in the fields on either side of the road. The lead tank was in flames fifty yards up the road. Men were down around it. Bullets snapped overhead and another high-velocity shell hit the rear tank. The explosion knocked the turret to one side, tipping the cannon down at an odd angle. Dark, greasy smoke poured from the tank; nobody got out.

The two tanks in the middle were now trapped. The tank in front fired once before a direct-fire antitank weapon hidden nearby set it ablaze. The other tank backed a few feet toward us before a shell blew off its track on the side away from me. The tank shuddered, surged backward awkwardly, and tilted to a stop.

I peeked over the edge of the ditch. German machine guns chattered away on my left but I couldn't see where they were, no emplacements, no pillboxes, though they couldn't be far away. Several men were down in the road, some killed, others wounded and screaming. I couldn't see anybody else. Tracers passed over us and I felt a flutter of panic. We were pinned down, taking fire and returning none that I could see or hear.

Another round hit the crippled tank with a sharp crack, rocking it on its suspension. A shell fragment buzzed angrily, and the bright flash of impact gave way to orange flames and roiling black smoke. The acrid smell of cordite and burning fuel filled the air. The turret stayed closed. The men inside never had a chance.

A volley of mortar rounds landed on both sides of the road in a series of booming explosions. Sizzling fragments cut through the air with metallic zings and twangs.

My runner lay at my feet with his rifle pointed along the ditch. "Don't let any Germans come down toward us," I yelled.

My walkie-talkie guy, another young private, lay close by my side. I grabbed the bulky handset and yelled into it, trying to reach my weapons platoon for mortar support. Nobody answered. Down in the ditch, we must have been out of their line of sight, which made the walkie-talkie useless. I looked back toward Lammersdorf but couldn't see anybody.

We were in a terrible spot, with no big guns to support us. All four tanks were burning in the middle of the road, the nearest one crackling and popping as metal expanded and rivets gave way. I needed the SCR-300 so I could try to reach our artillery.

I yelled across the road. "Get over here! I need that radio." Better for one man to move than three.

Crouching low, the bulky radio flopping in its harness on his back, the sergeant ran across and skidded into the ditch. Still holding the walkie-talkie in my right hand, I grabbed the SCR-300 handset with my left, toggled them both on, and yelled my call sign into the mikes.

"Come in! This is Charlie. Come in!"

Nobody answered.

I tried again. "Come in, goddamn it! We need help!"

Still nobody answered.

Another volley of mortar shells whirred in and explosions boomed around us, kicking up sod and debris. Jagged shards of hot metal whizzed through the air. Dirt and gravel and tiny fragments rained down as I pressed against the ground and continued screaming into both handsets.

Suddenly, my world went dark and silent. I didn't see it or hear it coming. I didn't feel anything. There was just nothing for I don't know how long. Then I noticed I couldn't see. I tried to move my right arm but it didn't seem to be working. I thought for a moment that maybe I was dead.

I reached up with my left hand and wiped wetness off my face. I could see blood on my hand with my left eye. My radio sergeant lay on his side a foot away from me, his pants shredded, his uniform soaked in blood. The sergeant's right leg was gone, blown off at the hip. I reached over and shook him gently. He didn't respond, and it occurred to me he was dead.

I looked down along my body and saw my runner leaning against the other side of the ditch, his head slumped on his chest. His bowels erupted out of a blackened gash, past a large steaming sliver of metal lodged in his lower abdomen. My runner was dead.

I felt no pain but couldn't move my right arm and couldn't see out of my right eye. Maybe this is what it's like to be dead, I thought. I twisted my head to the right and rolled slightly until I saw what was left of the walkie-talkie. It was still in my hand, case peeled open, wiring snarled, looking like a handful of worms. My index finger was flopped back on my wrist at an impossible angle. I dropped the radio. The finger dangled from my bloody hand by a string of gristle. Still, I didn't hurt.

I turned a little more to the right and saw the body of my other soldier. His head was missing, the neck stuck up between his shoulders like a red stump. It didn't shock or surprise me. Nothing did anymore. The three men around me were dead, and I relaxed. There was nothing left to struggle for.

I began to think of my family. God, take care of my wife, my mother, and my brother. Keep them safe. I offered no prayers for my own salvation. Still feeling no pain, I lay back and waited to go to heaven or hell, whichever God had chosen for me, whenever He got around to it. He had so many to take care of right now.

Then a single bullet cracked over my head, automatically starting me to count. Before my mind could say "thousand," I heard the thumping sound of the gun. Crack and thump. Someone not far away was shooting in my direction.

Crack and thump pulled me out of limbo and back to earth. I began hurting down my right side. I could see blood where fragments had chewed into the right leg of my trousers. More blood oozed from a large hole in the right bicep of my field jacket. I felt blood trickling down my face, and I still couldn't see out of my right eye.

I was alive but I knew I was in big trouble. I was losing too much blood. I rolled onto my right side enough to reach the first aid kit on my left hip. I needed to get some sulfa tablets out of it to protect against infection. I laid the kit on my stomach and fumbled it open. Tearing the sulfa packet with my teeth, I choked down as many tablets as I could, washing them down with blood running down my face. I needed water, but my canteen was on my right hip, out of reach.

I was really hurting now, my hand, my head, my whole right side. And I was scared. The sounds of battle pressed in on me again, the rattle of machine guns, the muffled thud of explosions. The tanks continued to burn. If the Germans counterattacked, I was dead. If they didn't, I would bleed to death anyway. I had to move. I crawled across my dead sergeant, keeping as low as possible, and dragged myself along the bottom of the ditch back toward Lammersdorf.

While the war raged on all sides, I fell into a slow, painful rhythm. Pull forward with my left arm. Rest a moment and catch my breath. Gather strength. Reach forward. Pull. Rest. Do it again. I concentrated on the task at hand to keep the pain at bay, grunting and moaning with the effort. Move your arm. Now pull. Again.

I crawled up to a medic crouched in the bottom of the ditch, a Mexican kid assigned to one of the following platoons. I tried to look past him but we seemed to be alone.

"Where the hell is everybody?"

The medic leaned down, looking me over. "I don't know, Sir. I need to stop this bleeding."

He rolled me over and I groaned with the pain.

"Do you want morphine?"

Yes, I did. The medic punctured the little syrette and gave me a shot in my left arm. While he worked on my wounds, I listened to occasional explosions and German rifles and machine guns firing toward us. I still couldn't hear our guys shooting back. What a mess. My pain was not lessening, either. And morphine was supposed to work fast.

"Give me another shot. This stuff's not working."

The medic gave me the shot even though, according to the book, it was way too soon. I think he'd given up on me because he stopped working on my wounds. Or maybe he had run out of bandages. Anyway, he began shouting for help back toward Lammersdorf. "The old man's hit!" I heard him yell.

I was on my back in the bottom of the ditch, my double dose of morphine finally beginning to kick in. I closed my eyes. When I opened them again, the medic's face was close to mine.

"I'm going to get you out of here," he yelled.

How is he going to do that? The battle noise was still intense; it sounded like some of our guys were now firing back.

"Stay down," I said. "Don't do anything stupid. You'll get killed trying to help me."

But he kept rising up and calling back down the road while I faded in and out. A few minutes later, the kid shook me awake. "Here they come," he said.

A litter jeep skidded to a halt on the road next to us. As the medics rolled me onto a litter, I noticed the silence. I couldn't hear any explosions or gunshots. Apparently, the Red Cross flag on the front of a jeep had caused both sides to cease firing. The war stayed on hold while the medics strapped me onto the stretcher rack hanging over the jeep.

"Let's get the hell out of here," one of them said.

The driver wheeled the jeep around and sped back to Lammersdorf. As we turned a corner behind a building, the firing started up again. My executive officer stopped the jeep as we passed our rear command post. My wounding left him in charge.

"Jesus Christ, Charlie," he said when he saw me.

"You're it," I said. "Get the sonsabitches."

Then I passed out again.

34
The Journey Home

I woke up and saw a chandelier hanging over me. I was on my back on a table, and two 1st Battalion doctors I knew were working on my wounds. I was in the battalion aid station in a large house with high ceilings, probably somewhere in Lammersdorf, because I could hear muffled explosions and small arms firing in the distance. I hurt like hell.

"There you are. How do you feel?" The doc smiled.

"Not so good."

"Do you want a drink? It's not homemade."

Medics always had liquor around, but alcohol was never a big part of my life. Still, I thought about it for a long pause. With my good left eye, I looked directly at the battalion surgeon.

"Am I going to make it?"

He smiled again. "I believe you will. They didn't seem to hit any vital organs."

"Then, no thanks. Save it for somebody else."

I got a shot of morphine instead. Later that afternoon, I began hurting again. My right hand and arm, bandaged and immobilized, seemed to be on fire, same as my right leg. Half wrapped in gauze, my head was pounding. Someone finally gave me another shot.

The next thing I heard was the loud, ripping sound of a German burp gun firing not too far away. I opened my good eye and saw I was in an ambulance. We were not moving. Two other wounded soldiers lay in stretchers on racks across from me. There was probably another GI above me.

I heard two short bursts from the German weapon again. This guy knew what he was doing. I didn't hear anybody shooting back. I reached over my head for the handle of the closed rear door, but I couldn't find it. One of the men shifted in his rack.

"Where the hell's our driver?" I asked.

"They bailed out when the shooting started. They're not far away. I can hear them talking."

I couldn't hear them but I figured our medics must have known they had an officer on board. "Hey, you guys!" I yelled as loud as I could.

No answer. Only another short burst from the German automatic weapon in the near distance.

"Hey, out there!" I yelled again. "You sonsabitches get your asses back in here and let's get moving."

After a moment, I heard, "Yes sir, we're coming."

Soon we were bumping along a rough road, the last thing I remember before losing consciousness again.

When I awoke, I was still on a litter. Above me, daylight filtered through the slanted canvas of an olive-drab tent ceiling. My left hand slipped off the litter and touched grass. My whole right side was hurting so I rolled slightly onto my left hip to try to get more comfortable. Less than two feet away, on another low stretcher, I saw a German soldier, still wearing his field gray uniform. Oh, hell. All that firing by the burp guns back at the ambulance. It jumped into my mind that they had captured me. I was now a prisoner of war in a German hospital somewhere.

I sank back and began to think about being a prisoner, wondering what that would be like. At least I was still alive, but what would happen next? I began to envision camps and barbed wire and starving in some freezing barracks deep in Germany. Would they even treat my wounds?

A figure coming from the left interrupted my thoughts. It was a woman, wearing a nurse's cap, a shapeless white smock, and a red cross on her right arm. No rank or other insignia.

As she approached the foot of my stretcher, I raised my head. "Do you speak English?"

She smiled. "What the hell do you think I speak?"

"Where am I?"

"You're in an Army field hospital near Liege."

Just like that, the German and I traded places. He was the prisoner, not I. "What day is it?"

"Sunday, the seventeenth."

I had been out for three days. "What happened to Friday and Saturday?"

"We didn't think you were going to make it. I'll go get the major."

The doctor looked me over and said they'd done all they could for me. "Do you think you can stand to fly back to England this afternoon?"

"You have planes?"

"There was an air drop in Holland this morning. We've asked for a plane to evacuate some of our most seriously wounded. Do you feel like going?"

I didn't have to think about it. My war was over. "Get me out of here as quick as you can."

A short while later, I heard a plane land, taxi, and shut down. Two men carried my litter into bright sunshine and set me in the shade of the fuselage, near the cargo door. I recognized the plane's tail markings. My friend from semipro baseball days back in Oklahoma flew for the same outfit. He had been a lieutenant colonel and a squadron commander when I visited him on leave in England after the Sicilian Campaign. I stopped the loadmaster, a sergeant, and asked if he knew my friend.

The sergeant glanced at me, then hurried on without answering.

"Sergeant, I asked you a question," I yelled in my best command voice.

That stopped him. "Sir," he said, "I'll get the pilot to answer your question."

A couple minutes later, the pilot, a lieutenant, walked up and stood over my stretcher. "Can I do something for you, Captain?"

I asked him the same question.

"You know the colonel?" he asked.

"Yes, I know him."

"How well do you know him?"

What the hell's going on here? "I played ball with him," I said. "My wife and his wife live a couple blocks apart in Enid, Oklahoma."

"What's his wife's name?"

I told him.

"Captain, I've got some sad news for you," he said. "I was right behind the colonel's plane at about 500 feet this morning when he got hit by flak and went straight in. Nobody got out that I could see. I'm sorry."

Operation Market Garden, memorialized in *A Bridge Too Far*, claimed many lives. The Army listed my friend as missing in action for a long time. This meant nobody could discuss his combat death outside the European Theater until the Army officially notified his family that he had been killed in action. This was to keep the family's hopes alive. Later, the Air Force named a street after the colonel at a base near Enid.

"If I get back to Oklahoma," I assured the lieutenant, "I will visit his wife."

On convalescent leave in Enid a few months later, when I first saw my friend's widow, the Army still officially had him listed as missing in action. By this time she had convinced herself he had survived, holding onto the hope that he was in a German prison camp somewhere. She spoke excitedly of plans for their life together after the war, as if saying it would make it true. Uncomfortable with what I couldn't tell her, I cut my visit short. It was many years after the war before I finally got a chance to tell her what I knew about how her husband died.

The shadows lengthened before the medics at last lifted me aboard the C-47. Two nurses tended us on the flight across the Channel, and after an hour of shivering in the unpressurized cabin, we landed in England.

Ambulances convoyed us to Bournemouth, where I checked into the 90th General Hospital for the first in a series of long hospital stays during my extended convalescence.

In England, I stayed drugged up for weeks while doctors worked on me. First, they unwrapped the bandage on my hand and the doctor looked at my barely-attached trigger finger.

"I don't think we can hook that back on," he said. "Why don't we take it off? Okay with you?"

His bluntness shocked me. "Do whatever you think is necessary," I said finally. What else could I say?

Instead of cutting the finger off even with my hand like surgeons would today, they left me with a little one-inch stub that gets in the way of everything I do. It stayed red and angry for a long time and I remained too self-conscious to shake hands with anyone for many years. Even now, it's tender if I bump it.

My other wounds slowly healed. Every day they removed shell fragments in my right leg from the calf all the way up to my butt. The huge rip in my right bicep rendered that arm pretty much useless for a while, but I was alive.

They couldn't do anything about the fragment behind my right eye. I thought I'd never see out of it again, but one morning a gauzy light came through. Within another week, I could make out colors and fuzzy objects.

After a month, I could see again and walk without a cane. This lifted my spirits so much I asked for a pass to go into London. I wanted to get away from the hospital for a few hours and see a play. I got off the train at a station near the theater district and found a ticket for the evening performance.

The Germans had started firing their new supersonic V-2 rockets at London in September, but the Brits were not about to let it bother them much. Rockets fell without warning and were so powerful that only the deepest tube stations offered any real protection. London might still be blacked out, but the Brits went on with their lives. The Germans could go to hell.

The theater, a favorite escape for many, was crowded with civilians and people in uniforms of all kinds, mostly American. I ate an early supper and settled into my seat to enjoy the play. The playbill had that familiar notice. In case of attack, the performance would continue if possible, and those who wished to leave should please exit in an orderly fashion.

Sometime in the second act, a tremendous explosion not far away shook the building enough that dust sifted down from the ceiling. There was no panic and only a few people left. The play continued.

I sat there for a few minutes but couldn't concentrate. All I could think of was that I had already lived through too many things I couldn't get out of to die now in a theater where I didn't have to be. I walked to the station and took the first train back to Bournemouth, but I had to admire the British. They were tough.

By the end of October I was well enough to travel to the States. I was more than ready. I even had a choice. I could go by ship or I could fly. I thought about all the problems I'd had on ships. That German warship chasing us on the *Queen Elizabeth* in the North Atlantic. The *Scythia* torpedoed under me going into North Africa. The LST running aground on that sandbar during the Sicily invasion. The *Empire Lance* getting sideswiped and strafed off Normandy.

I decided I'd take my chances flying.

I was one of two ambulatory patients on the C-47 flight to Prestwick, south of Glasgow on the west coast of Scotland. Other men were flat on their backs, missing arms or legs, hooked up to bags. After we landed, the two of us who could walk became "gofers" and ran errands to get the seriously wounded soldiers squared away as best we could. It felt good to do something useful for a change, and helped pass the time while waiting for a flight.

Near the terminal, two civilian C-54s sat just off the runway, big four-engine transports with red crosses on their tails. I watched them as I walked around the airfield. Late in the afternoon, I noticed rolling stairs had been moved up to the open loading door of the plane on the left. It would soon be taking off.

From being around trains in Oklahoma, I remembered that if two were leaving at about the same time, always catch the first one, because the second might never leave. I hurried to the operations office and introduced myself to a British sergeant standing behind the counter.

"I guess those two Pan Am C-54s out there are going to the States," I said. "Can I get on the first plane?"

"No, it's full."

I leaned forward on the counter. "Come on, sergeant, you can always squeeze on another ambulatory. I'm not litter-bound. There's always one more seat on a big plane."

"No, it's filled up."

I thought about that plane leaving without me and kept pushing the sergeant.

"Oh, come on. I know you've got an extra seat."

By this time he was a little pissed. "Look, Captain," he said with a tight smile, "you can't get on now."

I turned around and saw two men pulling the rolling stairs away from the plane. The door closed and the engines revved. I was too late. Watching that C-54 taxi away and rise into the evening sky hurt more than I would have thought. The plane was on its way across the northern rim of the Atlantic to the States via Iceland, Greenland, and Newfoundland.

I went next door to the NAAFI exchange to have a beer and wait for the next flight. Two hours later, I walked back into the operations office and found the room almost deathly silent, the air heavy and still.

I walked up to the sergeant I'd argued with earlier. He was busy behind the desk, but subdued.

"What's going on?" I asked.

"Be glad you didn't get on that plane, Captain."

The C-54 never reached Iceland. Perhaps German fighters flying from Norway shot it out of the sky, as they had done to other planes in the past few months. Maybe they wouldn't have shot down a hospital plane if it had been daytime, but who knew for sure.

Before dawn, I was on the other C-54, climbing over the Irish Sea, headed for the Azores, first leg of the longer southern route across the Atlantic. Filled mostly with patients on litters and two nurses, the plane flew at 10,000 feet because it wasn't pressurized. I tried to stay out of the way as the nurses scurried about checking on their patients.

All was quiet for an hour, and then I heard a muffled explosion; the plane banked sharply up and to the right. The evasive maneuver threw a nurse across the cabin and had me straining against my seat belt. Outside my window I could see orange flashes of explosions. Tracers curved past us as the plane's engines revved hard to gain altitude and change direction. The straining seemed to go on forever.

"Come on, come on, come on," I kept muttering to myself.

Somehow, we weren't hit, and the plane finally leveled off and throttled back. After things calmed down, one of the crew told us we had crossed over a U.S. convoy that mistook us for the enemy. They hadn't gotten notice of our changed flight plan.

We refueled in the Azores and again in Bermuda before heading for Mitchel Field on Long Island. It was dusk when we approached New York City. The pilot tipped a wing and circled to give us all a look. Lights were on in buildings, and cars moved down the streets with headlights shining, a sight I hadn't seen since October 1942. I'd been in blackout conditions for over two years.

As the pilot circled the city, letting us look out on the lights, there was little cheering. Men wiped their eyes silently, lost in their own thoughts.

Others, too wounded to move, wept openly. We had been through so much. A mass of emotions rushed in on me and threatened to spill over. A lump rose in my throat. We were so happy to be home again.

At Mitchel Field, after being put in a barracks, we got to call our families. It felt strange talking to Ruth after all this time. Neither of us was the same. I was almost dumbstruck and barely said more than one of those canned telegrams. "I love you and will see you soon."

The next day I learned I would be transferred to Brooke General Hospital in San Antonio. I finally got hold of Ruth at Enid High School and told her I would be in San Antonio in two days.

"Quit your job as soon as you can," I said.

The next morning they loaded us on a C-47 with some litter patients and we took off on a milk run through the South. We landed several times to let off soldiers going home on leave and finally stopped for the night at a small airport in Mississippi. I kept thinking about Ruth, hoping she would quit her job without giving notice and be in San Antonio when I got there.

But she wasn't. I checked into Fort Sam Houston and went over to the hospital, one of the Army's major treatment centers for the increasing flow of casualties coming out of the war zones. The place was massive. The Army had converted over 200 enlisted barracks to medical use early in the war. I was assigned to a crowded ward in a new section that, until a few months before, had been home to a cavalry battalion.

I called Ruth again, the third time since I'd been back, and after two years of being away, could still not say much more than "Your husband is home. Quit your job. Come on down."

To my tongue-tied delight, she replied, "I'll be on the three-o'clock train the day after tomorrow."

I had two days to find us a hotel room in a town that had no vacancies. I put on my uniform and spent every spare minute looking. San Antonio was a bustling military town, filled with soldiers, their families, and all sorts of civilians hurrying in and out of the city.

I went from hotel to hotel, asking the desk clerks if there were any cancellations. I finally told the hospital ward chief that if I didn't find a room by the time my wife arrived, I was going to sneak her into the hospital and hide her there with me.

I sat slumped in a chair in the busy lobby of the St. Anthony Hotel in downtown San Antonio an hour before Ruth's train came in, wondering what I was going to do. I'd been badgering the clerk every few minutes about cancellations and there was still nothing. I sat there lost in thought, trying to figure out how I was going to sneak Ruth into the hospital ward.

"Captain?"

I looked up and saw a distinguished-looking older gentleman standing in front of me.

"You look like someone who needs a room, Captain," he said.

"Yes, sir, I sure do. My wife is coming in on a train from Oklahoma in an hour. I haven't seen her in over two years."

"Let me see what I can do," he said, and walked over to the desk. A few minutes later he came back and handed me a key. "Welcome home, soldier. Stay as long as you need."

His generosity overwhelmed me. He wouldn't let me pay and wouldn't tell me his name. I mumbled a thank you and rushed off to the station to meet Ruth.

The train was on time and I was never so happy to see anyone in my life. I held her there on the platform, and we kissed and stared unbelieving into each other's face, smiling through our tears.

35
Epilogue

After extended stays for specialized treatment at various military and veterans hospitals, Charlie Scheffel retired in January 1946 from disabilities caused by combat wounds at Lammersdorf, Germany. During his military service, he earned the Combat Infantry Badge, two Purple Hearts, the Bronze Star, and for his actions at Cherence le Roussel, the Silver Star and the French Croix de Guerre.

Like millions of others after the war, Charlie and Ruth began a family and got on with their lives. They asked for little. They knew life itself was a gift and they sought to be happy. They worked hard and prospered. Their daughters, Susan and Elaine, and their son, Lee, grew up to become productive members of society and raise families of their own.

While building a successful insurance business in Oklahoma City, Charlie and Ruth found time to travel extensively throughout America and the world. On a dare from his son, Charlie became an instrument-rated pilot in his fifties, which added to his urge to see the world. After retirement, he and Ruth continued to travel as long as her health permitted.

Charlie has been a widower for several years now, but his enthusiasm for travel endures. Hanging on his bedroom wall is a map of the world with a pin sticking in each of about a dozen countries he has yet to visit. He pulled another pin out of his map recently after he sailed to Antarctica on an ex-Soviet icebreaker with one of his granddaughters. His goal is to visit every country in the world and remove every pin from his map.

Besides visiting the more exotic corners of the globe, Charlie has also walked the ground where he fought during World War II, trying to come to some understanding of what happened during those uncertain times when tyranny stalked the earth.

At the la Gallerie farm, near the village of Cherence le Roussel, he told his story of the four-day battle to the current owner, a woman whose family owned the farm during the war when she was a little girl. She presented Charlie with a bottle of la Gallerie's *Calvados*, which he shared with other members of his unit at a 9th Infantry Division reunion.

Later, outside Lammersdorf, Charlie knelt in a ditch at the site of his final battle and prayed for the men who died around him there. They are never far from his mind.

Maps

North Africa 227
Sicily... 228
Northern France 229
la Gallerie 230
Belgium 231

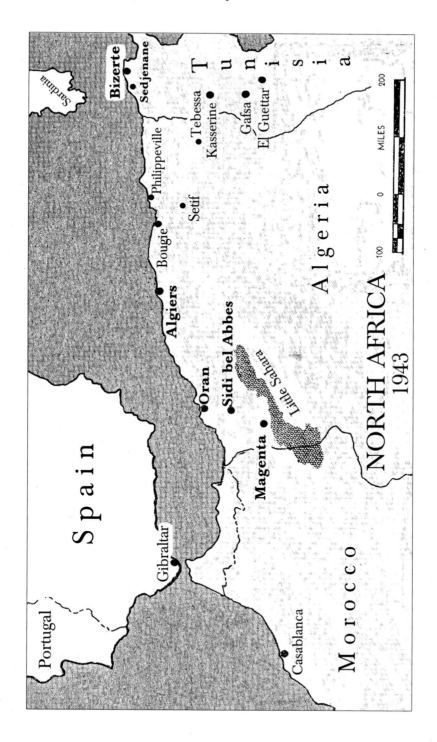

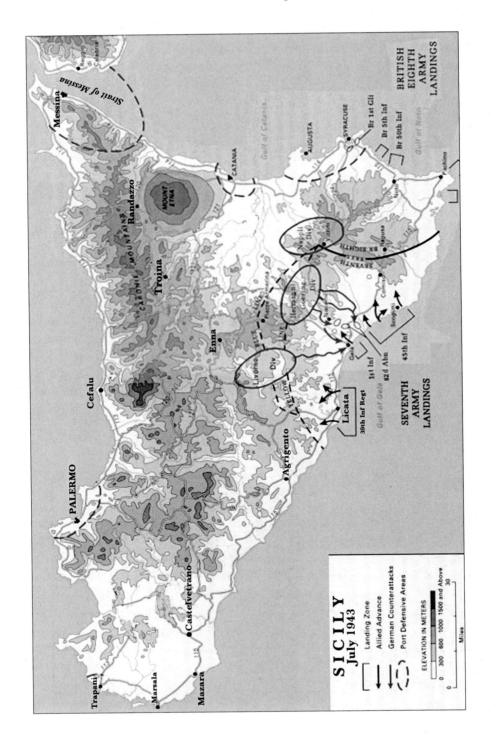

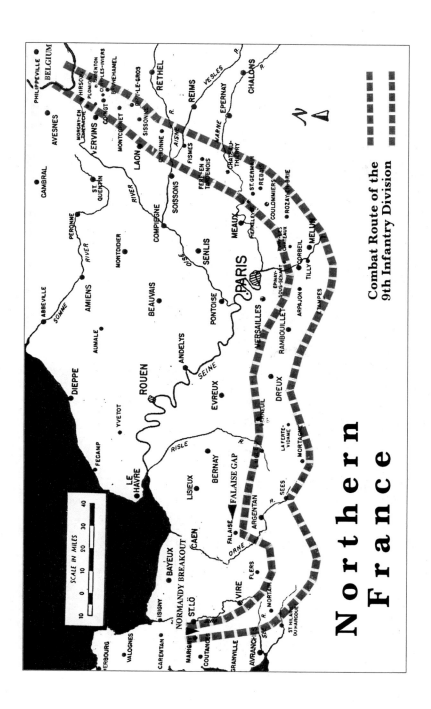

Northern France

Combat Route of the
9th Infantry Division

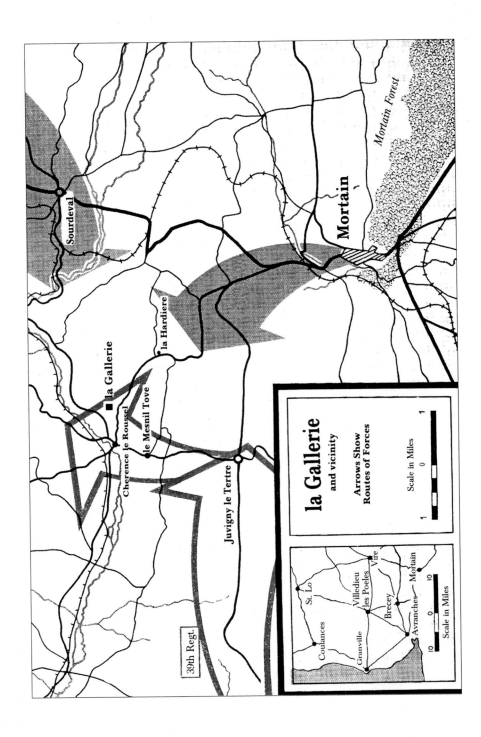

la Gallerie
and vicinity

Arrows Show
Routes of Forces

Scale in Miles
1   0   1

Sourdeval

Mortain

Mortain Forest

la Gallerie

la Hardiere

Cherence le Roussel

le Mesnil Tove

Juvigny le Tertre

39th Regt.

St. Lo
Coutances
Granville
Villedieu
les Poeles
Brecey
Avranches
Vire
Mortain

Scale in Miles
10   0   10

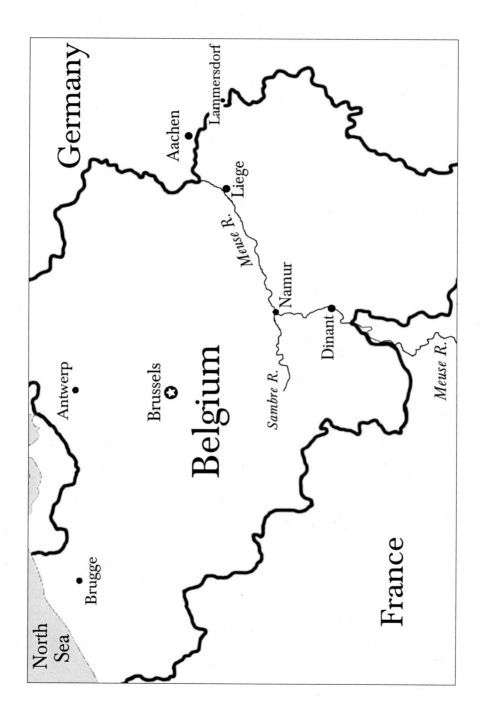